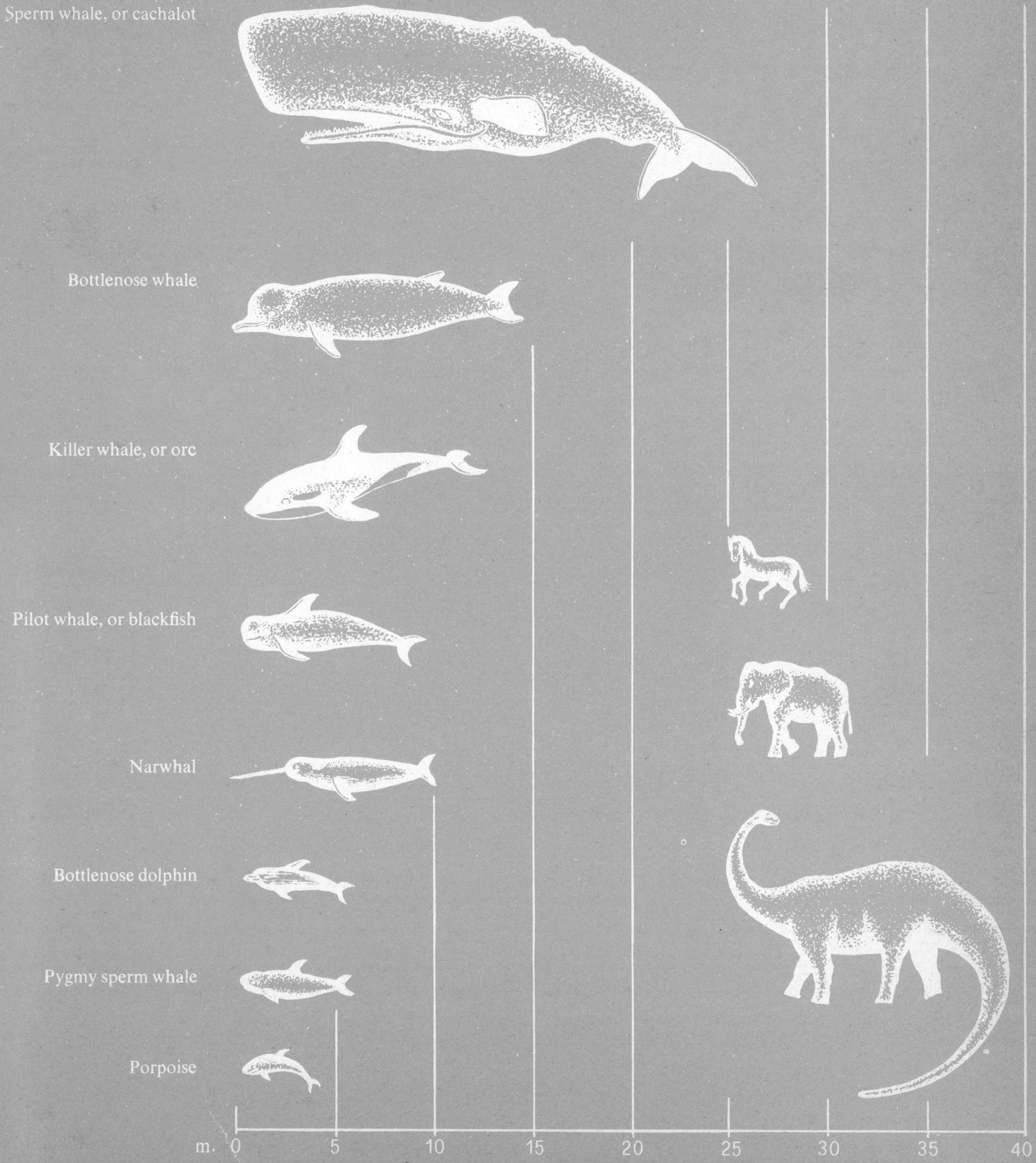

Sperm whale, or cachalot

Bottlenose whale

Killer whale, or orc

Pilot whale, or blackfish

Narwhal

Bottlenose dolphin

Pygmy sperm whale

Porpoise

m. 0 5 10 15 20 25 30 35 40

MAMMALS IN THE SEAS

FAO Fisheries Series No. 5, Volume II

Mammals in the seas

Volume II

Pinniped Species Summaries and Report on Sirenians

Being the Annex B Appendixes VI and VII of the Report of the

FAO ADVISORY COMMITTEE ON
MARINE RESOURCES RESEARCH
WORKING PARTY ON MARINE MAMMALS

with the cooperation of the
UNITED NATIONS ENVIRONMENT PROGRAMME

FOOD AND AGRICULTURE ORGANIZATION OF THE UNITED NATIONS

Rome, 1979

The designations employed and the presentation of material in this publication do not imply the expression of any opinion whatsoever on the part of the Secretariats of the Food and Agriculture Organization of the United Nations and the United Nations Environment Programme concerning the legal status of any country, territory, city or area or of its authorities, or concerning the delimitation of its frontiers or boundaries.

P-43
ISBN 92-5-100512-5

Printed in Italy

PREPARATION OF THIS REPORT

The Report of the ACMRR Working Party on Marine Mammals was approved at the Working Party's final session held in La Jolla, USA, 21-25 January 1977. The Report, and its Annexes, which have been edited as agreed at the session, together with selected papers of the Scientific Consultation on the Conservation and Management of Marine Mammals and their Environment held in Bergen, 1976, are being published as follows:

MAMMALS IN THE SEAS

FAO Fisheries Series No. 5

Volume 1

Report of the ACMRR Working Party on Marine Mammals

Annex A	- Terms of Reference and Members of the Working Party and of its *ad hoc* Groups
Annex B	- Proceedings of the Scientific Consultation on the Conservation and Management of Marine Mammals and their Environment
Appendix I	- List of Documents
Appendix II	- List of Participants and Organizations Represented at the Scientific Consultation
Appendix III	- Tasks and Conveners of Working Groups
Appendix IV	- Report of *ad hoc* Group IV on Ecological and General Problems
Appendix V	- Opening Plenary Meeting

Volume 2

Annex B

Appendix VI	- Pinniped Species Summaries
Appendix VII	- Report on Sirenians

Volume 3

General papers, and large cetaceans

Selected papers of the Scientific Consultation on the Conservation and Management of Marine Mammals and their Environment

Volume 4

Small cetaceans, seals, sirenians, and otters

Selected papers of the Scientific Consultation on the Conservation and Management of Marine Mammals and their Environment

Contents

Page

REPORT OF THE ADVISORY COMMITTEE ON MARINE RESOURCES RESEARCH WORKING PARTY ON MARINE MAMMALS

Annex B Appendix VI

PINNIPED SPECIES SUMMARIES

Selected papers of the Scientific Consultation on the Conservation and Management of Marine Mammals and their Environment will be published in subsequent volumes.

Annex B - Appendix VII, Report on Sirenians, is also issued as a separate reprint in view of its particular interest to specific groups of users.

Annex C - Programme of Research Relating to Marine Mammals, is a working document and has been published separately as FAO Fisheries Technical Paper, No. 177, for limited distribution.

The Report of the Working Party, included in Volume 1, has already appeared separately as *FAO Fisheries Report,* No. 194.

Bibliographic entry:

FAO. Advisory Committee on Marine Resources Research.
Working Party on Marine Mammals (1979).
FAO Fish. Ser., (5) Vol. 2:152 p.
Mammals in the seas. Volume 2.
Pinniped species summaries and report on sirenians.
Being the Annex B Appendixes VI and VII.
of the Report of the FAO Advisory Committee
on Marine Resources Research, Working Party
on Marine Mammals
Pinnipeds. Sirenians. Geographic distribution.
Life History. Population structure. Feeding behaviour.
Interspecific relationships. Exploitation.
Management. Pollution effects. Conservation.

ANNEX B APPENDIX VI OF THE REPORT OF THE

FAO ADVISORY COMMITTEE ON MARINE RESOURCES RESEARCH WORKING PARTY ON MARINE MAMMALS

PINNIPED SPECIES SUMMARIES

PREFACE

In an attempt to carry out the task given it by the Advisory Committee on Marine Resources Research (ACMRR) of the Food and Agriculture Organization of the United Nations (FAO), the Working Party on Marine Mammals established four *ad hoc* groups of specialists. Prior to the meeting of *ad hoc* Group III on Pinnipeds and Marine Otters in Seattle, Washington, in September 1975, summaries of the knowledge of some species of pinnipeds were prepared according to a standard scheme. These were slightly modified during the meeting and new summaries for other species were written by individuals or by small groups. Subsequently and up to the convening by FAO of the Scientific Consultation on the Conservation and Management of Marine Mammals and their Environment in Bergen, Norway, 31 August - 9 September 1976, O.A. Mathisen, a member of the Working Party and its contact with *ad hoc* Group III, attempted to complete the coverage and increase the authority of the summaries by contacting a number of specialists chosen for their knowledge of individual species; they were requested to revise and add to existing summaries all additional knowledge called for in the outline, to prepare summaries for species not yet covered and to add a bibliography of pertinent references. Compliance with these requests varied. The names of the specialists who completed the final reviews or compilations appear at the head of each summary. A.W. Erickson, F.H. Fay, H.D. Fisher, D.E. Sergeant and D.B. Siniff also contributed to various drafts. Editing of the final versions was completed by W.N. Bonner, a member of the Working Party and convener of the working group on pinnipeds during the Scientific Consultation, following the conclusion of that meeting.

The species summaries have value as a collection of contemporary knowledge of all species of pinnipeds. This value extends beyond the need they fulfilled for *ad hoc* Group III. Finally, in the review of the summaries undertaken during the meeting of *ad hoc* Group III, a new level of summaries based on taxonomic groupings and geographical distribution was provided. These group summaries form sections 5.1.1-5.1.6 of the Proceedings of the Scientific Consultation.

NORTHERN (STELLER) SEA LION

B. Mate & R.L. Gentry

1 Description

1.1 *Species identification*

1.1.1 Family: Otariidae
Species: Eumetopias jubatus (Schreber 1776)

1.1.2 Size

- Newborn pups ca 1 m; 16-23 kg.
- Adult males to 3 m; to 900 kg.
- Adult females to 2 m; to 300 kg.

Males are buff or tan with coarse heavy pelage about the neck of adults; subadults may appear silver to light brown when wet. Females buff to light brown. Pups are dark brown until age 4 to 6 months when they moult to a somewhat lighter brown.

1.2 *Stocks*

1.2.1 Identification

Although this species covers a large range, no isolated or subspecific populations have been identified, but this has not been given extensive study.

1.2.2 Seasonal Distribution

Northern (Steller) sea lions occur in the North Pacific from the Sea of Japan (43°N), northward around the Pacific rim (66°N), and then southward to San Miguel Island, California (34°N).

Some seasonal movements have been noted among the Bering Sea populations. In the southern extent of the species' range in the eastern North Pacific, adult males undergo a distinct postbreeding season northward migration. Some females may also participate in latitudinal movements during winter months.

1.2.3 Structure of stocks

The males are polygynous and begin forming territories in early May on rocky semi-exposed areas. Bachelor haulout grounds are often located near the main breeding rookeries.

2 Vital Parameters

2.1 *Population size*

2.1.1 Methods of estimation

Boat, air and ground counts have been used, often in conjunction with photographs, over the species' range with varying degrees of success. Most censusing has occurred during the breeding season. Tagging studies have been initiated at various rookeries with no published reports to date. Branding and dye markings have been used in individual study areas.

2.1.2 Results

Populations in the Californian Channel Islands have been historically reduced until, at present, the species is located only on and near San Miguel Island in numbers of less than 100. Ano Nuevo Island, the largest and most studied population in California, has apparently maintained a stable population numbering 1,600-2,000 for half a century.

California Department of Fish and Game has found, from aerial surveys of California, fairly stable numbers (5,000 to 7,000 individuals) from 1958 to 1973. Oregon breeding populations number approximately 2,000, while Washington populations are estimated at 600. British Columbia populations number approximately 5,000 (2,500 around Vancouver Island, 2,000 in the area of Cape St. James and the Queen Charlotte Islands, and 500 distributed along the northern British Columbia coast).

The major breeding areas are the Kerouard Islands and Scott Islands, which are traditional rookery areas. Alaskan populations have been estimated in excess of 200,000. Japanese populations are seasonal. Animals start to appear in northern Hokkaido during late January, peak in numbers during March at approximately 10,000-13,000, and depart by late May (presumably for the Kurile Islands to breed). No breeding occurs in Japanese waters. Estimates of Soviet populations are unconfirmed at 20,000 to 50,000.

2.1.3 Trend in abundance

The range of *Eumetopias* appears to be receding northward during this century, with reduced numbers in the southern extent of the range.

2.2 Rates

2.2.1 Reproductive

Age of sexual maturity:

- females, age 4-5
- males, age 5-7; socially and physically competitive at age 7-9.

Pregnancy rate: The pregnancy rate seems to vary with the tendency to wean pups of the year, which varies in different parts of the range. At some rookeries most females wean their young before 11 months and pregnancy rates are highest at such sites. At other rookeries most females fail to wean and here the lowest pregnancy rates are found (e.g. Lewis Island). Pregnancy rates ranging from 85 % to 6 % have been reported. Birth season: mid-May through June.

Lactation period: typically 8-11 months. Individual females are occasionally observed nursing both a newborn pup and a yearling (more common in northern populations) and a newborn, yearling and two-year old are rarely seen suckling from a single female in Alaskan waters.

Mating time: 8-14 days after parturition.

Gestation: one year (delay of implantation about 3 months).

Longevity: 23 years.

2.2.2 Natural mortality

Adults - unknown

Pups - highly variable (10 %-100 %) due principally to weather and also crowding effects (crushing and terrain). Natural predators include sharks and killer whales.

2.2.3 Harvesting

None known in U.S. and Canadian waters except by Alaskan natives in limited numbers. Small numbers are harvested annually in northern Japan for human consumption. Fishermen kill some animals each year in fishing gear conflicts throughout its range.

3 Trophic Relationships

3.1 Food and feeding

3.1.1 Food base and habits

This species is an opportunistic feeder, taking primarily non-commercial species of fish and cephalopods. Some competition with man for commercial fishes exists associated with trolling, gill nets and less frequently, trawling. Some individuals ascend rivers in pursuit of prey species which include salmon, shad and lampreys. Seasonally, and perhaps only regionally, *Eumetopias* males have been observed to kill and consume *Callorhinus ursinus* pups.

3.1.2 Requirements and utilization

Various estimates have been made for *Eumetopias* food requirements. The reported range is 2-6 % of body weight per day.

3.1.3 Changes in abundance of food supply unknown

4 Relation to man

4.1 Values

4.1.1 Consumptive

Small numbers are taken for human consumption and animal food in Alaska, Japan and possibly the Soviet Union. A few are taken by natives in the Bering Sea for traditional arts and crafts.

4.1.2 Low-consumptive

A small number are taken annually for display and scientific purposes.

4.2 Effects of human activities other than exploitation

Significant levels of heavy metals and chlorinated hydro-carbons have been found in individuals from the southern extent of the eastern Pacific range. Effects of pollutants, if any, are as yet unknown. Harassment of breeding areas was a " local " problem for some populations prior to the Marine Mammal Protection Act 1972 in the United States, but appears to be of little significance since.

Unintentional harassment occurs to varying degrees from sport and commercial fishing boats, divers, photographers and tourists, which has unknown consequences.

4.3 Management and conservation

Management agencies in Alaska feel that the numbers of *Eumetopias* have increased to levels approaching carrying capacity. No systematic study has been made to determine total population numbers and movements. The U.S. Marine Mammal Protection Act has prevented the application of any management practices to U.S. populations. Japan allows the taking of sea lions without permit and has a current bounty of 1,000 yen per animal. Regulation in the U.S.S.R. is unknown at this time.

5 Threats to stocks

Populations in the southern extent of the eastern Pacific range are probably threatened by toxicants, increased unintentional harassment and reduced suitable habitat, although the effect of these is presently unknown. It is hard to understand how these relatively small populations have managed to survive over such a long documented period with consistently high observed pup mortality and (until the last few decades) such heavy human predation and harassment. Natural recruitment may be supplemented by immigrants from the more populated segments of the species range, but this is unknown.

The greatest threat to the northern populations would appear to be diseases.

6 Research

6.1 Current status

Behavioural studies focusing on population dynamics and feeding are currently being carried out by the U.S. National Marine Fisheries Service. University studies on behaviour, population structure, physiology and parasitology of *Eumetopias* are continuing in California, Oregon, British Columbia and Alaska. Monitoring of Soviet and Japanese populations is carried out by their respective governmental agencies.

6.2 Future research

Stock assessment in the northern part of the species' range appears necessary, if management is to be successful. This will require further development of censusing techniques and/or sampling statistical estimators. Study of population-limiting factors in the southern extent of the range including behaviour, toxicants and pathology would be desirable. Feeding behaviour, migratory status, and reproductive biology of northern populations are appropriate topics to determine the impact of this species on its environment and possible competition with man for mutually desirable prey species. A study of the relationship between weaning tendency and pregnancy rate is needed to understand differences in recruitment in different parts of the range.

References

DAILEY, M.D., and B.L. HILL, A survey of metazoan
1970 parasites infesting the California (*Zalophus californianus*) and Steller (*Eumetopias jubatus*) sea lion. *Bull. South. Calif. Acad. Sci.*, 69:126-32.

FISCUS, C.H., and G.A. BAINES, Food and Feeding be-
1966 havior of the Steller and California sea lions. *J. Mammal.*, 47:195-200.

GENTRY, R.L., Social behavior of the Steller sea lion.
1970 Ph.D. Thesis, University of California, Santa Cruz, California.

KENYON, K.W., and D.W. RICE, Abundance and distri-
1961 bution of the Steller sea lion. *J. Mammal.*, 42:223-34.

MATE, B.R., Annual migrations of the sea lions' *Eume-*
1975 *topias jubatus* and *Zalophus californianus* along the Oregon coast. *Rapp. P.-V. Réun. CIEM*, 169:455-61.

MATHISEN, O.A., T. BAADE and J. LOPP, Breeding habits,
1962 growth and stomach contents of the Steller sea lion in Alaska. *J. Mammal.*, 43(4):469-77.

CALIFORNIA SEA LION

B. Mate

1 Description

1.1 Species Identification

1.1.1 Family: Otariidae
Species: *Zalophus californianus* (Lesson 1828)

1.1.2 Size

- Newborn pups 75 cm; 5-6 kg.
- Adult males 2.2 m; 275 kg.
- Adult females 1.8 m; 91 kg.

Both sexes are generally a dark brown although females frequently appear a tan colour. The mature males (5 years and older) have a characteristically enlarged sagittal crest with a corresponding area of lighter-coloured pelage.

1.2 Stocks

1.2.1 Identification

This species has been divided into three subspecific groups: *Zalophus californianus californianus* which breeds from the tip of Baja California (23°N) north throughout the Sea of Cortez and north to San Miguel Island, California (34°N).

During the non-breeding season *Zalophus* can be found along the west coast of Mexico from 19°N northward to the southern coast of British Columbia (51°N). *Z. c. wollebaeki* breeds on the Galapagos Islands. *Z. c. japonicus* inhabited the Sea of Japan and may now be extinct.

1.2.2 Seasonal Distribution

Male *Zalophus californianus* on the Pacific side of Baja California (and northward) undergo a post-breeding seasonal migration during the fall, moving from the northern extent of breeding range (34°N) as far as southern British Columbia (51°N). Some males from the Sea of Cortez and/or Pacific appear to migrate south following the breeding season along mainland Mexico at least as far as Manzanillo (19°N). Some males may be found north of the breeding range during the breeding season.

1.2.3 Structure of stocks

The animals are polygynous with males establishing territories on rocks and sandy or gravel beaches in early May. Females move freely about the rookeries.

2 Vital parameters

2.1 Population Size

2.1.1 Methods of estimation

Population counts have been made from the ground, boats, aircraft, and resulting photographs. Tagging, mainly of pups, has been done at several rookeries. Although most counts have been made during the breeding season, some non-breeding seasonal data are available for some regions.

2.1.2 Results

There are only limited data available for

populations in Mexican waters. Counts of several major areas in the Sea of Cortez during 1966 yielded 5,411 animals. Estimates, made during 1975, of the entire Gulf place the population near 8,500. 1965 estimates of Cedros, Benitos and Guadalupe Islands indicated just over 16,000 animals during winter. An estimate of the total breeding population during 1975 for the Pacific side of Baja California was 15,000. The Californian Channel Islands have been censused rather regularly during the last fifty years and the population is known to have expanded considerably during that time both in numbers and range. Recent data from 1961, 1965 and 1969 seems to indicate a fairly stable population of approximately 20,000. One very complete aerial photographic survey in 1964 indicated as many as 35,000 animals present.

Seasonally, as many as 14,000 animals may be found in northern California, 2,500 in Oregon, 500 in Washington and 1,000 in British Columbia. The total number of *Z. c. californianus* is probably near 50,000.

The Galapagos population is estimated at 20,000.

2.1.3 Trends in abundance

Numbers of *Zalophus* appear to have increased in the last few decades and a northward range expansion has occurred (perhaps at the expense of *Eumetopias* populations) after some history of exploitation. Except for the 1964 census figures, the Californian Channel Islands populations appear fairly stable at 20,000-25,000. An apparent epizootic of leptospirosis in 1970 produced regional-seasonal changes in distribution during 1970-1971 and a noticeable increase in beach-cast and sick animals. The data are inadequate to judge stability or trends of Mexican populations at this time.

2.2 Rates

2.2.1 Reproductive

Age of sexual maturity: unknown
Pregnancy rates: unknown
Birth season: end of May to end of June in Mexico and California; October to December on Galapagos Islands
Lactation time: 5-12 months
Mating time: about 14 days after parturition
Gestation: 50 weeks (delay of implantation not known)
Longevity: 17 years.

2.2.2 Natural mortality

In recent years an increase in the number of premature births has been observed, with the possible causative agents being: 1) chemical residues (polychlorinated biphenyls, DDT and metabolites): 2) a bacterium (*Leptospira*); and 3) a virus. Lungworm is a common parasite and may be responsible for significant mortality. An increased mortality rate for migrant males occurred during 1970-1971 and was attributed to leptospirosis. Sharks and killer whales are natural predators.

2.2.3 Harvesting

Although commercially harvested in the past for hides and animal food, no known harvest occurs except incidental take by fishermen in gear conflicts and harassment activities in violation of current laws.

3 Trophic relationships

3.1 Food and feeding

3.1.1 Food base and habits

Little is known of the food habits of *Zalophus.* It appears to be a shallow water opportunistic feeder, eating mainly squid, including *Loligo*, and various small fishes, including *Engraulis, Merluccius,* various rock-fishes and *Clupea.* Both night and daytime feeding occur.

3.1.2 Requirements and utilizations

No data available

3.1.3 Changes in abundance of food supply

Overexploitation of *Engraulis* and *Clu-*

pea during the 1960's caused declines in commercial catch of both species. Recently these species appear to be increasing in number.

3.2 *Competition and predation*

Competition with *Eumetopias* for food, habitat, and other resources may significantly affect the distribution of both species. Mutual shifts in breeding range, short periods of cohabitation, use of similar prey species indicate this may be of some significance. Predation by sharks and killer whales occurs.

4 Relation to man

4.1 *Values*

4.1.1 *Consumptive*

Zalophus is a protected species throughout its range and only a few are taken annually for display purposes.

4.1.2 *Low-consumptive*

This species is the most " popular " circus and zoo pinniped. There are also several areas through the species range where they are a tourist attraction. The U.S. Navy has recently been using *Zalophus* in underwater object retrieval programs.

4.2 *Effect of human activities, etc.*

The major conflict between man and *Zalophus* is resource allocation. In certain areas damage is done by sea lion to fishing gear and " caught " fish. As mentioned in 2.2.2, environmental contaminants (DDT and polychlorinated biphenyls) may be causing an increase in premature births and in mortality rate of young and subadult animals. Human disturbance of some breeding areas occurs and may cause some problems of reduced suitability as rookery sites.

4.3 *Management and conservation*

This species is protected in Mexico, but small numbers are taken. Although a harvest program has been proposed, none has been initiated.

In the United States *Zalophus* is protected under the Marine Mammal Protection Act against any killing or harassment.

In British Columbia fishermen are permitted to shoot animals if they are found in the water in the area of active fishing. The numbers are relatively few and seasonal in British Columbia and as yet no management program has been established.

5 Threats to stocks

Significant levels of environmental toxicants and the introduction of new diseases appear to be the most serious problems. The species is certainly not endangered at this time, although some " local " populations appear to fluctuate significantly. Resource conflict may be the greatest ultimate concern.

6 Research

6.1 *Current research*

Mexico — unknown.

U.S. — NMFS study in conjunction with *Callorhinus* studies on San Miguel Island and on pelagic feeding. Numerous university and Navy studies principally on physiology. Limited work on behaviour and population assessment/movement are in progress.

British Columbia — some population and behavioural work in progress.

6.2 *Future research*

More information is needed on competition for man-shared prey species. A further refinement of population structure, dynamics and movements would be desirable because of the migration through several countries. Data on general biology and population numbers in Mexico, especially trends and migratory status, are poor at this time. Competition with *Eumetopias* and identification of resource limiting factors for both species requires more effort.

References

BARTHOLOMEW, G.A., Seal and sea lion populations of
1967 the California Islands. *In* Proceedings of the Symposium on the Biology of the California Channel Islands. Santa Barbara, Santa Barbara Botanic Garden, pp. 229-44.

BARTHOLOMEW, G.A., and R.A. BOOLOOTIAN, Numbers
1960 and population structure of the pinnipeds on the California Channel Islands. *J. Mammal.*, 41:366-75.

BUHLER, D.R., R.R. CLAEYS and B.R. MATE, Heavy
1975 metal and chlorinated hydrocarbon residues in California sea lions. *J. Fish. Res. Board Can.*, 32(12):2391-7.

CARLISLE, J.G., and J.A. ALPIN, Sea lion census for 1965
1966 including counts of other California pinnipeds. *Calif. Fish Game*, 52(2):119-20.

FREY, D.H., A winter influx of sea lions from Lower
1939 California. *Calif. Fish Game*, 25:245-50.

FREY, H.W., and J.A. ALPIN, Sea lion census for 1969,
1970 including counts of other California pinnipeds. *Calif. Fish Game*, 56(2):130-3.

HUBBS, C.L., Personal communication.
1975

KING, J.E., Seals of the world. London, British Museum
1964 (Natural History), 154 p.

MATE, B.R., Population kinetics and related ecology of
1973 the northern sea lion, *Eumetopias jubatus*, and the California sea lion, *Zalophus californianus*, along the Oregon coast. Ph.D. Thesis, University of Oregon, Eugene, 94 p.

—, Annual migrations of the sea lions *Eumetopias ju-*
1975 *batus*, and *Zalophus californianus* along the Oregon coast. *Rapp. P.-V. Réun. CIEM*, 169:455-61.

MOREJOHN, G.V., A northern record of a female Cali-
1968 fornia sea lion. *J. Mammal.*, 49:156.

ODELL, D.K., Premature pupping in the California sea
1970 lion. *In* Proceedings of the Seventh Annual Conference on the Biology of Sonar and Diving Mammals. Stanford Research Institute.

—, Censuses of pinnipeds breeding on the California
1971 Channel Islands. *J. Mammal.*, 52(1):187-90.

—, Studies on the biology of the California sea lion and
1972 the northern elephant seal on San Nicholas Island, California. Ph.D. Thesis, University of California, Los Angeles, 168 p.

ORR, R.T., and T.C. POULTER, The pinniped population
1945 of Ano Nuevo Island, California. *Proc. Calif. Acad. Sci.*, 32:377-404.

ORR, R.T., J. Schonewald and K.W. Kenyon, The Cali-
1970 fornia sea lion; skull growth and a comparison of two populations. *Proc. Calif. Acad. Sci.*, 37:381-94.

PETERSON, R.S., and G.A. BARTHOLOMEW, The natural
1967 history and behaviour of the California sea lion. *Spec. Publ. Am. Soc. Mammal.*, (1):79 p.

RICE, D.W., K.W. KENYON and D. LLUCH B., Pinniped
1965 populations of Islas Guadalupe, San Benito, and Cedros, Baja California, in 1965. *Trans. San Diego Soc. Nat. Hist.*, 14(7):73-84.

RIPLEY, W.E., K.W. COX and J.K. BAXTER, California
1962 sea lion census 1958, 1960 and 1961. *Calif. Fish Game*, 48:228-31.

SCAMMON, C.M., The marine mammals of the northwe-
1874 stern coast of North America. San Francisco, John H. Carmany Co., 319 p.

SCHEFFER, V.B., Seals, sea lions and walruses. Stanford,
1958 California, Stanford Univ. Press, 179 p.

SMITH, A.W., *et al.*, A preliminary report on potentially
1974 pathogenic microbial agents recently isolated from pinnipeds. *J. Wildl. Dis.*, 48:228-31.

VEDROS, N.A., *et al.*, Leptospirosis epizootic among
1971 California sea lions. *Science, Wash.*, 172:1250-1.

SOUTH AMERICAN SEA LION

R. Vaz-Ferreira

1 Description

1.1 *Species Identification*

1.1.1 Family: Otariidae
Species: *Otaria flavescens* (Blainville 1820)

1.1.2 Size

- Newborn pups — male 82 cm, (79-85), 14,2 kg (13.6-14.8) female 79 cm, (73-82), 11.5 kg (10.2-13.4) (Lobos Isl. Vaz-Ferreira in press)
- Adult males — 256 cm; 300-340 kg.
- Adult females — 200 cm; 144 kg.

(Falkland Islands — Hamilton, 1934, 1939 — Lobos Island — Vaz-Ferreira 1976)

Colour very variable: often adult males are dark brown to orange, the mane generally of a paler shade, and the belly lightening to a dark yellow; females dark to light brown-orange with part of the head and neck a dull yellow or different shade (Hamilton 1934; Vaz-Ferreira 1976); pups are black.

1.2 *Stocks*

1.2.1 Identification

No separate stocks have been identified.

1.2.2 Distribution

Areas inhabited or reached by the South American sea lion comprise the Atlantic and Pacific shores of South America from Rio de Janeiro, Brazil, about 23°S, to the southern tip of South America (at least as far as 55°S), and from there on the Pacific side to Zorritos, Peru, (4°S) (Scheffer 1958), wandering as far as Galapagos Islands (Wellington and de Vries 1976).

No established migration patterns have been observed, although local seasonal movements occur (Hamilton 1939; Vaz-Ferreira 1956a, 1975a; Vaz-Ferreira & Palerm 1961).

1.2.3 Structure of Stocks

Males are polygynous and establish territories on sand of gravel beaches and flat rock areas from the end of November through the end of February. The male-female ratio may be as high as 1:15, published averages are 1:7.8 (Falkland Islands, Hamilton 1934) and 1:7.6 (Lobos Island, Vaz-Ferreira 1975).

Bachelor male groups are often situated at the sides of the breeding groups (Vaz-Ferreira & Sierra 1961).

2 Vital parameters

2.1 *Population size*

2.1.1 Methods of estimation

Counts have been made from the ground (Uruguay and Falkland Islands), boats (Chile) and aircraft (Argentina and Falkland Islands).

2.1.2 Results

By adding together the most recent census data available obtained from the 1950's to 1973, an estimate of 273,000 individuals has been made for the whole range (except for the Chilean coast from Maiquillahue to the south, for which no counts or estimates have been as yet published).

Summarized Population of *Otaria*

Brazil	200-300 (1953)
Uruguay	30,000 (1954)
Argentina	168,270 (1953)
Falkland Islands	30,000 (1965)
Peru	20,000 (1966)
Chile (Northern)	25,000 (1965-1971)
	273,570

Sources: Aguayo & Maturana 1973; Carrara 1954; Grimwood 1968, 1969; Laws 1973; Piazza 1959; Strange 1972, 1973; Vaz-Ferreira 1976; Ximenez 1964.

2.1.3 Trends in abundance

In many areas, commercial exploitation by man and killing by fishermen have greatly reduced the number of animals. Many island and shore areas populated by sea lions in historic times are now deserted by them. Unknown causes have resulted in other populations being reduced. In 1964-1965 there was a maximum of 30,000 animals on the Falkland Islands (Strange 1972). In the early 1930's the number was estimated at 375,000 (Hamilton 1939). In some areas, however, increases have been reported. Populations of the Falkland Islands have been historically reduced, while Uruguay populations appear stable. There are no comparative data on populations of Chile and Argentina. Peruvian populations although historically reduced, have increased since the termination of extensive exploitation.

2.2 Rates

2.2.1 Reproductive

Age of sexual maturity:

- females, age 4
- males, age 5 and 6 (both unconfirmed).

Pregnancy rate: no data

Births: In Uruguay majority between 25 december and 15 January

Lactation: 6-12 months; rarely a female may nurse both a newborn pup and a yearling

Mating: a few days after parturition

Gestation: almost 1 year; delay of implantation — unknown

Longevity: 20 years (captivity records, Flower 1931).

2.2.2 Natural Mortality

Adults — no data

Pups — mortality from 2 % to 50 % depending on crowding and also the activity of subadult males aggressively killing pups on the rookery (Vaz-Ferreira 1965).

2.2.3 Harvesting

In Uruguay, where the number of pups born in 1956, was 9116 (Vaz-Ferreira, 1976) and present estimated number of births is 11,000 annually (I. Ximénez, Personal communication) there is an annual harvest of approximately 3,000 young sea lions for the garment industry (average 3.50 for the last five years).

The Argentine sea lion colonies are under the provincial administrations, and no killing is now allowed.

In the Falkland Islands the harvest has been stopped. In Chile, sea lion killing is not allowed without a special permit. In Peru, some exploitation is believed to occur.

Probably in all areas in which fishing occurs some sea lions are killed in fishing gear conflicts with fishermen.

3 Trophic Relationship

3.1 Food and Feeding

3.1.1 Food Habits

Some feeding takes place in shallow

water down to 30 m deep and within 5 miles of shore.

This species is known to take advantage of fish caught on commercial long line set gear and in gill nets.

3.1.2 Food base

The species is considered an opportunistic feeder and although little is known, stomach contents indicate that small schooling fish, such as anchovies, *Engraulis anchovita*, and bottom fish are important to the diet; squid are also frequently eaten. (Summary of references in Vaz-Ferreira 1976.)

Various people have observed sea lions eating penguins. (Hamilton 1934; Boswall 1972).

3.1.3 Requirements and Utilization

Not known.

3.1.4 Changes in abundance of food supply

The competition between man and sea lions for food resources is apparent, but unstudied.

3.2 Competition and Predation

Although *Arctocephalus australis* occupies the same approximate range, there appears to be little competition for habitat (seasonal differences in breeding, different feeding areas, etc.) (Vaz-Ferreira & Sierra 1963).

Young animals are often predated on (in southern waters) by leopard seals, *Hydrurga leptonyx*, and all ages are subject to attack by sharks while killer whales, *Orcinus orca*, may take the larger animals.

4 Relation to Man

4.1 Values

4.1.1 Consumptive

Hides are used for heavy leather goods, blubber for oil and the meat is used for animal food. Pelts of pups are used for the fur garment industry.

Artifacts are sometimes made from teeth.

4.1.2 Low-consumptive

Since these sea lions adapt easily to captivity, many are displayed in zoos throughout the world. In certain areas, sea lion colonies on islands or the mainland are accessible and are the basis of some tourism.

4.2 Effects of Human Activities etc.

No data.

4.3 Management and conservation

At present, Uruguay annually harvests this species under government regulation. Other countries in the species' range have occasionally issued permits for infrequent harvests.

5 Threats to Stocks

None known, although data on pollutants and industrial effects have not been collected.

6 Research

6.1 Current Status

Research on ecology and ethology in Uruguay; population dynamics studies in Argentina.

6.2 Future Research

Morphological differences should be examined to determine the existence of local populations. Continued investigations of population dynamics and stock management would be beneficial. The relationship of this species to the commercial fisheries and its impact on the near shore environment is little understood at this time and may be of considerable importance.

References

AGUAYO, A., and R. MATURANA, Presencia del lobo marino comun (*Otaria flavescens*) en el litoral chileno. *Biol. Pesq., Santiago*, (6):45-75.
1973

BOSWALL, J., South American sea lion *Otaria byronia* as a predator on penguins. *Bull. Brit. Ornithol. Club*, 92(5):129-32.
1972

CARRARA, I.S., Observaciones sobre el estado actual de las poblaciones de pinnipedos de la Argentina. La Plata, Universidad Nacional de Eva Perón, Facultad de Ciencias Veterinarias, 17 p.
1954

FLOWER, S.S., Contributions to our knowledge of the duration of life in vertebrate animals. 5. Mammals. *Proc. Zool. Soc. Lond.*, 1931 (1):145-224.
1931

GRIMWOOD, I.R., endangered mammals in Peru. *Oryx*, 9(6):411-21.
1968

—, Notes on the distribution and status of some Peruvian mammals. *Publ. Am. Comm. Int. Wild. Life Protect. N.Y. Zool. Soc.*, (21):1-86.
1969

HAMILTON, J.E., The southern sea lion *Otaria byronia* (De Blainville). *Discovery Rep.*, 8:269-318.
1934

—, A second report on the southern sea lion, *Otaria byronia* (De Blainville). *Discovery Rep.*, 19:121-64.
1939

LAWS, R.M., The current status of seals in the Southern Hemisphere. *IUCN Publ. (New Ser.) Suppl. Pap.*, (39):147-61.
1973

PIAZZA, L.A., Los lobos marinos en el Peru. *Publ. Pesca Caza Minist. Agric. Lima*, (9):1-29.
1959

SCHEFFER, V.B., Seals, sea lions and walruses. A review of Pinnipedia. Stanford, California, Stanford Univ. Press, 179 p.
1958

STRANGE, I., Sealing industries of the Falkland Islands. *Falkland Isl. J.*, 1972:9 p.
1972

—, The silent ordeal of a South Atlantic archipelago. *Nat. Hist.*, 82:30-9.
1973

VAZ-FERREIRA, R., Comportamiento antisocial en machos sub adultos de *Otaria byronia* (de Blainville), (" lobo marino de un pelo "). *Rev. Fac. Hum. Cienc. Montev.*, 22:203-7.
1965

—, Ecología terrestre y marina de los pinnipedios del Atlántico Sudoccidental. *An. Acad. Bras. Ciênc.*, 37 Supl.: 179-91.
1965a

—, Behaviour of the southern sea lions, *Otaria flavescens* (Shaw) in the Uruguayan Islands. *Rapp. P.-V. Réun. CIEM*, 169:219-27.
1975

—, Factors affecting numbers of sea lions and fur seals on the Uruguayan Islands. *Rapp. P.-V. Réun. CIEM*, 169:257-62.
1975a

VAZ-FERREIRA, R., *Otaria flavescens* (Shaw) South American sea lion. Paper presented to the Scientific Consultation on the Conservation and Management of Marine Mammals and their Environment, Bergen, Norway, 31 August-9 September, 1976. Rome, FAO, ACMRR/MM/SC 48:20 p.
1976

VAZ-FERREIRA, R., and E. PALERM, Efectos de los cambios meteorologicos sobre agrupaciones terrestres de pinnipedios. *Rev. Fac. Hum. Cienc. Montev.*, 19:281-93.
1961

VAZ-FERREIRA, R., and B. SIERRA, Estructura de una agrupación social reproductora de *Otaria byronia* (de Blainville) representación gráfica. *Rev. Fac. Hum. Cienc. Montev.*, 19:253-60.
1961

—, Tolerancia en grupos biespecificos de pinnipedios. *Proc. Int. Congr. Zool.*, 15:250 (abstr.).
1963

WELLINGTON, G.M., and TJ. DE VRIES, The South American sea lion, *Otaria byronia*, in the Galapagos Islands. *J. Mammal.*, 57(1):166-7.
1976

XIMENEZ, I., Estudio preliminar de la distribución geográfica actual de los pinnipedos en América Latina. *Bol. Inst. Biol. Mar., Mar del Plata*, (7):65-72.
1964

AUSTRALIAN SEA LION

J.B. King & B.J. Marlow

1 Description

1.1 Species identification

1.1.1 Family: Otariidae
Species: Neophoca cinerea (Peron 1816)

1.1.2 Size

- Newborn pups ca. 75 cm; 6.5 kg.
- Adult males ca. 2 m.
- Adult females ca. 1.5 m.

Newborn pups are chocolate brown with a pale fawn crown. Adult females are silver grey dorsally, creamy yellow ventrally when newly moulted. The grey colour fades during the year to brownish. Subadult males are larger than adult females but lack the white head of the adult male. Adult males are dark blackish brown; a mane of longer, coarser hairs covers the shoulder area. There is a cream coloured area from the level of the eyes to the back of the head.

1.2 Stocks

1.2.1 Identification

There are no known differences between the groups living on Australian coast.

1.2.2 Distribution

Occurs in small groups on many of the Australian islands from Houtman's Abrolhos (28°S) in Western Australia to Kangaroo Island (138°E) in South Australia (Marlow & King 1974). Present in Jurien Bay, W.A. (Ford 1963), Cheyne Beach W.A. (Storr 1965), the Islands of the Recherche Archipelago W.A. (Serventy 1953) and in the Spencer Gulf area S.A. (Marlow 1968), particularly on Dangerous Reef. A small colony on the mainland at Point LaBat S.A.

There is no evidence of migration, nor of any seasonal movement, the animals moving out to sea to feed from the rookery. Present in the area throughout the year.

1.2.3 Structure of stocks

Males polygynous. Individuals sometime wander several miles inland. Establish territories on sandy beaches or smooth rock. These territories are not fixed and can be altered by environmental factors and location of females. Harem 4-6 or average 3 at Dangerous Reef (Marlow 1975).

2 Vital Parameters

2.1 Population size

2.1.1 Methods of estimation

Ground counts and tagging.

2.1.2 Results

These sea lions are not abundant, but the scattered nature of their living places makes accurate estimation of their numbers difficult. Relatively recent figures for isolated populations are: Recherche Islands ca 300 (Serventy 1953), Jurien Bay 200 (Ford 1963), Seal Bay, Kangaroo Island 350 (Ling & Walker 1976) Dangerous Reef ca 170 (King unpubl.). Possibly a total population of between 2-3000 animals may be present.

2.1.3 Trends in abundance

Used to be more abundant in recent historic times. Current trend not known, though possibly decreasing. Decline noted on west coast of Western Australia.

2.2 Rates

2.2.1 Reproduction

Age of sexual maturity:

- adult male probably more than 6 years (Marlow 1975),
- adult female 3 years (?).

Birth season: variable from October — December (Marlow 1975) in contrast to all other sea lions

Mating time: ca 6-7 days after parturition

Gestation: ca 12 months

Longevity: not known.

2.2.2 Natural mortality

Not known.

Intraspecific aggression causes pup mortality (Marlow 1975). Some late foetuses lost through abortion.

2.2.3 Harvesting, commercial and incidental kill

No commercial harvesting. Fishermen kill sea lions that are caught damaging nets.

3 Trophic relationships

3.1 Food and feeding

3.1.1 Food habits

Feed out at sea. Habits when feeding not recorded.

3.1.2 Food base

Known to eat local fish and squid. Some references to penguin eating (Jones 1925, Troughton 1957) but penguins probably form only a very small part of diet. Occasionally seen to eat fiddler crabs (*Trygonorhina*) at the surface. This crab is common in shallow coastal waters of South Australia.

3.1.3 Requirements and utilization

Not known.

3.1.4 Changes in abundance of food supply

No information.

3.2 Competition and predation

In the area of the Recherche Archipelago and in the Eyre Peninsula — Kangaroo Island area the distribution of the New Zealand fur seal (*Arctocephalus forsteri*) and the Australian sea lion overlap (King 1969). No interaction between the two seals is recorded. Sharks are the greatest predators on the sea lions, especially in the Dangerous Reef, S.A. area which is known for record sized White Pointers (*Carcharodon carcharias*).

4 Relations to man

4.1 Values

4.1.1 Consumptive

No present exploitation.

4.1.2 Low-consumptive

This sea lion is a most significant species as a tourist attraction in South Australia whose economic value to the state will increase as tourism expands. This has been shown by estimates of tourist expenditure at Seal Bay, Kangaroo Island (Stirling 1972). A non-breeding population there has become so accustomed to humans that tourists are able to mingle with the seals on the beach. Conducted tours began in 1955 and have increased recently. *Neophoca* is held in many zoos and aquaria in Australia and seems to be hardy and adaptable in confinement.

4.2 Effects of human activities other than exploitation

Continual harassment by tourists and

fishermen disturbs sea lions, but detailed information is not available.

4.3 Management and conservation

This sea lion is fully protected by State Legislation. However, one of its main breeding grounds Dangerous Reef, S.A. is not designated as a Fauna Reserve. Permits to take sea lions for scientific purposes and for displays are issued.

5 Threats to stock

None known.

6 Research

6.1 Current status

The South Australian Museum is conducting a tagging programme and population survey. The Australian Museum is involved in long term behavioural and anatomical work (Marlow 1975, King, 1977).

6.2 Recommendations for future research

All aspects of the biology of this sea lion need attention, especially the anomalous extended breeding season.

References

FORD, J., The reptilian fauna of the islands between 1963 Dongara and Lancelin, Western Australia. *West. Aust. Nat.*, 8:135-42.

JONES, F.W., The mammals of South Australia. 3. 1925 Adelaide.

KING, J.E., The identity of the fur seals of Australia. 1969 *Aust. J. Zool.*, 17:841-53.

—, Comparative anatomy of the major blood vessels of 1977 the sea lions *Neophoca* and *Phocarctos*. *J. Zool., Lond.*, 181.

LING, J.K., and G.E. WALKER, Seal studies in South 1976 Australia: progress report for 1975. *S. Aust. Nat.*, 50(4):59-68.

MARLOW, B.J., The sea lions of Dangerous Reef. *Aust.* 1968 *Nat. Hist.*, 1968, June issue:39-44.

—, The comparative behaviour of the Australasian sea 1975 lions *Neophoca cinerea* and *Phocarctos hookeri* (Pinnipedia: Otariidae). *Mammalia, Paris*, 39(2):159-230.

MARLOW, B.J., and J.E. KING, Sea lions and fur seals of 1974 Australia and New Zealand — the gowth of knowledge. *J. Aust. Mamm. Soc.*, 1(2):117-36.

SERVENTY, V.N., Mammals. *In* The archipelago of the 1953 Recherche. Pt. 4. *Rep. Aust. Geogr. Soc.*, (1).

STIRLING, I., The economic value and management of 1972 seals in South Australia. *Publ. Dep. Fish. Adelaide*, (2):11 p.

STORR, G.M., Notes on Bald Island and the adjacent 1965 mainland. *West. Aust. Nat.*, 9:187-96.

TROUGHTON, E., Furred animals of Australia. London, 1957 Angus and Robertson, 376 p.

HOOKER'S (NEW ZEALAND) SEA LION

B.J. Marlow & J.B. King

1 Description

1.1 *Species identification*

1.1.1 *Family:* Otariidae
Species: Phocarctos hookeri (Gray 1844)

1.1.2 ***Size***

- Newborn pups: ca 75 cm
- Adult males ca 2.2 m; 400 kg.
- Adult females ca 1.8 m; 230 kg.

Newborn pups are light chocolate brown with a light stripe down the nose, the light colour extending to the top of the head and nape of the neck. Adult females are silver grey dorsally and pale yellow ventrally. Adult males are dark blackish brown all over, with thicker coarser hair forming a mane over the shoulders.

1.2 *Stocks*

1.2.1 *Identification*

There is only a single stock of these sea lions.

1.2.2 *Distribution*

The main centre of the population is on the Auckland Islands, about 300 miles south of New Zealand, and in this area Sandy Bay on Enderby Island, and Dundas Island have probably the largest breeding colonies (Marlow 1975). A few pups may also be born on the Snares (Crawley & Cameron 1972) and on Campbell Island (Bailey & Sorensen 1962), and the sea lion may occur as a straggler on Macquarie Island (Csordas 1963). There is no evidence of any migration or seasonal movement though concentration of numbers takes place at the breeding season.

1.2.3 *Structure of stocks*

Males polygynous establishing territories on open sandy beaches. Less aggressive than *Neophoca.* Large numbers of static bachelor bulls (Marlow 1975).

2 Vital parameters

2.1 *Population size*

2.1.1 *Methods of estimation*

Ground counts.

2.1.2 *Results*

On Enderby Island the population is about 1000 animals, and estimates suggest about 2000 animals on Dundas Island (Best 1974). Probably under 50 animals occur on the Snares (Crawley and Cameron 1972). Including animals hauled out at various other points on the Auckland Islands, and a maximum of about 100 on Campbell Island, the total population is about 4000.

2.1.3 *Trends in abundance*

Little evidence of population trend, though probably maintaining numbers.

2.2 *Rates*

2.2.1 Reproduction

Age of sexual maturity:

- females, not known,
- males, estimated 6 years

(Marlow 1975).

Birth season: December and beginning January

Gestation: ca 12 months

Longevity: not known.

2.2.2 Natural mortality

Not known.

Accident and starvation seem to be main causes of mortality amongst pups (Marlow 1975).

2.2.3 Harvesting, commercial and incidental kill

No commercial harvesting.

3 Trophic relationships

3.1 Food and feeding

3.1.1 Food habits

Habits when feeding not recorded.

3.1.2 Food base

Stomach contents indicate they eat local cephalopods, prawns, crayfish, crabs * and fish (Yaldwyn 1958). Have been known to eat penguins but these probably do not form a large part of diet.

3.1.3 Requirements and utilization

Not known.

3.1.4 Changes in abundance of food supply

No information.

3.2 Competition and predation

The New Zealand fur seal *Arctocephalus forsteri* occurs in the same area as the sea lion, but the fur seal occurs on more rocky coasts and there is little interaction with it, or with visiting Leopard seals (*Hydrurga leptonyx*) or Elephant seals (*Mirounga leonina*).

It is possible that Killer whales take these sea lions, though there is no evidence for this.

* Including *Nectocarcinus antarcticus.*

4 Relations to man

4.1 Values

4.1.1 Consumptive

No present exploitation.

4.1.2 Low consumptive

None — too remote.

4.2 Effects of human activities other than exploitation

Relatively little. The Auckland Islands are a fauna reserve, and uninhabited. Other places where this sea lion occurs have limited human population. However, because the Auckland Islands are remote and uninhabited it is impossible to police the reserve. Some sea lions may well be shot by fishermen, but the greatest danger is probably the accessibility of the sea lions for use as crab bait. An initial trial of Japanese commercial crab fishing using ca 1000 traps was attempted in late 1973.

4.3 Management and conservation

Protected under New Zealand legislation, but implementation may be difficult.

5 Threats to stock

None, unless crab fishing is increased or becomes permanent in the Auckland Islands area.

6 Research

6.1 Current status

Sporadic work may take place on animals close to the New Zealand mainland, e.g. Crawley & Cameron (1972), but the remoteness of the Auckland Islands makes any sustained study difficult. A recent (1972-73) expedition to the Auckland Islands under the auspices of the Wildlife Service of the New Zealand Department of Internal Affairs has provided information for several papers on various aspects of the behaviour of the sea lion (Best 1974, Marlow 1974, Marlow 1975) and much material was collected which is in the process of being worked on (King, 1977).

6.2 Recommendations for future research

Most aspects of the life and morphology of this sea lion would benefit from further work, though there are difficulties due to the remoteness of the habitat. Special watch should be kept on any possible human predation involving the taking of sea lions for crab bait.

References

BAILEY, A.M., and J.H. SORENSEN, Subantarctic Campbell Island. *Proc. Denver Mus. Nat. Hist.*, 1962 10:305 p.

BEST, H.A., A preliminary report on the natural history and behaviour of Hooker's sea lion at Enderby Island, Auckland Islands, New Zealand, December 1972 to March 1973. *Fish. Tech. Rep. N.Z. Minist. Agric.*, (132):1-15. 1974

CRAWLEY, M.C., and D.B. CAMERON, New Zealand sea lions, *Phocarctos hookeri* on the Snares Islands. *N.Z.J. Mar. Freshwat. Res.*, 6 (1/2): 127-32. 1972

CSORDAS, S.E. , Sea lions on Macquarie Island. *Vict. Nat.*, 80:32-5. 1963

KING, J.E., Comparative anatomy of the major blood vessels of sea lions *Neophoca* and *Phocarctos. J. Zool., Lond.*, 181. 1977

MARLOW, B.J., Ingestion of placenta in Hooker's sea lion. *N.Z.J.Mar. Freshwat. Res.*, 8(1):233-8. 1974

—, The comparative behaviour of the Australasian sea lions *Neophoca cinerea* and *Phocarctos hookeri* (Pinnipedia Otariidae). *Mammalia, Paris*, 39(2):159-230. 1975

YALDWYN, J.C., Decapod Crustacea from Subantarctic seal and shag stomachs. *Rec. Dominion Mus., Wellington*, 3(2):121-7. 1958

ALASKAN OR NORTHERN FUR SEAL

R.H. LANDER

1 Description

1.1.1 Family: Otariidae
Species: Callorhinus ursinus (Linnaeus 1758)

1.1.2 Size

- Newborn: male - 0.66 m, 5.4 kg. (average); female - 0.63 m, 4.5 kg. (average)
- Adult males: 2.13 m, 182-272 kg. (average, range)
- Adult females: 1.42 m, 43-50 kg. (average, range).

(Marine Mammal Biological Laboratory 1969; Baker, Wilke and Balzo, 1970).

1.2 Stocks

1.2.1 Identification

Bases of stocks are: Pribilof Islands (U.S., eastern Bering Sea), Commander Islands (U.S.S.R., western Bering Sea), Robben Island (U.S.S.R., Sea of Okhotsk), Kuril Islands (U.S.S.R., western N. Pacific) and San Miguel Island (U.S., eastern north Pacific).

1.2.2 Distribution

Except for the small San Miguel population, the animals leave the islands during October-December and migrate south. Most of the Commander seals move down the Japanese coast in winter, while most Pribilof seals move down the North American coast. Some intermixture occurs at sea and on land. The Robben Island stock winters mainly in the Sea of Japan. Southern limits of migration are about 32°N on both sides of the Pacific. Females and young seals of both sexes make the longest migrations. Adult bulls tend to remain near the breeding islands but few have been taken in pelagic research collections.

1.2.3 Structure of stock (Kenyon, Scheffer & Chapman, 1954; Baker, Wilke & Balzo, 1970)

Animals of all herd elements (except harem bulls) are extremely gregarious while on land. At sea, however, less than 1 % of the animals sighted are in groups of 7 or more, about 10 % in groups of 4-6, 12 % in groups of 3, 28 % in pairs, and 48 % single; the proportion of solitary animals (mainly nursing females) is even higher near the breeding islands in summer despite their high density (H. Kajimura, personal communication). The species is highly polygamous (but see pp. 35-39 of Peterson 1968). Breeding rookeries contain adult territorial harem bulls, adult females in harems ranging in size from one animal to over 100, and newborn pups. Sub-adult males appear on separate hauling grounds adjacent to the rookeries in generally decreasing order of age during June-October. Some non-harem females appear on the hauling grounds also. Most yearlings of both sexes and many two-year olds apparently spend the entire years at sea.

Sources: (North Pacific Fur Seal Commission 1962, 1969, 1971, 1975; Taylor, Fujinaga and Wilke, 1955).

2 Vital parameters

2.1 Population size

2.1.1 Methods of estimation

Only the pups are all on land at any one time, hence censusing from land counts is relatively straightforward and accurate on smaller rookeries. Pups on larger rookeries must be estimated by marking and by later counting of marked and unmarked animals. Aerial photography has not been successful because of high pup density and limited image resolution. Harem bulls are also counted.

Sources: (Kenyon, Scheffer and Chapman, 1954; Chapman, 1964; Chapman and Johnson, 1968; Nikulin, 1971).

2.1.2 Results

Pribilof stock	1,300,000
Commander stock	265,000
Robben stock	165,000
Kuril Stock	33,000
San Miguel stock	2,000
Total	1,765,000

Sources: (Chapman 1964; Johnson 1975; Lander & Kajimura, 1976).

2.1.3 Trend in abundance

All stocks were greatly reduced at the end of the 19th century. The 1911 Treaty prohibited pelagic sealing and permitted repopulation. Abundance of the Pribilof stock was experimentally reduced during 1956-63 by killing females to reduce overcrowding on the rookeries and to improve pup survival and yield. The yield did not increase and this practice was ended after 1968.

Sources: (Kenyon, Scheffer and Chapman, 1954; Nikulin 1971; NOAA, 1973).

2.2 Rates

2.2.1 Reproduction

Age at sexual maturity:

- females: three years - Asian; four years - N. American.
- males: four-five years, but sociological maturity and breeding is at 9-15 years.

Peak breeding is at 7-14 years for females.

Pregnancy rates, 60 per cent on N. American side; slightly higher on Asian side.

Birth season: late June-early August.

Lactation period: approximately four months.

Mating: late June and July (one week after birth of pup).

Gestation: 51 weeks, includes a delay of implantation of 3·5—4 months, to early November.

Longevity: about 25 years.

Sources: Baker, Wilke and Balzo, 1970; North Pacific Fur Seal Commission, 1962; Northwest Fisheries Center, Marine Mammal Division 1975; Craig, 1964; Peterson, 1965, 1968; Chapman, 1964).

2.2.2 Natural mortality

Pup mortality on land averages about ten per cent but can vary widely (Kenyon, Scheffer & Chapman, 1954; Marine Mammal Biological Laboratory 1971; North Pacific Fur Seal Commission 1962, 1969, 1971, 1975). Hookworms, apparent malnutrition and an infection (leptospirosis) caused by a spirochaete bacterium account for 2/3 of all pup mortality on the Pribilofs (Northwest Fisheries Center, Marine Mammal Division 1975). Mortality is about 50 per cent in the first year of life and 20 per cent annually for ages 1-3; 20 per cent has been used for males of 3-7 years in population modelling; mortality for adult females is about 11 per cent (Chapman 1964). Mortality is about 38 per cent annually for breeding males (Johnson 1968). From only the known numbers of pups in a year class and the resulting commercial kill by age and sex (i.e., mark recoveries from the kill are not required) a method is available for approximating total natural mortality until the age of first kill and average annual natural mortality during the ages of kill; for the 1961-66 year classes of Pribilof Islands males, natural survival was

31-42 % during ages 0-2 years and 84-89 %: annually during ages 2-5 years (Lander 1975).

2.2.3 Harvesting

Rates for Robben Island are 22-44 per cent of male pups born; for Commander Islands, 32-42 per cent, and for Pribilof, 20-31 per cent. The commercial kill of males of ages 2-5 averages about 30,000 on the Pribilofs. Because of a decline in number of pups born and of adult males on the Commanders and Robben Islands in recent years, the kill has been restricted from about 9,000 to 2,000 and from about 7,000 to 3,000, respectively.

(North Pacific Fur Seal Commission 1972, 1973, 1974, 1975, 1975a).

3 Trophic relationships

3.1 Food and feeding

3.1.1 Food habits

Fur seals feed during the evening, night and early morning and usually sleep during the day. They have been recorded to depths of 240 feet with the presence of " seal fish " (*Bathylagus collorbinus*) remains indicating that at least some food is otained in deep water. The most commonly eaten items are squid, herring, pollack, and lantern fish. Other species are also frequently found.

3.1.2 Food base

Food varies with season, age, and area. The principal items by volume are squid, hake, anchovy, herring, sandlance, capelin, walleye pollack, Atka mackerel and deepsea smelt.

3.1.3 Requirements and utilization

Fur seals eat about ten per cent of their body weight per day. The total annual consumption of the Pribilof stock is estimated to be 965,000 tonnes of fish.

3.1.4 Changes in abundance of food supply

Major changes in the Bering Sea are recognized to be taking place through intensive fisheries. Research to clarify the relationship of this to fur seal food habits and survival is in an early stage.

3.2 Competition and predation

Fur seals prey at times on the same items as sea lions and harbor seals, particularly on herring and salmon along the British Columbia coast in winter. No firm data exist however, on the competitive aspects of this feeding. Nothing definite is known on predators of fur seals, although sharks and killer whales are probably involved. Steller sea lions are known to prey on fur seal pups.

(North Pacific Fur Seal Commission 1962, 1969, 1971, 1975; Sanger 1974; Spaulding 1964; Keyes 1968.)

4 Relation to man

4.1 Values

4.1.1 Consumptive

Pelts are auctioned publicly in the U.S.; they presently sell for about $89 (Personal communication, Pribilof Islands Programme Office, National Marine Fisheries Service, Seattle, Washington). Thus the annual *auctioned* value of these pelts is roughly 30,000 × 89 - $2,670,000. There is presently no trend in demand for U.S. pelts. The smaller (grey) skins of moulted male pups were taken experimentally on the Commander Islands and Robben Island in 1972 and 1973, and were auctioned in Leningrad for an average of $68; demand for these pelts is good (North Pacific Fur Seal Commission 1975a).

4.1.2 Low-consumptive

There is a developing tourist industry on the Pribilof Islands (St. Paul) where several hundred tourists view the rookeries annually. The animals have a high aesthetic and educational value.

4.2 Effects of human activities other than exploitation

Man-made debris such as scraps of fish nets, twine and plastic wrapping bands are having a gradually increasing effect. Between 1967 and 1973 the occurrence of seals entangled in fishery-related debris increased from 0.17 to 0.51 per cent of harvested seals on the Pribilof Islands (Sanger 1974a). Approximately 3,500 fur seals are reported (Fukuhara 1974) to be taken annually by high seas gill net fishing for salmon. Acquisition of accurate data is not good and needs improvement; there is some utilization of animals as food by Japanese fishermen and this accidental catch may be closer to 7,000 seals annually (Nishiwaki, personal communication).

4.3 Management and conservation (Baker, Wilke and Balzo, 1970)

Management is under rigid and well enforced control. It has, as noted above, included the killing of females as a management tool in striving for MSY. There are size limits for the most desirable pelts which restrict the kill mainly to ages 3-4 years. Drives on the Pribilofs are carefully carried out to ensure that stress is minimized; veterinary inspection to ensure humane and tidy killing occurs. The kill at present is not managed with a view to relating it to commercial fisheries. The resource is managed under international control and agreement through the North Pacific Fur Seal Commission, to which the U.S.A., U.S.S.R., Japan, and Canada belong.

5 Threats to stock

Reduction in abundance of food supply may pose a threat to continued present levels of fur seal abundance. Oil exploration is planned for the Bering Sea and could pose an ecological problem.

6 Research

6.1 Current status (North Pacific Fur Seal Commission 1973; NOAA, 1973)

A long term international research program is in effect under the auspices of the North Pacific Fur Seal Commission. The basis for a recently expanded research program is the fact that ocean survival to age 3 years has declined in recent year classes. The commission set aside St. George Island in 1973, as an area of intensive research.

6.2 Future

Studies are being planned to investigate the genetic effect of past management practices, i.e., of selection for small males. Future emphasis will be placed on trophic relationships with fisheries and other marine mammals. At an early stage is a long term study of growth rates (from stained sections of canine teeth) in different year classes.

References

BAKER, R.C., F. WILKE C.H. BALZO, The northern fur seal. *Circ. USFWS,* (336):19 p.
1970

CRAIG, A.M., Histology of reproduction and the estrus cycle in the female fur seal, *Callorhinus ursinus. J. Fish. Res. Board Can.*, 21(4):773-811.
1964

CHAPMAN, D.G., A critical study of Pribilof fur seal population estimates. *Fish. Bull. USFWS,* 63:657-69.
1964

CHAPMAN, D.G., and A.M. JOHNSON, Estimation of fur seal pup population by randomized sampling. *Trans. AM. Fish. Soc.*, 97(3):264-70.
1968

FUKUHARA, F.M., Estimated mortality of seabirds, fur seal, and porpoise in Japanese salmon drift net fisheries and sea lions in the eastern Bering Sea trawl fishery. Seattle, Wash., NOAA/NMFS, Northwest Fisheries Center, 12 p. (unpubl. MS).
1974

JOHNSON, A.M., Annual mortality of territorial male fur seals and its management significance. *J. Wildl. Manage.*, 72:94-9.
1968

—, The status of northern fur seal populations. *Rapp. P.-V. Réun. CIEM*, 169:263-6.
1975

KENYON, K.W., V.B. SCHEFFER and D.G. CHAPMAN, A
1954 population study of the Alaska fur seal herd. *Spec. Sci. Rep. USFWS (Wildl.)*, (12):77 p.

KEYES, M.C., The nutrition of pinnipeds. *In* The beha-
1968 viour and physiology of pinnipeds, edited by R.J. Harrison *et al.*, New York, Appleton-Century-Crofts, pp. 359-95.

LANDER, R.H., Method of determining natural mortality
1975 in the northern fur seal (*Callorhinus ursinus*) from known pup and kill by age and sex. *J. Fish. Res. Board Can.*, 32(12):2447-52.

LANDER, R.H., and H. KAJIMURA, Status of northern fur
1976 seals. Paper presented to the Scientific Consultation on the Conservation and Management of Marine Mammals and Their Environment, Bergen Norway, 31 August-9 September, 1976, Rome, FAO, ACMRR/MM/SC/34.

Marine Mammal Biological Laboratory, Fur seal inve-
1969 stigations, 1966. *Spec. Sci. Rep. USFWS (Fish.)*, (584):123 p.

—, Fur seal investigations, 1969. *Spec. Sci. Rep.*
1971 *USFWS (Fish.)*, (628):90 p.

NIKULIN, P.G., Present condition and growth perspecti-
1971 ves of the Commander Islands fur seal population. *In* Pinnipeds of the North Pacific, edited by V.A. Arsen'ev and K.I. Panin, Jerusalem, Israel Program for Scientific Translations, IPST Cat. No. 5798:28-38 (Transl. of *Tr. VNIRO*, 68(1968)).

NOAA, Administration of the marine mammal protec-
1973 tion act of 1972, December 21, 1972, to June 21, 1973. Washington, NOAA/NMFS (Reprint. from *U.S. Fed. Reg.*, 38(147):20564-601 (1973)).

North Pacific Fur Seal Commission, Report on investi-
1962 gations from 1958-1961. Tokyo, Kenkyusha Co., 183 p.

—, Report on investigations from 1964-1966. Tokyo,
1969 Kenkyusha Co., 161 p.

—, Report on investigations from 1962 to 1963. Tokyo,
1971 Kenkyusha Co., 96 p.

—, Proceedings of the fifteenth annual meeting. Wa-
1972 shington, D.C., NPFSC, 36 p.

—, Proceedings of the sixteenth annual meeting. Wa-
1973 shington, D.C., NPFSC, 36 p.

—, Proceedings of the seventeenth annual meeting.
1974 Washington, D.C., NPFSC, 47 p.

—, Report on investigations from 1967 through 1972.
1975 Hyattsville, Maryland, Dependable Printing Co., 212 p.

—,Proceedings of the eighteenth annual meeting. Wa-
1975a shington, D.C., NPFSC, 40 p.

Northwest Fisheries Center, Marine Mammal Division,
1975 Fur seal investigations, 1974. Seattle, Washington, NOAA/NMFS, Northwest Fisheries Center, 125 p. (processed).

PETERSON, R.S., Behaviour of the northern fur seal. Dr.
1965 Sci. Thesis, Johns Hopkins University, Baltimore, Maryland, 208 p. (processed).

—, Social behaviour in pinnipeds. *In* The behaviour and
1968 physiology of pinnipeds, edited by R.J. Harrison *et al.*, New York, Appleton-Century-Crofts, pp. 3-53.

SANGER, G.A., A preliminary look at marine mammal
1974 food chain relationships in Alaskan waters. Seattle, Washington, NOAA/NMFS, Northwest Fisheries Center, Marine Mammal Division, 129 P. (processed).

—, On the effect of fish net scraps and other oceanic
1974a debris on northern fur seals. Seattle, Washington, NOAA/NMFS, Northwest Fisheries Center, Marine Mammal Division, 4 p. (processed).

SCHEFFER, V.B., Seals, sea lions and walruses: a review
1958 of the Pinnipedia. Stanford, California, Stanford Univ. Press, 179 p.

SPAULDING, D.J., Comparative feeding habits of the fur
1964 seal, sea lion, and harbour seal on the British Columbia coast. *Bull. Fish. Res. Board Can.*, (146):1-52.

TAYLOR, F.H.C., M. FUJINAGA and F. WILKE, Distribu-
1955 tion and food habits of the fur seals of the North Pacific Ocean. Report of Cooperative Investigations by Governments of Canada, Japan, and United States of America, February-July 1952. Washington, D.C., U.S. Government Printing Office, 86 p.

GUADALUPE FUR SEAL

C.L. HUBBS

1 Description

1.1 Species identification

1.1.1 *Family:* Otariidae
Species: Arctocephalus townsendi Merriam 1897

Some authorities regard *Arctocephalus townsendi* as a synonym, or as subspecies, of *Arctocephalus philippii* (Peters, 1866), of the Juan Fernandes Islands far off Chile; Repenning, Peterson & Hubbs (1971), recognized both as species, though closely related.

1.1.2 *Size*

- Newborn pups 60 cm (?)
- Adult males definitely less than 200.6 cm (size of largest *Arctocephalus philippii* recorded).

Nearly black, becoming light colored below and on chest, especially in adult males. Snout elongate, so that face resembles that of a collie dog (especially in males). Flippers elongate, often held overlapping when animal lies at surface. Guard hairs, over fur, conspicuously long.

1.2 Stocks

1.2.1 *Identification*

Only one stock extant.

1.2.2 *Distribution*

Breeding range now restricted to central part of east coast of Isla Guadalupe, Baja California, at ca. 28°N, ca. 140 miles west of Baja California mainland (Peterson *et al.* 1968). Formerly occurred and presumably bred on Channel Islands of southern California. Increasing numbers of strays are being noted on these islands, especially on San Miguel, and there have been reports, none well substantiated, of some on the west coast and even the Cape region of Baja California.

1.2.3 *Structure of stocks*

Scattered, with concentrations becoming obvious only on the very narrow, exclusively rocky shoreline, especially in recesses and caves. Young largely congregate in " the Nursery ", in 3 small, connected tidepools just north of " Red Cinder Cone ". Almost never seen on open ocean.

2 Vital parameters

2.1 Population size

2.1.1 *Methods of estimation*

Direct counts, requiring *very* close inshore transport in small boats, with landing of party where rocky shore permits transit on foot, checking recesses and caves.

2.1.2 *Results*

Recent careful counts during the summer breeding period have yielded estimates of ca. 500 during breeding season, with minor allowance for some still, or temporarily, at sea. Some very recent observations suggest a larger population.

2.1.3 Trends in abundance

There appears to be scarcity of information on the abundance of the species prior to and during large-scale commercial sealing, though there are records of early sealing on North Pacific islands even south of Mexico, and of late commercial sealing in to the early occupation of California by Americans. The last reported kill for fur was in 1928. The population prior to the near extermination by the commercial sealers is thought to have been high, some think as high as 200,000, on Isla Guadalupe alone. The evidence stems in part from the much better documentation on fur seals in the Southern Hemisphere, especially of the teeming abundance of the elated *Arctocephalus philippii* on the Juan Fernandes Islands off Chile (Hubbs & Norris 1971). The recent rediscovery and initial resurgence of the two species, furthermore, is strikingly parallel. The other line of evidence, that of the widespread high polishing of the rock surfaces on Isla Guadalupe, close to sea level, definitely suggests vast early concentrations, comparable with those observed by early explorers on Juan Fernandez Islands.

Following the acquisition of 2 specimens for the San Diego Zoo and the reported intended extinction of the remnant on Isla Guadalupe in 1928, it was generally considered that *Arctocephalus townsendi* had become extinct. In 1949, however, Bartholomew (1950) photographed a single, rather emaciated bull, with sea lions, on San Nicolas Island, southern California. An effort by him and Hubbs to relocate the species on Isla Guadalupe in 1950 failed, but in 1954 14 individuals were found by Hubbs in one cave on this island (Hubbs, 1956, 1956a). Since then, the increase in population on the island has been documented, along with, quite recently, the discovery on shore of strays as far southward as Caleta Melpomene at the south end of the island, and very close to the extreme north end of the east shore.

2.2 Rates

No data.

3 Trophic relationship

No data.

4 Relations to man

4.1 Values

4.1.1 Consumptive

It has been assumed that the fur of this species is somewhat inferior to that of the northern fur seal (*Callorhinus ursinus*).

4.1.2 Low-consumptive

The Guadalupe fur seal supplements the northern elephant seal as a major tourist attraction, particularly on cruises from San Diego.

4.2 Effects of human activities other than exploitation

Effects very limited, because of protection by Mexican authorities and by tour leaders; also because the tour ships approach shore almost entirely to see the elephant seal rookeries, which are located along sandy to stony beaches, whereas the fur seals are restricted to the rough rock shores (with almost complete ecological segregation).

4.3 Management and conservation

No relaxation of the protection of the fur seal seems indicated. Probably it should be suggested to the Mexican authorities and to tour operators that it would be desirable (or even mandatory) to forbid operations very close to the rocky shorelines of Isla de Guadalupe, and particularly to prohibit landings there (except by scientific permit).

5 Threat to stock

Relatively small, but see 4.3.

6 Research

6.1 Current status

Plans are under consideration to carry on and expand the census operations by Hubbs and others. Others with marine mammals interests are also concerned with the species on Isla de Guadalupe and are keeping a watch on the increasing returns of the species to the Channel Islands of California.

6.2 Recommendations for future research

A continuation and expansion of activities mentioned under 6.1.

References

ANTHONY, A.W., Expedition to Guadalupe Island, Mexico, in 1922. The birds and mammals. *Proc. Calif. Acad. Sci.*, 14:306-8.
1925

BARTHOLOMEW, G.A., JR., A male Guadalupe fur seal on San Nicolas Island, California. *J. Mammal.*, 32:175-80.
1950

BOWER, W.T., Guadalupe fur seals. *In* Alaska fishery and fur seal industries in 1928. Appendix to Report of the U.S. Commissioner of Fisheries for Fiscal Year 1929. *U.S. Bur. Fish. Doc.*, (1064): 324-5.
1929

GRINNEL, J., Review of the recent mammal fauna of California. *Univ. Calif. Publ. Zool.*, (40):71-234.
1933

HANNA, G.D., Expedition to Guadalupe Island, Mexico, in 1922. General report. *Proc. Calif. Acad. Sci.*, 14:217-75.
1925

HANNA, G.D., and A.W. ANTHONY, A cruise among desert islands. *Nat. Geogr. Mag.*, 44:70-99.
1923

HUBBS, C.L., The Guadalupe fur seal still lives: *Zoonoz San Diego Zool. Soc.*, 29(12):6-9.
1956

—, Back from oblivion, Guadalupe fur seal: still a living species. *Pac. Discovery*, 9:14-21.
1956a

HUBBS, C.L., and K.S. NORRIS, Original teeming abundance, supposed extinction, and survival of the Juan Fernandez fur seal. *In* Antarctic Pinnipedia, edited by W.H. Burt. *Antarct. Res. Ser.*, 18:35-52.
1971

HUEY, L.M., Past and present status of the northern fur seal with a note on the Guadalupe fur seal. *J. Mammal.*, 11:188-94.
1930

LLUCH BELDA, D., L. IRVING and N. PILSON, Algunas observaciones sobre mamiferos acuáticos. Censo de la foca fina de Guadalupe *(Arctocephalus townsendi). Publ. Inst. Nac. Invest. Biol.-Pesq., Mex.*, (10B):71.
1964

MERRIAM, C.H., A new fur seal or sea-bear (*Arctocephalus townsendi*) from Guadalupe Island, off Lower California. *Proc. Biol. Soc. Wash.*, 11:175-8.
1897

PETERSON, R.S., *et al.*, The Guadalupe fur seal: habitat, behaviour, population rise, and field identification. *J. Mammal.*, 49:665-75.
1968

REPENNING, C.A., R.S. PETERSON and C.L. HUBBS, Contributions to the systematics of the southern fur seals, with particular reference to the Juan Fernandez and Guadalupe species. *In* Antarctic Pinnipedia, edited by W.H. Burt. *Antarct. Res. Ser.*, 18:1-34.
1971

STARKS, E.C., Records of the capture of fur seals on land in California. *Calif. Fish Game*, 8:155-60.
1972

THOBURN, W.W., Report on an expedition in search of the fur seal of Guadalupe Island, Lower California, June 1897. Including a survey of the island and notes on the animal and plant life of the region. *In* The fur seals and fur-seal islands of the North Pacific Ocean, edited by D.S. Jordan, Washington, Government Printing Office, Pt. 3:275-83.
1899

TOWNSEND, C.H., Pelagic sealing. With notes on the fur seals of Guadalupe, the Galapagos, and Labos Islands. *In* The fur seals and fur-seal islands of the North Pacific Ocean, edited by D.S. Jordan, Washington, Government Printing Office, Pt. 3:233-74.
1899

—, Mammals collected in Lower California, with descriptions of new species. *Bull. Am. Mus. Nat. Hist.*, 31:117-30.
1912

—, Voyage of the ALBATROSS to the Gulf of California in 1911. *Bull. Am. Mus. Nat. Hist.*, 35:399-475.
1916

TOWNSEND, C.H., The northern elephant seal and the Guadalupe fur seal. *Nat. Hist.*, 24:567-78.
1924

—, Reappearance of the Lower California fur seal. *Bull.*
1928 *N.Y. Zool. Soc.*, 31:173-4.

—, Guadalupe fur seal in 1929. *Bull. N.Y. Zool. Soc.*,
1930 33:32.

—, The fur seal of the Californian islands. *Zoologica,*
1931 *(N.Y.)*, 9:443-57.

Wegeforth, H.M., The Guadalupe fur seal *(Arctoce-*
1928 *phalus townsendi). Zoonoz, San Diego Zool. Soc.*, 3(3):4-9.

Anon., A trip to Guadalupe. *Zoonoz, San Diego Zool.*
1930 *Soc.*, 5(5):5-7.

JUAN FERNANDEZ FUR SEAL

A. AGUAYO L.

1 Description

1.1 Species identification

1.1.1 Family: Otariidae
Species: Arctocephalus philippii (Peters, 1866)

The taxonomic position of the Juan Fernandez Fur Seal is in dispute (Aguayo *et al.* 1971, Aguayo & Torres, in preparation); the view of Repenning, Peterson & Hubbs (1971) that the Juan Fernandez and Guadalupe Fur Seals belong to the genus *Arctocephalus* is accepted. Sivertsen (1954) showed that each of the animals belongs to a separate species namely, *A. philippii* and *A. townsendii*. Repenning, Peterson & Hubbs (1971) pointed out that the *philippii-townsendii* complex is in some ways distinctive from all oher members of the genus *Arctocephalus.*

1.1.2 Size

- Newborn pups: no data.
- Adult males: approx. 200 cm, 140 kg (estimated. See also Hubbs and Norris 1971)
- Adult females: approx. 140 cm, 50 kg (estimated).

1.2 Stocks

1.2.1 Identification
No separate stocks identified.

1.2.2 Distribution
Up to the present mainly confined to the three islands of the Juan Fernandez Archipelago (Hubbs & Norris 1971; Sivertsen 1954; Aguayo & Maturana 1970; Aguayo 1971; Repenning, Peterson & Hubbs 1971) Desventuradas Islands (San Ambrosio and San Felix Islands) off the coast of central Chile (Aguayo & Torres, in preparation).

1.2.3 Structure of stocks
No data.

2 Vital parameters

2.1 Population size

2.1.1 Method of estimation
Direct surface count (Aguayo & Maturana 1970; Aguayo 1971; Aguayo, Maturana & Torres 1971).

2.1.2 Results
The first complete census of this species gave a figure of about 427-259 animals on Juan Fernandez Archipelago in March 1969 (Aguayo & Maturana 1970; Aguayo 1971), and the second gave a figure of about 705-750 animals on the same Archipelago in February, 1970 (Aguayo, Maturana & Torres 1971; Aguayo 1973). However, the count in 1970 may not indicate the actual increase (Aguayo, Maturna & Torres 1971; Hubbs & Norris 1971).

The fur seals counted at San Ambrosio numbered only two and were the first reported there for perhaps a century and a half (Gilmore 1971). According to the fishermen on the coast of San Ambrosio Island there are some caves with underwater entrances; these may serve as a natural refuge to the fur seals, and may have been the reason why more animals were not found with Dr. Gilmore in June 1970 (Aguayo, unpublished).

2.1.3 *Trend in abundance*

Extremely abundant during the 16th and 17th centuries. No direct figures available, but several million were slaughtered up to the end of the first quarter of the 19th century (Hubbs & Norris 1971). Commercially extinct by 1824 (King 1964). Thought in recent years to be extinct (Luke 1953, cited by Scheffer 1958; and King 1964), but rediscovered by Prof. N. Bahamonde from Chile (Aguayo & Maturana 1970; Aguayo 1971) on 2 December 1965, and by Dr. O.T. Solbrig and Dr. J.W. Walker from U.S.A. (Hubbs & Norris 1971) on Isla Alejandro Selkirk (ex-Mas a Fuera); and by D.W. Bourne on the Isla Robinson Crusoe (ex-Mas a Tierra) on 27 January 1966 (Hubbs & Norris 1971). However, the fishermen of Juan Fernandez Archipelago always knew of the existence of the so-called " Lobo Fino ", which was present in small numbers on these islands (Aguayo, Maturana & Torres 1971; Hubbs & Norris 1971).

2.2 *Rates*

Aguayo, Maturana & Torres (1971) have calculated a provisional annual increase of about 70-80 animals for all the Juan Fernandez Archipelago, equivalent to about 16-17 % yearly, without taking into account the small illegal catch made by the fishermen.

3 Trophic relationship

According to the fishermen of the Juan Fernandez Archipelago this species feeds on several kinds of fish, cephalopods and on local lobster (*Jasus frontalis*). The only stomach examined by us in 1969 was empty (Aguayo, unpublished).

4 Relation to Man

4.1.1 *Consumptive*

No data on commercial value, but probably its fur is a little lower quality to other southern fur seals.

4.1.2 *Low-consumptive*

Aesthetic value for tourists.

4.2 *Effects of human activities other than exploitation*

There is a small catch for lobster bait and for illicit fur market (Hubbs & Norris 1971; Aguayo & Maturana 1973).

4.3 *Management and Conservation*

Prohibition of poaching enacted in 1965 (Aguayo 1971) and in 1970 (Aguayo, Maturana & Torres 1971).

5 Threats to stocks

Vulnerable, but the populations are recovering although do not yet approach optimum numbers.

6 Research

6.1 *Current status*

Dr. Götz Schürholz from FAO, Santiago, and Mr. G. Mann, Jr., have completed a study on the behaviour and habits of this species (D. Torres, personal communication, May 1976). On the other hand Aguayo and Torres have also in preparation a paper on this species since 1971.

6.2 *Recommendations*

All aspects of the Juan Fernandez fur seal biology need further investigations.

References

AGUAYO, L.A., The present status of the Juan Fernandez fur seal. *K. Nor. Vidensk. Selsk. Skr.*, 1971(1):1-4.
1971

—, The Juan Fernandez fur seal. *IUCN Publ. (New Ser.) Suppl. Pap.*, (39):140-3.
1973

AGUAYO, L.A., and R. MATURANA, Primer censo de lobos finos en el Archipielago de Juan Fernandez. *Biol. Pesq., Santiago*, (4):3-15.
1970

—, Presencia del lobo marino comun (*Otaria flavescens*) en el litoral chileno. 1. Arica a Punta Maiquillahue. *Biol. Pesa., Santiago*, (6):45-75.
1973

AGUAYO, L.A., and D, TORRES, Contribution to the present knowledge of the Juan Fernandez fur seal (in preparation).

AGUAYO, L.A., R. MATURANA and D. TORRES, El lobo fino de Juan Fernandez. *Rev. Biol. Mar., Valparaiso*, 14(3):135-49.
1971

GILMORE, R.M., Observations on marine mammals and birds off the coast of southern and central Chile, early winter 1970. *Antarct. J.U.S.*, 6(1):10-1.
1971

HUBBS, C.L., and K.S. NORRIS, Original teeming abundance, supposed extinction and survival of the Juan Fernandez fur seal. *Antarct. Res. Ser.*, (18):35-52.
1971

KING, J.E., Seals of the world. London, British Museum (Natural History), 154 p.
1964

REPENNING, C.A., R.S. PETERSON and C.L. HUBBS, Contributions to the systematics of the southern fur seals, with particular reference to the Juan Fernandez and Guadalupe species. *Antarct. Res. Ser.*, (18): 1-34.
1971

SCHEFFER, V.B., Seals, sea lions and walruses: a review of the Pinnipedia. Stanford, California, Stanford Univ. Press, 179 p.
1958

SIVERTSEN, E., A survey of the eared seals (family Otariidae) with remarks on the Antarctic seals collected by M/K NORVEGIA in 1928-1929. Det Norske Vedenskaps-Akademi i Oslo. *Sci. Result. Norw. Antarct. Exped.*, 36:1-76.
1954

GALAPAGOS FUR SEAL

T.W. CLARK

1 Description

1.1 Species identification

1.1.1 Family: Otariidae
Species: *Arctocephalus galapagoensis* (Heller 1904)

1.1.2 Size

This fur seal is the smallest of the southern fur seals but no external body measurements or weights are available. Condylobasal length of skull ranges from 201 to 210 mm for adult males and 171 to 186 mm for adult females (the largest known skull is that of the holotype). No other species of fur seal has an adult skull this small (Repenning, Peterson & Hubbs 1971). Little sexual dimorphism; males have a minimal development of cranial crest and there are only minor size differences between the sexes. Some adult female skulls are only 15 mm shorter than the smallest adult male skulls.

1.2 Stocks

1.2.1 Identification

There are no subspecies. This species was derived from *Arctocephalus australis* and has been considered in the past as a subspecies of this.

1.2.2 Distribution

Although once widespread in the Galapagos Islands, exploitation by sealers nearly eliminated the population toward the beginning of this century. Orr (1966) and Scheffer (1958) reviewed fur seal distribution up to the mid 1960's. After their discovery in 1535, the Galapagos Islands were often visited by whalers and sealers; exploitation greatly altered natural distribution. Morrell took about 5000 sealskins there in 1823 (Baur 1897). During a sealing expedition of five to six months's duration in 1898 and 1899, only 200 skins were taken, chiefly on Isla Wenman, Isla Fernandina, and Isla Isabela (Heller 1904). One seal was seen on Isla Culpepper and others were reported on Isla Genovesa and Isla Pinta. Heller thought each group to be resident and he commented: " The seals are so reduced in number and so scattered that no well-defined rookeries exist ... the seals being widely scattered and well concealed in holes and crevices" .

Townsend (1930) reported no sightings of fur seals. Banning (1933) in his account of the Hancock Expedition of 1933 mentioned the capture of six seals on Tower Island. Eibl-Eibesfeldt (1958) discovered " a large colony " in 1957 on James Island. Subsequently Leveque (1963) has shown that the species is presently much more widespread in the northern part of the archipelago than was previously suspected. He noted neraly 500 animals on the east coast of Isabela. Brosset (1963) observed 60 individuals at James Bay on James Island in 1962 and four on Santa Cruz Island at the entrance of the channel that separates it from Baltra Island. He also observed four on Tower Island.

Distributions from 1970 to 1973 were

summarized by Orr (1973). Perry (1970) indicated that well-established colonies were recently seen along the south and southwest coasts of Fernandina, between Punta Mangle and Cabo Hammond, and on Isabela at Cabo Marshall, south of Punta Garcia, Punta Essex and Punta Tortuga, as well as at Isla Pinta. The same report mentioned 200 to 300 fur seals at James Bay on James Island and probably up to 100 individuals at Buccaneer Bay on the same island. Other permanent but small colonies were reported on Wolf Island, on the east coasts of Seymour Island, in the south channel between Baltra and Santa Cruz islands, and 20 to 30 individuals on the northwest coast of Pinzon Island. Perry (1970) further noted a colony found in May on Isla Espanola at Pinta Suarez. This group contained 33 individuals, mainly males.

1.2.3 Structure of stocks

Prefer rocky areas with sea-caves. Not as approachable as the sea lions on land. None has been observed any distance at sea. They seem not to move or migrate much, but little is known on this.

2 Vital Parameters

2.1 Population size

2.1.1 Methods of estimates

Casual surface counts which have not been complete.

2.1.2 Results

Scheffer (1958) gave estimates of fur seal populations in the Galapagos to be between 100 and 500. Recent estimates of fur seal number are more than 1000 (Orr 1973) and some estimates are near 5000. However, Orr pointed out that the species is still within the " danger zone ".

2.1.3 Trends in abundance

There has been an increase in the Galapagos fur seal population during the past 30 to 40 years and presently, as a conservative estimate, there are considerably more than 1000 individuals distributed on at least 10 islands. From north to south, these islands are Wolf, Marchena (where a sick individual was observed and reported by Peter Kramer in 1971), Tower, Isabela, Fernandina, James, Pinzon, Seymour, Santa Cruz, and Hood.

2.2 Rates

2.2.1 Reproduction

The breeding season is thought (perhaps without foundation) to be indefinite (Scheffer 1958). Orr (1973) reported that the only evidence of reproduction seen by him in August 1971 was a small pup that had been dead for several months; all other animals seen were immature or adults.

2.2.2 Natural mortality

Nothing known. There is some indication that an epizootic causing a high die-off of sea-lions on the Galapagos in 1970-71 also affected some fur seals (Orr 1973).

2.2.3 Harvesting

Not presently harvested.

3 Trophic relationships

Nothing known.

3.1 Competition and predation

Nothing known. There presumably is resource sharing with the sea lion, *Zalophus californianus wollebaeki*, which numbers about 20,000, although the terrestrial habitat is separated.

4 Relations with Man

4.1 Values

4.1.1 Consumptive

None presently. Was a major fur resource for over 350 years; over-exploitation is cause for present low numbers.

4.1.2 Low consumptive

Some aesthetic value for Galapagos visitors, but limited because the animals are shy.

4.2 Effect of human activities other than exploitation

Contact apparently is very limited.

4.3 Management-Conservation

The species is protected by the Ecuadorean Fish and Game Service.

5 Threats to Stock

No data but see 2.2.2.

6 Research

6.1 Current status

None as far as known.

6.2 Recommendations for future research

Better stock assessment is needed, and studies on reproductive success, mortality rates and seasonal movements. Any addition to our knowledge of their ecology and ethology would be valuable.

References

BANNING, G.H., Hancock Expedition of 1933 to the 1933 Galapagos Islands. General report. *Bull. Zool. Soc. San Diego*, (10):1-30.

BAUR, G., On the distribution of marine mammals. 1897 *Science, N.Y.*, 5:956-7.

BROSSET, A., Statut actuel des mammifères des îles Galapagos. 1963 *Mammalia, Paris*, 27:323-38.

CLARK, T.W., *Arctocephalus galapagoensis. Mammal.* 1975 *Spec. Monogr. Am. Soc. Mammal.*, (64):1-2.

EIBL-EIBESFELDT, I., Wander of a Noah's Ark off the 1958 coast of Ecuador. *Unesco Cour.*, 11:20-3.

HELLER, E., Mammals of the Galapagos Archipelago, 1904 exclusive of the Cetacea. *Proc. Calif. Acad. Sci.*, 3:233-50.

KRAMER, P., and J. VILLA R., Conservation and scientific 1971 report. *Publ. Charles Darwin Res. Stn.*, (23):4.

LEVEQUE, R., Le statut actuel des vertébrés rares et me-1963 nacés de l'archipel des Galapagos. *Terre Vie*, 4:397-430.

ORR, R.T., Evolutionary aspects of the mammalian 1966 fauna of the Galapagos. *In* The Galapagos, edited by R.I. Bowman. Berkeley, University of California Press, 318 p.

—, Galapagos fur seal *(Arctocephalus galapagoensis).* 1973 *IUCN Publ. (New Ser.), Suppl. Pap.*, (39):124-8.

PERRY, R., Conservation and scientific report. *Publ.* 1970 *Charles Darwin Res. Stn.*, (18):1-6, (19):1-14.

REPENNING, C.A., R.S. PETERSON and C.L. HUBBS, Con-1971 tributions to the systematics of the southern fur seals, with particular reference to the Juan Fernandez and Guadalupe species. *Antarct. Res. Ser.*, (18):1-34.

SCHEFFER, V.B., Seals, sea lions, and walruses: a review 1958 of the Pinnipedia. Stanford, California, Stanford Univ. Press, 179 p.

TOWNSEND, C.H., The Astor Expedition to the Galapa-1930 gos Islands. *Bull. N.Y. ZOOL. Soc.*, 33:135-55.

SOUTH AMERICAN FUR SEAL

R. VAZ-FERREIRA

1 Description

1.1 Species identification

1.1.1 Family: Otariidae
Species: Arctocephalus australis (Zimmermann 1783)

1.1.2 Size

- Newborn pups: 3.5-5.5 kg.
- Adult males: 1.9 m, 159 kg.
- Adult females: 1.4 m, 48.5 kg.

(Specimens from Isla de Lobos, Uruguay — Vaz-Ferreira, unpublished — and from Falkland Islands — Repenning, Peterson & Hubbs 1971).

1.2 Stocks

1.2.1 Identification

Differences between populations of the Falkland Islands and the South American mainland have been summarized by King, 1954.

1.2.2 Distribution

This species is widely distributed: " Falkland Islands and coastal South America from Rio de Janeiro, Brazil, southward around Cape Horn and northward to Lima, Peru. All published records from nearby antarctic islands, such as the South Orkney Islands, are either not this species, or are not verifiable insofar as we can determine ". (Repenning, Peterson & Hubbs 1971). It breeds at colonies in Uruguay, Argentina, the Falkland Islands, Chile and Peru. There are no definite migrations, but seasonally there is wide seaward dispersion. The Uruguayan populations, and probably others, maintain contact with land all the year round.

1.2.3 Structure of stocks

Males polygynous. The breeding group is normally established in rocky places and lacks precisely defined harems, though it contains territorial males and a variable population of females and pups. Male to female ratio in the breeding rookeries varies from 1:1 to 1:13, average 1:6.5.

Territories mostly occupied by early November and December when non-breeding groups are chased away. Males without females, but making continuous reproductive attempts, are located mostly in front, more rarely to the rear of the reproductive groups. These non-breeding male sites are occupied by individuals which arrive there either directly from sea or after fighting and rejection from the breeding grounds. Immature males begin to arrive late in the season and reach maximum several months after the breeding periods has ended; in immature male areas, where most of the play is performed, there is no site adherence at all. (Vaz-Ferreira 1956, 1965; Vaz-Ferreira & Sierra 1961, and Vaz-Ferreira, unpublished).

2 Vital parameters

2.1 Population size

2.1.1 Methods of estimation

Direct surface counts of pups and breeding population; counts from aircraft or boats.

2.1.2 Results

Counts in Uruguay in 1953 totalled 9194 pups and 17,205 adults (Vas-Ferreira, unpublished).

In 1972 the Uruguayan population was estimated by Ximenez (1973a) at 252,000. Ximenez (personal communication) gives the figure of 101,470 for the pups born on the season 1972-1973.

The Argentinian population was estimated in 1954 to be 2,700 (Carrara 1954).

In the Falkland Islands counts in 1965-66 gave for the whole Archipelago 15,000 to 16,000 (Strange 1973).

In Chile 40,000 have been counted in 1976 (Lieutenant I. Petrowitsch - personal communication).

The Peruvian population in 1968 was 12,000 (Peruvian Department of Fisheries).

2.1.3 Trend in abundance

The population has increased in Uruguay since 1949; in the other areas, after killing was stopped, populations seem stable or slowly increasing, but no comparative data have been published.

2.2 Rates

2.2.1 Reproductive

Ages at sexual maturity:

- female - 3 Years
- male - 7 years (unconfirmed).

Pregnancy rates: of 40 females sampled in 1953 (before selective killing) - 82 %.

Birth Season: November-December.

Lactation period: six months to one year.

Mating time: late November and December.

Gestation: nearly one year (implantation March-April).

Longevity: unknown.

(Data from Vaz-Ferreira 1950 and Vaz-Ferreira, 1976, and unpublished; Ximenez 1973).

2.2.2 Natural mortality

Natural mortality of pups during the first three months of age varies for different islands and years from 4 % to 82.5 % (Ximénez 1973). In some years a big mortality of pups is produced by sudden increase of the sea level during storms.

2.2.3 Harvesting

Commercial exploitation takes place only in Uruguay under government management. This has been under the Servicio Oceanografico y de Pesca (SOYP), now being restructured as the Industrias Loberas y Pesqueras del Estado (ILPE). Sealing operations are performed during the winter. The annual harvest since 1970 has averaged 11,956 animals, (11,287 to 12,654), (data of I. Ximénez, sealing manager, ILPE). Mostly the animals killed have been males of 8 months and older.

3 Trophic relationships

3.1 Food habits

Food fishes found in a small number of stomachs from seals caught in trammel nets at sea were *Engraulis anchoita, Trachurus lathami, Cynoscion striatus, Pneumatophorus japonicus, Peprilus* sp., (R. Brownell, personal communication). Remains of invertebrates such as cephalopods, crustaceans, lamellibranchs and sea snails were found in specimens caught on land. The seals feed over a wide area of continental shelf and beyond. This species is not a fishing boat follower, like *A. pusillus* and *Otaria flavescens.*

4 Relation to man

4.1 Values

4.1.1 Consumptive

The fur seal constitutes a very important

resource for Uruguay, the revenue for the government being similar to that from fisheries.

4.1.2 Low-consumptive

In general the fur seal rookeries are in remote areas with poor access for viewing.

4.3 Management and conservation

Under government supervision, young animals are killed preferably on higher parts of the rookery where the majority of them are males, (Ximénez, 1962). Females are sorted out when recognized. No specific quota system or basis of management has been published.

5 Threats to stocks

Offshore oil wells are planned which may constitute an ecological hazard.

6 Research

6.1 Current status

Long-term research on the population dynamics is carried out by the government of Uruguay and Argentina. Research on ecology and ethology is carried out by the Department of Vertebrate Zoology of the Faculty of Humanities and Sciences, Montevideo, Uruguay.

6.2 Recommendations for future research

Much more information is required on vital parameters for population modeling, and on population changes. Studies of possible morphological differences between populations of different areas should also be encouraged.

References

CARRARA, I.S., Observaciones sobre el estado actual de 1954 las poblaciones de pinnipedos de la Argentina. La Plata, Universidad de Eva Peron, Facultad de Ciencias Veterinarias, 17 p.

KING, J.E., The otariid seals of the Pacific coast of 1954 America. *Bull. Br. Mus. (Nat. Hist.) (Zool.)*, 2(10):311-37.

REPENNING, C.A., R.S. PETERSIB and C.L. HUBBS, Con-1971 tributions to the systematics of the southern fur seals, with particular reference to the Juan Fernandez and Guadalupe species. *Antarct. Res. Ser.*, (18):1-34.

STRANGE, I., The silent ordeal of a South Atlantic ar-1973 chipelago. *Nat. Hist.*, 82:30-9.

VAZ-FERREIRA, R., Observaciones sobre la Isla de Lobos. 1950 *Rev. Fac. Hum. Cienc. Montev.*, 5:145-76.

—, Etología terrestre de *Arctocephalus australis* (Zim-1956 mermann) (" lobo fino ") en las islas uruguayas. Servicio Oceanográfico y de Pesca. *Trab. Isla Lobos Lobos Mar., Montev.*, (2): 22 p.

—, Ecología terrestre y marina de los pinnipedios del 1965 Atlántico Sudoccidental. *An. Acad. Bras. Ciênc.*, 37 Supl.: 179-91.

—, *Arctocephalus australis* Zimmermann South Ameri-1976 can fur seal. Paper presented to the Scientific Consultation on the Conservation and Management of Marine Mammals and their Environment, Bergen, Norway, 31 August-9 September, 1976. Rome, FAO, ACMRR/MM/SC/49:13 p.

VAZ-FERREIRA, R., and B. SIERRA, División funcional del 1961 habitat terrestre y estructura de las agregaciones sociales de *Arctocephalus australis* (Zimmermann), estudio gráfico. *Actas Congr. Sudam. Zool.*, 1:175-83.

XIMENEZ, I., Frecuencia y fluctuaciones estacionales en 1962 la población de *Arctocephalus australis* en algunas zonas de la Isla de Lobos. *Rev. Inst. Invest. Pesq.*, 1(2):141-58.

—, Nota preliminar sobre la repoblación de *Arctoce-*1973 *phalus australis* en la Isla Rasa. *Trab. Congr. Latinoam. Zool.*, 5(1):281-8.

—, *In U.S. Fed. Register*, 38(147):20572.

CAPE (SOUTH AFRICAN) FUR SEAL

P.D. SHAUGHNESSY

1 Description

1.1 *Species Identification*

1.1.1 Family: Otariidae
Species: *Arctocephalus pusillus* (Schreber 1776)
Sub-species: *Arctocephalus pusillus pusillus* (Schreber 1776)

Repenning, Peterson & Hubbs (1971) have shown that this form is conspecific with the Australian fur sea *A. b. doriferus* (WP 34).

1.1.2 Size

- Newborn pups: 60-70 cm; 6 kg.
- Adult males: 2.34 m; 700 kg.
- Adult females: 1.8 m; 122 kg.

1.2 *Stocks*

1.2.1 Identification

No separate African stocks identified.

1.2.2 Distribution

Breeds in South West Africa and South Africa. No definite migratory movements. Individual movements up to several hundred km recorded.

1.2.3 Structure of stocks·

The species is polygamous. The total population of breeding bulls has been calculated at 13,000. Harem size ranges from 7 to 66 with an average of 28.

2 Vital parameters

2.1 *Population size*

2.1.1 Methods of estimation

Aerial photography for counts of pups; tag recaptures of pups; and collection of tags during winter harvest.

2.1.2 Results

Pup production is about 211,000. Total population estimated at 850,000.

2.1.3 Trend in abundance

The pre-exploitation pup abundance estimated at 291,000 pups, so that current production is about 73 % of its initial value. Recorded kills have increased from about 3,200 to a current kill of 78,000 pups and 2,200 bulls.

2.2 *Rates*

2.2.1 Reproductive

Age at sexual maturity:

- females, age 3 (Rand 1955) or later
- males, unreported.

Pregnancy rate: 74 %.

Birth season: early October to January with median date of 1st December. Ninety per cent of pups born in a 34 day period.

Lactation period: up to 12 months or longer. If a cow loses her pup the pup of the previous year may continue sucking until well into its second year of life.

Mating time: six days after birth

Gestation: almost a year; delay of implantation of about 4 months.

2.2.2 Natural mortality

Unknown.

2.2.3 Harvesting

25-50 % of pups are taken depending on accessibility of colonies. The current model in use indicates that a harvesting rate of 35 % of the newborn female pups will give MSY. A higher male pup exploitation rate may be possible - up to 40 %.

Calculations indicate that optimum sustainable population level has been achieved.

Unknown but apparently considerable numbers are taken by pelagic purse seine fisheries for pilchard and anchovy. A natural kill sometimes occurs from stranding of pups by gales which wash them away from rookeries.

3 Trophic Relationship

3.1 Food and feeding

3.1.1 Food habits

Primarily pelagic shoaling fish and cephalopods are taken. Small fish are brought to the surface. The seals have learned to feed around fishing boats, especially pilchard and anchovy purse seiners, and hake (*Merluccius capensis*) trawlers. They frequently jump into purse seines, consume the fish therein, and sometimes chase fish from the net during pursing.

3.1.2 Food base

The contents of 245 stomachs examined from Cape Province during 1954-56 was, by volume, 70 % fish, 20 % cephalopods, 2 % crustaceans and 8 % miscellaneous matter. Squid (*Lolico* spp.) maasbanders (*Trachurus trachurus*) and pilchards were the most numerous items.

3.1.3 Requirements and utilization

Seals other than yearlings are estimated to consume 600 lb. of fish annually per head. The annual consumption of the 634,000 of these seals is approximately 190,000 tonnes of fish, compared to the commercial fishery by South African and South West African vessels of 2.4 million tonnes.

3.1.4 Changes in abundance of food supply

Since the 1954-56 food habit study, pelagic fish populations off Cape Province have changed. Maasbanker and pilchard populations have decreased, anchovy have increased. A similar change has occurred off South West Africa. Thus availability of food presumably has also changed. The significance of food availability relative to occurrences of seals 80-100 miles out to sea is unclear. Bulls tend to move further out than other age groups.

3.2 Competition and predators

Species that share the same prey are the cape gannet (*Morus capensis*), jackass penguin, various cormorants and porpoises. Natural predators include sharks and possibly the killer whale. The black-backed jackal preys on pups.

An increase in Cape fur seal population size since 1940 has resulted in displacement of some sea bird colonies.

4 Relation to Man

4.1 Values

4.1.1. Consumptive

Pelts, after the completion of the first moult, from the 6-1/2 to 10-1/2 month old seal, are used in the fur market. About 60,000-80,000 pups are taken annually. Blubber from most of these seals is processed for oil. About 2,000 bulls are also taken for pelts and blubber oil.

There is no indication of any future change in current demand or utilization, except possibly for a declining emphasis on skins of adult males.

4.1.2 Low-consumptive

Four colonies are visited regularly by tourists. In 1975, 17,000 people viewed Seal Island, Mossel Bay, in a 5 week period. Annually some 68,000 people view seal colonies, with monetary takings from this exceding R 70,000.

Cape fur seals do well in captivity and are commonly displayed in zoos.

4.2 Effects of human activities other than exploitation

Seals feeding on fish in seine and trawl nets are shot by fishermen.

4.3 Management and conservation

Sealing is under control of the Sea Birds and Seal Protection Act of 1973. Permits issued under this Act specify methods of killing, age, and season and area of killing.

A quota system has recently gone into effect on most harvests. These are based on a maximum sealing rate of 40% of pups born. There has been a gradual shift in emphasis in the last 25 years from State sealing to private sealing under a concession system, controlled by the State. Quotas are determined according to a population model predicting effects of various harvesting notes on yearling females in a stable population of females.

5 Threats to Stock

Nothing known.

6 Research

6.1 Current

A new study of food habits is in progress to determine any changes suggested by changes in abundance of prey fish species. The current research programme to determine the accurate figures of the pup population size on each rookery is being implemented. Research on underwater sound deterrents for fishing boats is underway.

6.2 Recommendations

Many of the vital parameters used in population modeling are those of the Northern or Alaska fur seal, which are presumably similar. Research to establish the vital parameters of the Cape fur seal for this purpose needs to be completed.

References

Best, P.B., Seals and sealing in South and South West
1973 Africa. *S. Afr. Shipp. News Fish. Ind. Rev.*, 28(12):49-57.

Best, P.B., and R.W., Rand, Results of a pup-tagging
1975 experiment on the *Arctocephalus pusillus* rookery at Seal Island, False Bay, South Africa. *Rapp. P.-V. Réun. CIEM*, 169:267-73.

Rand, R.W., Reproduction in the Cape fur seal, *Arcto-*
1955 *cephalus pusillus* (Schreber). *Proc. Zool. Soc. Lond.*, 124:717-40.

—, The Cape fur seal *Arctocephalus pusillus* (Schreber).
1956 Its general characteristics and moult. *Invest. Rep. Sea Fish. Branch S. Afr.*, (21):52 p.

—, The Cape fur seal (*Arctocephalus pusillus*). Distri-
1959 bution abundance and feeding habits off the south western coast of the Cape Province. *Invest. Rep. Sea Fish Branch S. Afr.*, (34):75 p.

—, The Cape fur seal (*Arctocephalus pusillus*). 3. Gene-
1967 ral behaviour on land and at sea. *Invest. Rep. Sea Fish. Branch S. Afr.*, (60):39 p.

—, The Cape fur seal *Arctocephalus pusillus*. 4. Estima-
1972 tes of population size. *Invest. Rep. Sea Fish. Branch S. Afr.*, (89):1-28.

—, Management of South African fur seals. *J. S. Afric.*
1973 *Wildl. Manage. Assoc.*, 3:85-7.

Repenning, C.A., R.S. Peterson and C.L. Hubbs, Contributions to the systematics of the southern fur seals, with special reference of the Juan Fernandez and Guadalupe species. *Antarct. Res. Ser.*, (18):1-34.
1971

Shaughnessy, P.D., and P.B., Best, The pupping season of the Cape fur seal *Arctocephalus pusillus pusillus.* Sea Fisheries Branch, South Africa, 8 p. (unpubl. rep.).
1975

—, A simple population model for the South African fur seal, *Arctocephalus pusillus pusillus.* Sea Fisheries Branch, South Africa, 8 p. (unpubl. rep.).
1975a

Anon., Phantom killer whales. SPCA backs project to overcome seal problem in purse seine fishery. *S. Afr. Shipp. News Fish. Ind. Rev.*, 30(7):50-3.
1975

AUSTRALIAN FUR SEAL

R. WARNEKE

1 Description

1.1 *Species identification*

1.1.1 Family: Otariidae
Species: *Arctocephalus pusillus* (Schreber 1776)
Sub-species: *Arctocephalus pusillus doriferus* Wood Jones 1925

1.1.2 Size

- Newborn pups 64-81 (av. 72.9) cm
male: 5-12.5 (av. 8.1) kg.
62-79 (av. 69.7) cm
female: 4.5-10 (av. 7.1) kg.
- Adult 201-227 (av. 215.6) cm
male: 218-360 (av. 278.6) kg.
125-171 (av. 157.2) cm
female: 36-110 (av. 76.5) kg.

Marked sexual dimorphism in size and form. Males generally darker than females, greyish brown to dark brown and slightly paler ventrally; mane of coarse hairs over neck and shoulders, which may be paler than rest of dorsum. Colour of females varies from pale fawn through greys to greyish brown, with contrasting pale throat but not sharply defined; brown belly. Newborn pups black, some with silver tones, moulting after several months to greyish fawn with pale throat.

1.2 *Stocks*

1.2.1 Identification

Australian population geographically isolated from South African (Cape fur seal), and distinguished on the basis of minor cranial differences. Recognized as the sub-species *Arctocephalus pusillus doriferus* (Repenning, Peterson & Hubbs 1971).

1.2.2 Distribution

Breeding range extends from Seal Rocks, New South Wales, to southern Tasmania and throughout Bass Strait to Lady Julia Percy I. in the west, i.e. from 32°28′ to 43°52′S and from 152°33′ to 142°00′E. Breeding colonies occur on Judgement Rocks, Kanowna I., Lady Julia Percy I., Maatsuyker Is., Moncoeur Is., Moriarty Rocks, Pedra Branca, Reids Rocks, Seal Rocks (N.S.W.), Seal Rocks (Victoria), Tenth I. and The Skerries.

No evidence of migration, but ranges westward to about 138°E.

1.2.3 Structure of stocks

Highly gregarious and polygynous; ratio of males to females at breeding sites about 1:10. Non-territorial males and subadult males are segregated in areas adjacent to the breeding sites, but males less than 4 yr of age congregate in the breeding territories. No large (>200) isolated aggregations of nonbreeding seals are known.

2 Vital Parameters

2.1 *Population size*

2.1.1 Methods of estimation

Direct counts, and interpretation of aerial photographs.

2.1.2 Results

Estimates from an aerial survey in 1975 give 20,000 for the entire population, range 19,000 to 24,000 of which half is concentrated at Lady Julia Percy I. and Seal Rocks (Victoria).

2.1.3 Trends in abundance

Historical records do not reveal a wider distribution in the past, and the paucity of these data do not permit any direct estimate of original abundance. Sealing in the 19th century eliminated or drastically reduced all seal colonies within the range of this subspecies (including *A. forsteri* and *Neophoca cinerea*), but most of the favoured sites have been repopulated. All but one of the largest colonies (Lady Julia Percy I., Kanowna I., Reids Rocks and Seal Rocks) had reached stable levels by 1945 (estimates from aerial photographs, CSIRO Division of Fisheries & Oceanography) and that one, Judgement Rocks, may now be at its maximum size.

One major breeding site, Albatross I., has not been recolonized.

2.2 Rates

2.2.1 Reproduction

Age at sexual maturity:

- female 3-6 yr
- puberty in male 4-5 yr but not socially mature until 9-12 yr or even later.

Pregnancy rate: 68 percent.

Birth season: November-December.

Lactation period: 11-12 months; a small percentage of young are suckled through a second or even a third year.

Mating: 5-6 days post partum.

Gestation: 51 weeks (implantation delayed approx 3 months).

Longevity: not known.

2.2.2 Natural mortality

Little data available on mortality in relation to age or sex. Minimum loss (by direct count) of 15 % for first 2 months of life.

2.2.3 Harvesting

There is no commercial exploitation of this subspecies. The last harvest, for control purposes, was of 619 in 1948-49 (McNally and Lynch, 1954).

3 Trophic relationships

3.1 Food and feeding

3.1.1 Food habits

This fur seal apparently disperses widely and preys on a variety of near-surface, mid-water and bottom-dwelling organisms.

Recoveries from traps and nets indicate that it is able to dive to at least 120 m and this suggests that the whole of the Continental Shelf is available as a feeding area. Recent reports of seals congregating at nets brought up from 500+ m at the edge of the Shelf suggest that this zone may be a rich feeding area for this subspecies.

3.1.2 Food bases

Few quantitative data are available (McNally and Lynch, 1954), however this seal appears to feed predominantly on squid (*Notodarus, Sepioteuthis*) and octopus (*Octopus*), and a wide range of fishes depending on seasonal availability and local opportunity. Of these barracouta (*Thyrsites*) often occurs in large shoals off southern and southeastern Australia in summer, and is an important item in its diet. Other occasional items are whiting (*Sillaginodes*), flathead (*Platycephalus*), red mullet (*Upeneichthys*), parrot fish (*Pseudolabrus*), leather jackets (Aluteridae) and small fishes such as pilchards (Clupeidae). Rock lobsters (*Jasus*) are taken from time to time.

3.1.3 Requirements and utilization

Captive females of average size: approx. 5 kg/day.

3.1.4 Changes in abundance of food supply

No detailed data. Barracouta (*Thyrsites*) is migratory and highly variable in its seasonal occurrence and abundance in local waters, as are other shoaling species such as salmon (*Arripis*) and mackerel (*Trachurus*).

3.2 Competition and predation.

Tagging studies indicate that immatures are relatively sedentary (Warneke, 1975) and thus competition for food may occur, however, adults appear to disperse widely and may exploit the entire region of the Continental Shelf and its edge.

Cooperative feeding on fish shoals has been reported. Competition from *A. forsteri* and *Nephoca cinerea* is unlikely as there is no evidence of significant overlap of their ranges with *A. p. doriferus*. Both the white shark (*Carcharodon*) and the killer whale (*Orcinus*) have been observed to prey on this fur seal and many individuals carry scars of wounds that could only have been inflicted by the former. The extent of this predation is unknown.

4 Relations to man

4.1 Values

4.1.1 Consumptive

The pelt is of commercial quality (refer use of *A. p. pusillus* from South Africa for fur skins).

4.1.2 Low consumptive

Two accessible colonies near the Victorian coast (Lady Julia Percy I., and Seal Rocks) are well known tourist attractions of significant potential. Groups of captives are prominent exhibits at Australia's two largest zoos, in Melbourne and Sydney.

4.2 Effects of human activities other than exploitation

Increasing boat traffic to accessible colonies is a cause for concern as repeated disturbance of one breeding site (by biologists) caused abandonment.

Significant numbers of immatures are lost (40 % of tag returns) by accidental drowning in nets and rock lobster traps and by shooting. Oil/gas platforms in eastern Bass Strait and fixed navigation markers in Port Phillip Bay provide places of security for resting seals in areas otherwise lacking in suitable hauling sites.

4.3 Management and conservation

All known colonies lie within State territorial waters and the subspecies is protected by State laws. Most islands are under some form of protective legislation and access to some is prohibited.

5 Threats to stock

Pesticide and heavy metal pollution. High levels of chlorinated hydrocarbons and mercury have been recorded (J. Bacher, unpublished).

6 Research

6.1 Current status

General studies of social and reproductive behaviour, growth, reproductive physiology, population structure and movement were carried out by the Victorian Fisheries and Wildlife Division, 1966-74 (Warneke, 1966, 1968, 1973, 1975; Stirling and Warneke, 1971), but much data is as yet unpublished.

6.2 Recommendations for future research

In depth studies on all aspects of the biology of the subspecies on the marked population at Seal Rocks, Victoria, which includes individuals to 12 yr of age.

Detailed surveys of all known colonies, and especially those at the periphery of the range whose status is doubtful.

References

McNally, J., and D.D. Lynch, Notes on the food of
1954 Victorian seals. *Fauna Rep. Fish. Game Dep. Vict.*, (1):16 p.

Repenning, C.A., R.S. Peterson and C.L. Hubbs, Con-
1971 tributions to the systematics of the southern fur seals, with special reference to the Juan Fernandez and Guadalupe species. *Antarct. Res. Ser.*, (18):1-34.

Stirling, I., and R.M. Warneke, Implications of a
1971 comparison of the airborne vocalisations and some aspects of the behaviour of the two Australian fur seals, *Arctocephalus* spp., on the evolution and present taxonomy of the genus. *Aust. J. Zool.*, 19:227-41.

Warneke, R.M., Seals of Westernport. *Vict. Resour.*,
1966 5:24-5.

—, The fur seal. *In* Wildlife in southeastern Australia.
1968 *Wildl. Circ. Fish. Wildl. Dep. Aust.*, (25): 16-22.

—, *Arctocephalus pusillus doriferus* — the survivor.
1973 *B.H.P. (Broken Hill Propriet. Co.) J.*, Summer issue.

—, Dispersal and mortality of juvenile fur seals *Arcto-*
1975 *cephalus pupillus doriferus* in Bass Strait, southeastern Australia. *Repp. P.-V. Réun. CIEM*, 169:296-302.

NEW ZEALAND FUR SEAL

M.C. CRAWLEY, R. WARNEKE

1 Description

1.1 Species identification

1.1.1 Family: Otariidae
Species: Arctocephalus forsteri (Lesson 1828)

1.1.2 Size

- Newborn pups: 40-45 cm; 4.3 kg (av).
- Adult males: 1.45-2.50 m; 120-185 kg.
- Adult females: 1.25-1.50 m; 40-70 kg.

There is a marked sexual dimorphism in size and appearance. Adult males have distinctive thick manes and are generally darker than females, varying from a dark brown to almost black with a lighter belly; females brown to dark brown with greyish tones. Newborn pups black, moulting after several months to greyish brown. Sexual dimorphism in size is evident in pups only a few weeks old. Between birth and 240 days old, pups gain an average of 24 g and 0.86 cm per day, irrespective of their sex.

1.2 Stocks

1.2.1 Identification
Geographically isolated populations occur off southern Australia and in New Zealand waters. At present distinguished only by slight differences in serum proteins (Shaughnessy 1970).

1.2.2 Distribution
The Australian population is widely distributed among islands off the southern coast from 117° to 136°E (King 1969). In South Australia the largest known colonies are at the South Neptunes; smaller concentrations of unknown status occur at Althorpe I., Casuarina Is., Four Hummocks, Gambier I., Greenly I., Kangaroo I. (Cape du Couedic), and Thistle I. In Western Australia fur seals are widely distributed throughout the Recherche Archipelago but nowhere, apparently, in large numbers. Colonies have been reported from Boxer I., Capps I., Christmas I., Daw Is., Figure of Eight I., Hood I., Kermadec I., Middle I., Mondrain I., Round I., Salisbury I., Seal Rock, and Termination Is. To the west of the Archipelago a single colony occurs on Eclipse I.

In New Zealand fur seals breed at many places on the coast of South Island and adjacent islets, south of 43°S. To the west, large colonies occur on Chalky I. and Five Fingers Peninsula in Fiordland, on Open Bay Is. and at Karamea River. In Westland, while on the east coast and to the north only small non-breeding colonies occur, the most significant being at Kaikoura and on the Otago Peninsula. Significant breeding colonies occur at all the major islands and island groups to the south and in subantarctic waters: Antipodes Is., Auckland Is., Bounty Is., Campbell I., Chatham Is., Macquarie I., Snares, Stewart I. and Solander Is. (Wilson 1974). Both stocks are non-migratory. In Australia there is little movement beyond the breeding range. In New Zealand the winter range extends north along the coasts of North Island to 34°S (Wilson 1974).

1.2.3 Structure of stocks

The New Zealand fur seal is highly polygynous and congregates at specific breeding sites in late October to early January. From February to September, adult females, pups and some subadults remain on, or near, the rookeries but adult males and other subadults occupy hauling grounds elsewhere which are of two types (Wilson 1974).

2 Vital parameters

2.1 Population size

2.1.1 Methods of estimation

Direct surface counts of all seals present, corrected according to season (Wilson 1974).

2.1.2 Results

The Australian stock may be as low as several thousand animals (King 1969). The New Zealand population totals about 38,500 (range: 30-50,000), comprising about 25,000 on the New Zealand mainland and offshore islands, and the remainder on the Chatham Islands and the subantarctic islands. The main concentrations are in Fiordland (8,500), Westland (6,500), Solander Island (5,500), around Stewart Island (3,100), the Bounty Islands (5,500), Campbell Island (2,000), and the Chatham Islands (2,100) (Wilson 1974).

2.1.3 Trends in abundance

During the 19th Century, both stocks were harvested almost to extinction. The New Zealand population was partially protected from 1875 to 1916 and fully protected thereafter. There has been an increase in the New Zealand population, but there is no evidence that the Australian population is recovering.

Some of the sub-antarctic islands provide considerable scope for increase above current numbers:

	Minimum yield		Current population
Antipodes	60,000	in 1804-6	1100
Auckland	13,000	1823	750-1500
Campbell	15,000	1810	2000
Macquarie	57,000	1810	900-1000

2.2 Rates

2.2.1 Reproduction

Age at sexual maturity:

- female, 4-6 yr (est.)
- male, similar but not socially mature until 10-12 yr (est.).

Birth season: November-January (Stirling & Warneke 1971).

Lactation period: 10-11 months approx.

3 Trophic relations

3.1 Food and feeding

3.1.1 Food habits

Data from near South Island, New Zealand, indicate that *A. forsteri* feeds principally in near-surface water on squid and barracouta but takes octopus on the bottom at any time. In southern waters, off Campbell Island, the main diet is penguins and squid. There are no data on the species' food preferences in Australian waters, but squid, octopus and barracouta are all abundantly available. Mutton birds and presumably other small sea birds are occasionally taken.

3.1.2 Food base

Analysis of contents of stomachs from seals taken off South Island, New Zealand, showed that barracouta (*Thyrsites*) comprised 38 % by weight of the diet, with octopus (*Octopus*), squid (*Notodarus* and *Sepioteuthis*) and other small fish in the percentages 27, 24 and 9, respectively (Street 1964).

3.1.3 Requirements and utilization

Not known.

3.1.4 Changes in abundance of food supply

Not known.

3.2 *Competition and predation*

In Australian waters fur seals appear to disperse widely, so competition may not occur; on the other hand cooperative feeding of fish shoals has been reported. Predation by sharks (especially *Carcharodon*) and killer whales (*Orcinus*) occurs but its extent is not known.

4 Relation to man

4.1 *Values*

4.1.1 *Consumptive*

Produced the highest quality pelt of any Australian seal (Dunderdale, 1898).

4.1.2 *Low-consumptive*

Tourist attraction where non-breeding colonies are near human population centres. The remoteness of most sites limits their potential for this use.

4.2 *Effects of human activities other than exploitation*

Not known, but repeated disturbance at breeding sites may cause abandonment. Some incidental losses due to net and rock lobster fisheries probably occurs through accidental drowning.

4.3 *Management and conservation*

This species is protected by legislation throughout its range and is not exploited. Many breeding and hauling sites are under some form of protective reservation.

5 Threats to stock

None known.

6 Research

6.1 *Current status*

In New Zealand, detailed studies are in progress on distribution, abundance, population structure, population dynamics, breeding biology, behaviour, activity budgets, and thermoregulation. No active research in Australia.

6.2 *Recommendations for future research*

Detailed studies of reproductive biology, population structure and dynamics. In Australia baseline surveys of distribution and status are urgently required.

References

CRAWLEY, M.C., Distribution and abundance of New
1972 Zealand fur seals on the Snares Islands, New Zealand. *N.Z.J. Mar. Freshwat. Res.*, 6(1):115-26.

—, Growth of New Zealand fur seal pups. *N.Z.J. Mar.*
1976 *Freshwat. Res.*, 9(4):539-45.

CRAWLEY, M.C., and D.L. BROWN, Measurements of
1971 tagged pups and a population estimate of New Zealand fur seals on Tawnaka, Open Bay Islands, Westland. *N.Z.J. Mar. Freshwat. Res.*, 5(3/4):389-95.

CRAWLEY, M.C., and G.J. WILSON, The natural history
1976 and behavior of the New Zealand fur seal (*Arctocephalus forsteri*). Tuatara, 22(1):1-29.

DUNDERDALE, G., The book of the bush. London, Ward
1895 Lock.

KING, J.E., The identity of the fur seals of Australia.
1969 *Aust. J. Zool.*, 17:841-53.

McNAB, A.G., and M.C. CRAWLEY, Mother and pup
1975 behavior of the New Zealand fur seal. *Mauri Ora*, 3.

MILLER, E.H., Social behavior between adult male and
1974 female New Zealand fur seals, *Arctocephalus forsteri* (Lesson), during the breeding season. *Aust. J. Zool.*, 22:155-73.

—, Body and organ measurements of fur seals, *Arcto-*
1975 *cephalus forsteri* (Lesson), from New Zealand. *J. Mammal.*, 56(2):511-3.

—, Social and evolutionary implications of territoriality
1975a in adult male New Zealand fur seals, *Arctocephalus forsteri* (Lesson, 1828), during the breeding season. *Rapp. P.-V. Réun. CIEM*, 169:170-87.

SHAUGHNESSY, P.D., Serum protein variation in sou-
1970 thern fur seals, *Arctocephalus* spp., in relation to their taxonomy. *Aust. J. Zool.*, 18:331-43.

SORENSEN, J.H., New Zealand fur seals with special re-
1969 ference to the 1946 open season. *Fish. Tech. Rep. N.Z. Mar. Dep.*, (42):80 p.

STIRLING, I., Diurnal movements of the New Zealand
1968 fur seal at Kaikoura. *N.Z.J. Mar. Freshwat. Res.*, 2:375-7.

—, Observations on the behavior of the New Zealand
1970 fur seal *Arctocephalus forsteri. J. Mammal.*, 51:766-78.

—, Studies on the behavior of the South Australian fur
1971 seal, *Arctocephalus forsteri* (Lesson). 1. Annual cycle, postures and calls and adult males during the breeding season. *Aust. J. Zool.*, 19:243-66.

—, Studies on the behavior of the South Australian fur
1971a seal, *Arctocephalus forsteri* (Lesson). 2. Adult females and pups. *Aust. J. Zool.*, 19:267-73.

STIRLING, I., and R.M. WARNEKE, Implications of a
1971 comparison of the airborne vocalizations and some aspects of the behavior of the two Australian fur seals *Arctocephalus* spp., on the evolution and present taxonomy of the genus. *Aust. J. Zool.*, 19:227-41.

STREET, R.J., Feeding habits of the New Zealand fur
1964 seal, *Arctocephalus forsteri. Fish. Tech. Rep. N.Z. Mar. Dep.*, (9):20 p.

WILSON, G.J., The distribution, abundance and popu-
1974 lation characteristics of the New Zealand fur seal (*Arctocephalus forsteri*). M.Sc. Thesis, Univ. Canterbury, Christchurch, New Zealand, 204 p.

ANTARCTIC (KERGUELEN) FUR SEAL

W.N. Bonner

1 Description

1.1 *Species identification*

1.1.1 *Family:* Otariidae
Species: *Arctocephalus gazella* (Peters 1875)

1.1.2 *Size*

- Newborn pup: 60-66 cm; 5-6 kg.
- Adult male: 175-200 cm; 125-200 kg.
- Adult female: 113-145 cm; 25-50 kg.

Coat colour on back and sides grey to brownish, depending on the length of time the seal has been ashore; throat and breast creamy; belly a dark gingery colour. In adult males there is development of a heavy mane around neck, shoulders and breast which presents a grizzled appearance owing to presence of many white hairs. Underfur dark fawn, but reddish in adult males. Pups very dark brown or black. Occasional specimens (ca 0.1 %) lack pigment in the guard hair and appear white or, in the case of adult bulls, honey-coloured.

1.2 *Stocks*

1.2.1 and ***1.2.2*** Identification and distribution
A. gazella occurs on islands south of the Antarctic convergence and north of about 65°S. A major breeding population is found at South Georgia; smaller groups are found at the South Sandwich Islands and Bouvetøya, the South Shetland Islands, The South Orkney Islands, Heard and McDonald Islands, and perhaps Kerguelen.

The colonies disperse in autumn, but a definite migration has not been recorded.

1.2.3 *Structure of stocks*

The species is gregarious and polygamous during the breeding season. Breeding males are territorial and maintain harems of 5-15 females. Non-breeding males occupy area peripheral to the breeding rookeries. Non-breeders are, for the most part, absent from the breeding islands.

2 Vital parameters

2.1 *Population size*

2.1.1 *Methods*

Direct surface counts, capture/recapture estimates and aerial sample counts.

2.1.2 *Results*

The total population is estimated (1976) at about 350,000 and is increasing rapidly.

Locality	Stock size	Reliability
South Georgia	350,000	good
South Orkney	1000	poor
South Sandwich	5000	poor
Bouvetøya	1000	poor
South Shetland	3000	poor
Kerguelen	not known, but if present, few	?
Heard McDonald	3000	?

2.1.3 Trend in abundance (historical development)

This species was exploited almost to extinction in the 19th century. The general picture now is of a rapidly expanding stock centered on South Georgia, where numbers have increased from about 100 in the 1930's to about 15,000 in 1957 and to about 350,000 in 1976. If conditions remain unchanged the population may be expected to continue to increase, perhaps to between one and two million.

2.2 Rates

2.2.1 Reproductive

Ages at sexual maturity:
- females first pup at 3-4 yr.
- males 6 or 7 yr.

Pregnancy rates: not known but high.
Birth season: November-December.
Lactation period: 100-120 days.
Mating time: 8 days post partum.
Gestation: presumably 51 weeks, period of delay in implantation not known.
Longevity: male, 13+; female, 23 (breeding).

2.2.2 Natural mortality

Breeding cows, c. 10 %.

2.2.3 Harvesting, commercial and incidental kill

The species is protected at the present time, except in international waters north of 60°S.

3 Trophic relationships

3.1 Food and feeding

3.1.1 Food habits

The staple diet of this species at South Georgia is krill (*Euphausia superba*), but fish are occasionally eaten mostly by juveniles and non-breeders. Items include squid and birds.

3.1.2 Food base

No quantitative data available.

3.1.3 Requirements and utilization

Not known.

3.1.4 Change in abundance of food supply

Reduction of krill-eating whales implies a krill surplus of c. 153 million tons, which may have facilitated expansion of *A. gazella.*

3.2 Competition and predation

Leopard seals known to prey on young *A. gazella*, but effect probably insignificant.

4 Relation to man

4.1 Values

4.1.1 Consumptive (present and future)

There is currently no commercial exploitation of this species, however it yields a high quality pelt and the stocks could be managed in the same way as *Callorhinus*, by utilizing surplus males.

4.1.2 Low-consumptive

No data available.

4.2 Effects of human activities other than exploitation

No data available.

4.3 Management and conservation

Fur seals are protected in South Georgia and the South Sandwich Islands by the Falkland Islands Dependencies Conservation Ordinance. Norway bans the taking of fur seals at Bouvetøya and France at Kerguelen. South of 60°S the Antarctic Treaty and the Convention for the Conservation of Antarctic Seals (once it is ratified by sufficient nations) prohibit the taking of fur seals on land or at sea, by signatory nations.

5 Threats to Stock

A major expansion of commercial krill fishing could have adverse effects on this fur seal.

6 Research

6.1 Current status

Current research is centred on population dynamics and reproductive biology, mainly by British Antarctic Survey at South Georgia.

6.2 Recommendations for future research

Investigations of mortality rates and regulating factors, particularly colony density.

Study of factors determining the establishment of new colonies.

Study of feeding behaviour and energetics.

Continued monitoring of status.

References

AGUAYO, L.A., Census of Pinnipedia in the South Shet-
1970 land Islands. *In* Antarctic ecology, edited by M.W. Goldgate. London, Academic Press, vol. 1:395-7.

BONNER, W.N., Notes on the southern fur seal in
1958 South Georgia. *Proc. Zool. Soc. Lond.*, 130(2):241-52.

—, Population increase in the fur seal *Arctocephalus*
1964 *tropicalis gazella*, at South Georgia. *In* Biologie antarctique, Premier Symposium organisé par le S.C.A.R., Paris, 2-8 Sept., 1962, edited by R. Carrick, M.W. Holdgate and J. Prevost. Paris, Hermann, pp. 433-43.

—, The fur seal of South Georgia. *Brit. Antarct. Surv.*
1968 *Sci. Rep.*, (56).

BUDD, G.M., and M.C. DOWNES, Population increase
1969 and breeding in the Kerguelen fur seal, *Arctocephalus tropicalis gazella*, at Heard Island. *Mamalia, Paris*, 33:58-67.

—, Rapid population increase in the Kerguelen fur seal,
1970 *Arctocephalus tropicalis gazella*, at Heard Island. *Mammalia, Paris*, 34-410-4.

—, Breeding of the fur seal at McDonald Islands and
1972 further population growth at Heard Island. *Mammalia, Paris*, 36:423-7.

CSORDAS, S.E., The Kerguelen fur seal on Macquarie
1962 Island. *Vict. Nat.*, 79:1-4.

—, The history of fur seals on Macquarie Island. *Vict.*
1963 *Nat.*, 80:255-8.

GWYNN, A.M., Notes on the fur seals at Macquarie
1953 Island. *Inter. Rep. ANARE (Aust. Natl. Antarct. Res. Exped.)*, (4).

HOLDGATE, M.W., Fur seals in the South Sandwich Is-
1962 lands. *Polar Rec.*, 11:474-5.

HOLDGATE, M.W., P.J. TILBROOK and R.W. VAUGHAN,
1968 The biology of Bouvetøya. *Brit. Antarct. Surv. Bull.*, (15):1-7.

KING, J.E., The northern and southern populations of
1959 *Arctocephalus gazella. Mammalia, Paris*, 23:19-40.

—, A note on the specific name of the Kerguelen fur
1959a seal. *Mammalia, Paris*, 23:381.

LAWS, R.M., Population increase of fur seals at South
1973 Georgia. *Polar Rec.*, 16(105):856-8.

MACKINTOSH, N.A., Estimates of local seal populations
1967 in the Antarctic, 1931/37. *Norsk Hvalfangsttid.*, 3:57-64.

O'GORMAN, F.A., Fur seals breeding in the Falkland
1961 Islands Dependencies. *Nature, Lond.*, 192:914-6.

ØRITSLAND, T., Fur seals breeding in the South Orkney
1960 Islands. *Norsk Hvalfangsttid.*, 49:220-5.

PAYNE, M.R., Growth of a fur seal population. *Philos. Trans. R. Soc., (B)* (in press).

REPENNING, C.A., R.S. PETERSON and C.L. HUBBS, Con-
1971 tributions to the systematics of the southern fur seals, with particular reference to the Juan Fernandez and Guadalupe species. *Antarct. Res. Ser.*, 18:1-34.

SUBANTARCTIC FUR SEAL

W.N. BONNER

1 Description

1.1 Species identification

1.1.1 *Family:* Otariidae
Species: Arctocephalus tropicalis (Gray 1872)

1.1.2 *Size*

- Newborn: average length 63 cm, 4.9 kg.
- Adult male: to 180 cm, 165 kg.
- Adult females: 145 cm, 55 kg.

Adults brown to dark grey or black on the back and sides, throat and chest yellow, belly dark brown. Bulls generally darker than cows. Mane less well developed than in *A. gazella* and with fewer white hairs. The yellow colour of the chest interrupts the grizzled colour of the mane. Bulls with a crest of longer hair on the top of the head. Pups black.

1.2 Stocks

1.2.1 *Identification*

Shaughnessy (1970) considers that three main stocks occur, at the Tristan da Cunha-Gough group, the Prince Edward Islands, and New Amsterdam and St. Paul Islands. No attempts have been made to differentiate between these stocks; however, some blood samples have been collected for protein analysis and comparison.

1.2.2 *Distribution*

This species is known to breed on Gough I, New Amsterdam I, St. Paul I, Prince Edward I, and Marion I. (where it breeds sympatrically with *A. gazella*). It has been recorded as breeding on Nightingale and Inaccessible Is., and occasionally (1962, 1974) on nearby Tristan da Cunha. Stragglers have been reported at the Crozet Archipelago, the South African coast, Macquarie I. and South Georgia.

1.2.3 *Structure of stocks*

No details available.

2 Vital parameters

2.1 Population size

2.1.1 *Methods of estimation*

Direct surface counts.

2.1.2 *Results*

Stock	Estimate
Tristan da Cunha	13,500 (1956)
Gough Group	100,000 (1976, Nel, personal commun.)
Prince Edward Is.	4,600 (1973, 1974)
St. Paul I. and New Amsterdam I.	5,300 (1970)

2.1.3 *Trends in abundance (historical)*

Indiscriminate and uncontrolled sealing in the subantarctic, which began at the end of the 18th century and continued well into the 19th, quickly reduced all the colonies of this fur seal. Pre-exploitation levels are not known, but it is clear that the population was severely depleted and some colonies eliminated. The stock centred on Gough Island is recovering from a residual population of about 300 in 1892. In the Prince Edward Group the Marion Island colony was eliminated or at least greatly reduced by 1872 but recovery has apparently stemmed from the other island in the group where fur seals were harvested during the early years of this century. In St. Paul and New Amsterdam Islands the population may have been reduced to less than 100 by the early 1900's: Fur seals, presumably of this species, existed on all the islands of the Crozet Archipelago up to about 1825. Recent records there are of stragglers only.

2.2 *Rates*

2.2.1 *Reproductive*

Ages at sexual maturity: no data.
Pregnancy rates: no data.
Birth season: November-December.
Lactation period: 7 months.
Mating time: 3-7 days after birth.
Gestation: presumably 51 weeks, but no direct data.
Longevity: no data.

2.2.2 *Natural mortality (New Amsterdam Island)*

At birth: 0.9 per cent.

1-3 weeks: varied between colonies, from 32 to 63 per cent 3 weeks — 5 months: 1-2 per cent.

(For all colonies, to age 5 months, mortality averaged 47 per cent).

Weaning — 2 years: estimated at 40-50 per cent.

2.2.3 *Harvesting*

Prince Edward Islands: no harvesting.
Gough Island: no harvesting.
New Amsterdam/St. Paul Islands: no harvesting, but small numbers taken by French expeditions and others (1964).

3 **Trophic relationships**

3.1 *Food and feeding*

3.1.1 *Food habits and food base*

At Marion I. stomach contents comprised fish, cephalopods and euphausiids. At New Amsterdam I, squid was found in 11 of 12 stomachs examined and penguin remains in 2 stomachs, but no remains of fish or euphausiids.

3.1.2 *Requirements and utilization*

No data.

3.1.3 *Change in abundance of food supply*

No data.

3.2 *Competition and predation*

Sharks and killer whales are suspected of predating on this fur seal, but no positive data.

4 **Relation to Man**

4.1 *Values*

4.1.1 *Consumptive*

Pelt said to be better than that of *A. pusillus*, but not as good as that of *Callorhinus.*

4.1.2 *Low-consumptive*

A small number have been taken for display in zoos and oceanaria.

4.2 *Effects of human activities other than exploitation*

No data.

4.3 *Management and conservation*

All the colonies of this fur seal are protected; Marion and Prince Edward islands under the Sea Birds and Seal Protection Act of the Republic of South Africa, Gough and Tristan da Cunha Islands under the Tristan da Cunha Conservation Ordinance, 1976, and New Amsterdam and St. Paul Islands by the French Chamber of Deputies.

5 Threats to Stock

No data.

6 Research

6.1 Current status

The Mammal Research Institute, University of Pretoria, South Africa, is conducting biological studies at Marion and Gough Islands. The Museum National d'Histoire Naturelle, Paris, has recently conducted studies at the French subantarctic islands.

6.2 Recommendations for future research

Continued monitoring of status; general life history studies.

References

DESPIN, B., J.L. MOUGIN, and M. SEGONZAC, Regions of
1972 the French austral and antarctic lands: birds and mammals of the Ile de L'Est, Crozet Archipelago. *Rapp. Com. Natl. Fr. Rech. Antarct.*, (31).

HOLDGATE, M.W., *et al.*, The Hough Island Scientific
1956 Survey, 1955-56. *Nature Lond.*, 178:234-6.

KING, J.E., The northern and southern populations of
1959 *Arctocephalus gazella. Mammalia, Paris*, 23:19-40.

—, A note on the specific name of the Kerguelen fur
1959a seal. *Mammalia, Paris*, 23:381.

PAULIAN, P., Pinnipèdes, cetacés, oiseaux des Iles Ker-
1953 guelen et Amsterdam. Mission Kerguelen, 1951. *Mém. Inst. Sci. Madagascar (A Biol. Anim.)*, 8:111-234.

—, Note sur les phoques des Iles Amsterdam et Saint
1957 Paul. *Mammalia, Paris*, 21:210-25.

—, Note préliminaire sur la systématique de l'otarie de
1957a l'Ile Amsterdam. *Mammalia, Paris*, 21:9-14.

—, Contribution à l'étude de l'otarie de l'Ile Amster-
1964 dam. *Mammalia, Paris*, 28 Suppl. 1:146.

RAND, R.W., Notes on the Marion Island fur seal. *Proc.*
1956 *Zool. Soc. Lond.*, 126, (1):65-82.

REPENNING, C.A., R.S. PETERSON and C.L. HUBBS, Con-
1971 tributions to the systematics of the southern fur seals, with particular reference to the Juan Fernandez and Guadalupe species. *Antarct. Res. Ser.*, 18:1-34.

SEGONZAC, M., Données récentes sur la faune des Iles
1972 Saint-Paul et Nouvelle Amsterdam. *Oiseaux Rev. Fr. Ornithol*, 42:3-68.

SHAUGHNESSY, P.D., Serum protein variation in sou-
1970 thern fur seals, *Arctocephalus* spp., in relation to their taxonomy. *Aust. J. Zool.*, 18:331-43.

WALRUS

C. Brenton

1 Description

1.1 Species identification

1.1.1 Family: Odobenidae
Species: Odobenus rosmarus (Linnaeus 1758)

1.1.2 Size

• Calves	Atlantic	1.4 m;	50 kg.
	Pacific	1.4 m;	60 kg.
• Adult males	Atlantic to	3 m;	1200 kg.
	Pacific to	3.6 m;	1600 kg.
• Adult females	Atlantic to	2.5 m;	750 kg.
	Pacific to	2.6 m;	1250 kg.

1.2 Stocks

1.2.1 Identification

Two subspecies are recognized: *Odobenus rosmarus rosmarus*, the Atlantic walrus and *O.r. divergens*, the Pacific walrus. It has also been suggested that the walrus population of the Laptev Sea is of subspecific status (*O.r. laptevi* Chapskii 1940).

1.2.2 Distribution

Walruses are found in four areas as follows: (a) the east coast of Greenland, Spitzbergen (Svalbard), Franz Joseph Land and the Barents and Kara Seas; (b) the eastern Canadian Arctic and western Greenland; (c) the Bering and Chukchi Sea; (d) the Laptev Sea. (a) and (b) are the range of the Atlantic walrus, (c) and (d) are the range of the Pacific walrus. The extent of migration varies among populations and where it does occur the pattern is generally associated with seasonal movements of pack ice.

1.2.3 Structure of Stocks

Walrus are polygamous and partial segregation by sex is evident through most of the year. The breeding segments may have a male: female ratio of 1:5 or greater. Males are gregarious out of the breeding season.

2 Vital parameters

2.1 Populaltion size

2.1.1 Methods of estimation

Estimates are based on counts from aircraft and aerial photographs.

2.1.2 Results

a) eastern Greenland coast, Spitzbergen, Franz Joseph Land and Barents and Kara Seas — no accurate estimate but likely in the low thousands.

b) eastern Canadian Arctic and western Greenland — no accurate estimate but likely about 10,000.

c) Laptev Sea — no recent data but in excess of 3,000 in 1954.

d) Bering & Chukchi Seas — upwards of 140,000.

2.1.3 Trends in Abundance

Walrus populations were reduced by harvesting during the late 19th and early 20th centuries. However, as a result of regulation, and possibly other factors such as decreased need by natives, the take of walruses has been decreased sufficiently to allow the population to increase in most areas. An exception to this is south-west Greenland and where catches declined at the beginning of this century and remained at a low level for the last 20 years. The most important hunting area in Greenland is the Thule district, but information on the trend of catches there is insufficient.

2.2 *Rates*

2.2.1 *Reproductive*

Age of sexual maturity:

- females: some at age 5, most at 6 or 7 years
- males: some at age 5, most by 8-10 years.

Birth season: mid April - mid June.

Pregnancy rate: mature females: 80 % calve every 2 years, 15 % every 3 years, remainder less frequently.

Lactation: at least one year but most probably to 2 years.

Mating season: February and March

Gestation period: about 15 months; 3 to 3.5 month delay of implantation

Longevity: about 40 years.

2.2.2 *Natural mortality*

About 5 % in the Pacific walrus; no estimates for other population.

2.2.3 *Harvesting*

For the Pacific walrus, the total annual mortality was estimated in the early 1960's to be 13 %, with harvesting rate estimated to be near 8 %. The present rate is near 5 % (6,000 animals). Unretrieved kill is high, about 30-50 % of total numbers removed from the population.

Recent harvest rates are not available for other populations.

3 Trophic Relationships

3.1 *Food and feeding*

3.1.1 *Food base and habits*

The walrus feeds in shallow waters. About 65 species of benthic invertebrates, principally mollusks, echinoderms, tunicates, crustaceans, priapulids and echiuroids are eaten.

3.1.2 *Requirements and Utilizations*

As much as 45 kg of food may be consumed in a single day.

3.1.3 *Changes in abundance of food supply*

No evidence of changes.

3.2 *Competition and Predation*

There is a potential for competition among walruses and other ice inhabiting pinnipeds, particularly the bearded seal, *Erignathus barbatus.*

Predation is apparently an insignificant cause of mortality among walruses.

4 Relation to Man

4.1 *Values*

4.1.1 *Consumptive*

The utilization of the carcasses varies in different areas. About 35 % of the carcass is fit for humann consumption. The remainder of the animal is usually used for dog food. The skin is commercially used in the manufacturing of billiard-cue tips. Of primary commercial importance is the tusk ivory. It appears that most of the animals are harvested for this product.

4.1.2 *Low-consumptive*

These animals are generally remotely located and as such offer little recreational value except for those animals now in zoos.

4.2 *Effects of Human Activities Other than Exploitation*

At present extensive exploration for oil and minerals is underway throughout the walrus' range. This increased influx of people is likely to increase the harrassment problem and any major oil spills may have adverse effects.

There have also been studies on the potential mollusk resources in the Arctic with exploitation of this food source for human consumption in mind. This may have an adverse effect on the walrus population. The main problem at the moment is continual harrassment, particularly by low-flying aircraft, of herds near sites of human habitation.

4.3 Management and Conservation

Prior to 1972 in Alaska, hunting permits were issued only north of Cape Newenham (58°39′N). Licensed residents who depend on the walrus for food could take up to 5 adult cows or subadults of either sex and an unlimited number of adult bulls per year. Other licensed hunters were allowed one bull per year. Since 1972 in Alaska only Eskimoes, Aleuts, and Indians have been allowed to take walruses for subsistence; however, there has been no limit on the number that can be taken.

In the Soviet Union (Pacific region) only animals on the ice and land may be hunted and a total quota of 2,000 is imposed.

In Canada a bag limit of 7 animals per Eskimo family is practiced and exportation of walrus hides and uncarved tusks is prohibited.

In Greenland, hunting in Davis Strait and Baffin Bay is restricted to resident Danish citizens. There are also seasonal restrictions enforced in various areas along the Greenland coast.

No regular harvesting has taken place since about 1952 on the northeast Atlantic populations.

In the Laptev Sea walruses can be taken only by participants of some Arctic expeditions and native people for subsistence.

5 Threats to Stocks

With the protection offered the species at this time, no threats of serious depletion of numbers are foreseen. A possible exception to this would be a disastrous oil spill or extensive exploitation of the mollusk resources of the north.

6 Research

6.1 Current Status

Population assessments, reproductive biology, pathology and behaviour are presently being studied in some areas. Many populations, however, are not being studied.

6.2 Recommendations for future research

Although the practicality of obtaining useful population estimates of large and widely distributed walrus populations from aerial surveys is questionable, this method is probably the best one available. It may give useful results when applied to small populations. With this in mind, the highest priority for research should be population assessment studies of small populations for which there is now little information. This would apply to all populations except the Pacific walrus in the Bering and Chukchi Seas. Continuous monitoring and sampling of harvested animals is needed to provide additional biological data and to improve estimates of population parameters. Studies of activity and behaviour are needed to provide the basic knowledge on which to base improved methods of population assessment.

HARBOUR (COMMON) SEAL

W.N. Bonner

1 Description

1.1 Species identification

1.1.1 Taxonomic.
Family: Phocidae
Species: Phoca vitulina Linnaeus 1758

1.1.2 Size

		Source
• Newborn pups	70- 90 cm	United Kingdom (Bonner, unpublished)
	9- 11 kg	
• Adult males	130-170 cm	
	55-105 kg	
• Adult females	120-155 cm	
	45- 87 kg	
• Males	-195 cm	Scandinavia (Curry-Lindahl 1975)
	253 kg	
• Females	-168 cm	
	150 kg	
• Newborn pups	81.6 ± 6.2 cm	British Columbia (Bigg 1969)
• Adult males	161.1 ± 4.9 cm	
	87.6 ± 6.6 kg	
• Adult females	147.7 ± 2.4 cm	
	64.8 ± 4.4 kg	
• Newborn pups	98.2 ± 3.2 cm	Hokkaido (Naito and Nishiwaki 1975)
• Adult males	186 cm (average)	
• Adult females	169 cm (average)	

Coat colour and pattern very variable. Basically a mottle of dark spots on a lighter ground but in some seals spots coalesce, particularly on back, to give a pale interrupted reticulation on a dark ground. In the western North Pacific specimens with white ringmarks are common (Naito and Nishiwaki 1972); elsewhere ringmarks rare. Some evidence that seals from estuarine areas are not so brightly marked as seals from rocky coasts. Pups born in adult-type spotted pelage, very rarely in white lanugo.

1.2 Stocks

1.2.1 Identification

Many names have been applied to the *Phoca vitulina* seals. Those with the greatest currency are *P. vitulina vitulina* from the eastern Atlantic; *P. v. concolor* from the western Atlantic; and *P. v. richardi* from the western coast of North America. The name *P. v. kurilensis* (= *P. kurilensis, P. insularis*) has been used for the land-breeding seals of the Asiatic Pacific coast but these are doubtfully distinct from *P. v. richardi.* The sub-specific status of all these forms is based mainly on geographical isolation and a serious taxonomic study of the species is required.

1.2.2 Distribution

In the eastern Atlantic *P. vitulina vitulina* breeds around the coast of Iceland, chiefly in the west and south east (Arnlaugsson 1973; Hook 1961); around the shores of the British Isles, with major populations at the Hebrides, the west coast of Scotland, Orkney and Shetland, and at the Wash (Bonner 1976); the European continental coast from the Netherlands, German Bight, Danish and Norwegian coasts as far as Cape North (Summers, Bonner and van Haafton, in press; Øynes 1964); sparsely in the Baltic Sea as far north as Gotland, but not in the Gulfs of Bothnia and Finland (Hook and Johnels 1972). It no longer occurs as a breeding species in the Faroe Islands (Joensen in Bigg 1969a), but a small group has been reported from Svalbard. The status and distribution on the North Russian coast is unknown.

In the western Atlantic *P. vitulina concolor* breeds from Maine in the eastern United States as far north as Ellesmere Island in the Canadian Arctic and west to western Hudson's Bay (Mansfield 1967). The distribution is very discontinuous. A form described as *P. v. mellonae*, doubtfully distinct from *P. v. concolor*, (Mansfield 1967a) is found in freshwater lakes in the Ungava Peninsula, Quebec (Doutt 1942). *P. vitulina* seals are found on the coast of south-west Greenland from Kap Farvel to the Polar Circle, now and then north to Upernavik and to Angmagssalik in south east Greenland, in which areas it was previously more common.

P. vitulina richardi is found on the west coast of North America from Baja California to the northern side of Bristol Bay on the Alaska Peninsula and around Alaska eastwards to Herschel Island. A large form (see sect. 1.1.2), *P. vitulina kurilensis* is found in northern Hokkaido, the Kurile Islands, and the Aleutian Islands, where it meets the *P. v. richardi* seals. It is doubtful whether these two forms are distinct and it is probably a clinal variation.

An ice-breeding form from the western North Pacific is regarded as specifically distinct and is considered separately.

1.2.3 Structure of stocks

Harbour seals tend to occur in small groups, often around 30-80 individuals, though where food is plentiful, as in salmon estuaries, much larger groups may be found. There is little social structure in the group on land and no evidence of aquatic gregariousness (Bigg 1969, Bonner 1972). They are non-migratory but tend to spend more time offshore in the winter. There is no marked aggregation at the pupping season and *Phoca vitulina* does not form harems and is probably promiscuous (Bigg 1969, Bonner 1972). It is possible that the seals in northern Hokkaido are adopting a more terrestrial role in the breeding season and this may be associated with incipient polygyny.

2 Vital parameters

2.1 Population size

2.1.1 Methods of estimation

This is an extremely difficult seal to count. Methods have included direct counts from the shore, from boats, or from aircraft (Vaughan 1971); or capture/recapture techniques and interpretation of hunting effort (Summers and Mountford 1975).

2.1.2 Results

North-east Atlantic	*Thousands*	
U.K.	10.4-13.7	Summer, Bonner & Van Haaften, in press
Ireland	2?	
German Bight (including Wadden Sea and Denmark)	3.8	
Iceland	28	Summer, Bonner & van Haaften, in press; Arnlaugsson, 1973
Baltic	no data	
	48.2-51.5	

Northern-west Atlantic		
Canada, exluding Labrador, Hudson Bay and east Arctic	12.7	Boulva, 1975
Total Canada	20-30	
Greenland	no data	
Eastern USA	no data	

Alaska	260	Bigg, pers. comm. Mate, pers. comm.
British Columbia	35	
Washington	2.5	
Oregon	2	
California	2	
Baja California	1	
East of date-line	10-15	
	312.5-317.5	
Total	380.7-399.0	

2.1.3 Trends in abundance

No clear data, probably fairly static on a global basis (but see 2.2.3), local populations generally decreasing around areas of human habitation (Summers, Bonner and van Haaften, in press).

2.2 Rates

2.2.1 Reproductive

Age at sexual maturity:

- female 2-5 years
- male 3-6 years

Pregnancy rate (weighted for age): 88 % (for British Columbia seals, Bigg, 1969).

Birth season: generally lasts 1 ½-2 months in any one area and extends from late January to September over the range of the species. Bigg, 1969a, demonstrated clines in the pupping season in the Pacific and western Atlantic, but not in Europe. In Alaska most births from early March to April, later south to Washington and then earlier going south to Mexico. On Asiatic Pacific coast late March to late May. In western Atlantic March to June and in eastern Atlantic May to August, majority end of June and July.

Lactation: 4-6 weeks

Mating: within 2 weeks of end of lactation

Gestation: 10.5-11 month (delay, 2 months)

Longevity: 40 years.

2.2.2 Mortality (includes natural and hunting mortality)

First-year		20 %	
1-5 years:	males	20 %	British
	females	20 %	Columbia seals
6+ years:	males	26 %	(Bigg, 1969)
	females	15 %	
Preweaning		17 %	Eastern Canada
Subsequent		16 %	(Boulva, 1975)

2.2.3 Harvesting, commercial and incidental kill

Have been hunted in all areas of distribution for pelts, local consumption and fisheries predation control. Hunting losses are often high. Locally, hunting has radically reduced or eliminated populations but average harvests on a global basis do not approach MSY level. Very approximate annual catch figures are given below. The catch is made up predominantly of underyearling animals.

	Catch (thousand)
Europe	1
Iceland	5-7
E. Canada	1
Pacific (other than Alaska)	1
Alaska	8-12
Greenland	0.2-0.1
	16-22

No data available on incidental kill but this is believed to be negligible.

3 Trophic relationships

3.1 Food and Feeding

3.1.1 Food habits

Generally feed close in-shore or in shallow water. Highly opportunistic feeders with catholic tastes and the ability to change from one type of food to another.

3.1.2 Food base

Pelagic, demersal, anadromic and catadromic fishes, cephalopods and Crustacea. Gadids, clupeids, pleuronectids and salmonids are fishes of commercial importance eaten by these seals.

3.1.3 Requirements and utilization

2-3 kg fish/day for adult females (about 60 kg) in captivity at University of British Columbia (Bigg, pers. comm.).

5 kg/day for 120 kg seal in captivity in Japan (Naito, pers. comm.).

3.1.4 Change in abundance of food supply

No data.

3.2 Competition and predators

No data on competition. Newborn seals are preyed on by sea-eagles, golden-eagles and foxes; predators on older animals include sharks, killer whales, bears and walruses.

4 Relation to man

4.1 Values

4.1.1 Consumption

Phoca vitulina seals are hunted primarily for skins (produce a high quality fur), oil and meat (mainly by aboriginal hunters). Minor uses of local importance include the manufacture of trinkets and handicrafts and meat for mink feeding.

4.1.2 Non-consumptive

Locally these seals may be an important tourist attraction. They are commonly kept in aquaria and are the most widely utilized seal for experimental research.

4.2 Effects of human activities other than exploitation

Because it often inhabits relatively closed waters of bays and estuaries, the land-breeding seals are more prone to be affected by environment pollution. For example, high concentration of mercury and organo-chlorine compounds have been found in seals from the Wadden Sea, Netherlands. The seals are sensitive to disturbance and may desert an area if harried by people, boats or aircraft. Land reclamation in estuarine areas may result in habitat destruction (e.g. Delta region of Netherlands).

4.3 Management and conservation

Eastern Atlantic: in Iceland there is no regulation of hunting. In the British Isles *Phoca vitulina* is protected by law (not in northern Ireland) but in U.K. licenses can be issued to take surplus stock for commercial purposes or to protect fisheries. Hunting either strictly controlled or prohibited elsewhere in European range. Western Atlantic: protected in U.S.A.; subject to bounty payment in Canada; hunted by aborigines in Greenland (prohibited in summer months).

Pacific: protected in California, Oregon, Washington and Canada; recently bountied, but now protected in Alaska; full protection for land breeding seals in Japan. No data from Mexico.

5 Threats to stock

No data, but see 4.2.

6 Research

6.1 Current state

East Atlantic: regular population assessment and feeding and behavioural studies in U.S.; population assess and pollution studies in Netherlands; population studies in Iceland; studies of occurrence and pollution in Denmark.

West Atlantic: population dynamics, trophic relations and behaviour in Canada.

Pacific: studies of population dynamics, movements, stock identification, reproduction biology, feeding habits, growth, physiology and ecology in U.S.A., Canada, U.S.S.R. and Japan.

6.2 *Recommendations for future research*

There is a strong need for taxonomic information, based on morphometry, comparative anatomy, serology, etc. Better stock assessment methods need to be developed, and haulout behaviour must be studied to interpret on-land counts. General studies should be continued.

References

ARNLAUGSSON, T., Selir vid Island. Rannsóknastofnun 1973 fiskidnadarins. 25 p. (mimeo).

BIGG, M.A., The harbour seal in British Columbia. *Bull.* 1969 *Fish. Res. Board. Can.*, (172):33 p.

—, Clines in the pupping season of the harbour seal 1969a *Phoca vitulina. J. Fish. Res. Board Can.*, 26(2):449-55.

BONNER, W.N., The grey seal and common seal in Eu- 1972 ropean waters. *Oceanogr. Mar. Biol.*, 10:461-507.

—, The stocks of grey seals (*Halichoerus grypus*) and 1976 common seals (*Phoca vitulina*) in Great Britain. *Publ. Natl. Environ Res. Counc. (C)*, (16).

BONNER, W.N., The status of seals in the U.K. Paper 1976a presented to the Scientific Consultation on the Conservation and Management of Marine Mammals and their Environment, Bergen, Norway, 31 August-9 September, 1976. Rome, FAO, ACMRR/MM/SC 43:11 p.

BOULVA, J., Temporal variations in birth period and 1975 characteristics of newborn harbour seals. *Rapp. P.-V. Réun. CIEM*, 169:405-5.

CURRY-LINDAHL, K., Däggdjur i färg. Stockholm, 1975 Almqvist and Wiksell, 307 p.

DOUTT, J.K., A review of the genus *Phoca. Ann. Carne-* 1942 *gie Mus.*, 29:61-125.

HOOK, O., Notes on the status of seals in Iceland, Ju- 1961 ne-July, 1959. *Proc. Zool. Soc. Lond.*, 137:628-30.

HOOK, O., and A.G. JOHNELS, The breeding and distri- 1972 bution of the grey seal, (*Halichoerus grypus* Fab.) in the Baltic Sea with observations on other seals of the area. *Proc. R. Soc. Lond. (B. Biol. Sci.)*, 182: 37-58.

MANSFIELD, A.W., Seals of Arctic and eastern Canada. 1967 *Bull. Fish. Res. Board Can.*, (137):35 p.

—, Distribution of the harbour seal, *Phoca vitulina*, 1967a Linnaeus, in Canadian waters. *J. Mammal.*, 48:249-57.

NAITO, Y., and M. NISHIWAKI, Ecology and morphology 1975 of *Phoca vitulina largha* and *Phoca kurilensis* in the southern Sea of Okhotsk and north east of Hokkaido. *Rapp. P.-V. Réun. CIEM*, 169:379-86.

ØYNES, P., Sel på norskekysten fra Finmark til Møre. 1964 *Fisk. Gang*, (48):694-707.

SØNDERGAARD, N.O., A.H. JOENSEN and E.B. HANSEN, 1976 Saelernes forekomst og Saeljazten i Danmark. *Dansk Vildtunders.*, 26(131).

SUMMERS, C.F., and M.D. MOUNTFORD, Counting the 1975 common seal. *Nature, Lond.*, 253:670-1.

SUMMERS, C.F., W.N. BONNER and J. VAN HAAFTEN, Changes in the seal population of the North Sea. *Rapp. P.-V. Réun. CIEM*, (in press).

VAUGHAN, R.W., Aerial survey in seals research. *In* The 1971 application of aerial photography to the work of the Nature Conservancy, edited by R. Goodier, Edinburgh, Nature Conservancy, pp. 88-98.

LARGHA SEAL

W.N. BONNER

1 Description

1.1 *Species identification*

1.1.1 Taxonomic. Family: Phocidae
Species: Phoca largha (Pallas 1811)

1.1.2 Size

- Newborn pups 76-81 cm, 78 cm av.
  6.9-7.3 kg., 7.1 kg. av.
- Adult males 168 cm av.
  (185 cm max)
- Adult females 162 cm av.
  (182 cm max)

Bering Sea (Tikhomirov 1971)

- Newborn pups 85 cm
- Adult males 169.9 ± 4.0 cm
- Adult females 159 ± 3.1 cm

Southern Sea of Okhotsk (Natio & Nishiwaki 1975)

- Newborn pups 76-90 cm
  (1-5 days) 7-10 kg.
  167-169 cm
- Adults (both sexes) (214 cm max)
  90-114 kg.
  (150 kg max)

(Popov 1976)

Coat colour and pattern variable and similar to *P. vitulina* though Naito & Nishiwaki (1975) considered they could generally distinguish *P. largha* (paler) from *P. vitulina* (darker) in southern Sea of Okhotsk. Generally small black or white spots on a paler ventral side. Ring-shaped spots, if present, not so clear as in *P. v. kurilensis.* Pups born in white or smoky-grey lanugo.

1.2 *Stocks*

1.2.1 Identification

No separate stocks positively identified but the seals of the Po Hai Sea would seem to be reproductively isolated from the remainder.

1.2.2 Distribution

Bering and Chukchi Seas and Arctic Ocean coast of Alaska; Sea of Okhotsk south to Hokkaido, the Po Hai Sea and the northwestern parts of the Yellow Sea (Shou-jen Huang 1962) and occasionally off the Japanese and Korean coasts. As far as is known breeding is restricted to the Bering Sea, the Sea of Okhotsk and the Po Hai Sea.

1.2.3 Structure of Stocks

Very closely associated with ice and seasonally dependent on it for the birth and rearing of their pups.

During winter and early spring concentrated along edge of pack. Move northwards and towards coasts as ice retreats and disintegrates. During summer and autumn seals are cqastal and form large groups on shore. At breeding season males and females pair and remain in family groups (Burns *et al.* 1972).

2 Vital Parameters

2.1 Population size

2.1.1 Methods of estimation

Counted by USSR and USA from aerial and boat surveys using indirect methods and relative indices of abundance.

2.1.2 Results

No firm estimates but Bering Sea population variously estimated at 133,000 and 200,000-250,000. Sea of Okhotsk 135,000-200,000. No data for Po Hai Sea.

2.1.3 Trends in Abundance

No data. No reason to suppose man-made change in population.

2.2 Rates

2.2.1 Reproductive

Age at sexual maturity:

- females 3-4
- males 4-5

Pregnancy rate: no data.

Birth season: late March - mid April (extremes: late January - early May).

Lactation: 4 weeks.

Mating: no data.

Gestation: 10.5 months.

Longevity: 35 years.

2.2.2 Mortality

First year 45 % (Popov
Subsequent 8 %-10 % 1976.)

2.2.3 Harvesting

USSR (Bering Sea and Sea of Okhotsk): 10,000-15,000.

Alaska: 3,000.

No data on incidental kill, but believed negligible.

3 Trophic relationships

3.1 Food and Feeding

3.1.1 Food habits

No data.

3.1.2 Food base

Feed mainly on fish, cephalopods and crustacea during association with ice; in autumn, where seals near land, feed largely on salmonids. Young seals feed on amphipods, shrimps and sand eels (Popov 1976). In Po Hai Sea eat " dace " (*Leuciscus?*) (Shoujen Huang 1962).

3.1.3 Requirements and utilisation

No data.

3.1.4 Change in abundance of food supply

No data.

3.2 Competition and Predators

No data on competition. Bears, and to lesser extent, wolves and foxes predate seals (Popov 1976).

4 Relationship to man

4.1.1 Consumptive

Hunted for pelts and locally for food. Hunting pressure not heavy.

4.1.2 Low-consumptive

No data.

4.2 Effects of human activities other than exploitation

Not known.

4.3 Management and conservation

USSR sets limits for ship sealing of 5,000 seals in Sea of Okhotsk and 6,000 in Bering Sea with a land-based catch limit of 2,000 from each area. Alaska permitted hunting north of 58°30′ with no restriction of season or bag limits. Average harvest around 3,000. A bounty of $3 is authorised but no funds for payment of bounty have been allocated.

5 Threats to stocks

No data.

6 Research

6.1 Current status

Both USSR and USA have made investigations on general biology and population dynamics.

No data from Po Hai Sea.

6.2 Recommendations for future research

Existing programmes should continue with a major emphasis on reproductive potential and stock assessment. A general investigation of the seals of the Po Hai Sea should be made.

References

BURNS, J.J., *et al.*, Adoption of a strange pup by the
1972 ice-inhabiting harbour seal, *Phoca vitulina largha*. *J. Mammal.*, 53:594-8.

NAITO, Y., Comparison in colour pattern of two species
1973 of harbour seal in adjacent waters of Hokkaido. *Sci Rep. Whales Res. Inst., Tokyo*, (35):301-10.

NAITO, Y., and M. NISHIWAKI, Ecology and morphology
1975 of *Phoca vitulina largha* and *Phoca kurilensis* in the southern Sea of Okhotsk and north east of Hokkaido. *Rapp. p.-V. Réun. CIEM*, 169:379-86.

POPOV, L.A., Status of main ice-form of seals inhabiting
1976 water of the USSR and adjacent to the country marine areas. Paper presented to the Scientific Consultation on the Conservation and Management of Marine Mammals and Their Environment, Bergen, Norway, 31 August-9 September, 1976. Rome, FAO, ACMRR/MM/SC/51:17 p.

SHOU-JEN HUANG, Economically important animals of
1962 China. Seals. Peking, Kexue Chubanshe Scientific Publishing Co., pp. 414-7 (Transl. by Foreign Language Division, Department of the Secretary of State of Canada).

TIKHOMIROV, E.A., Body growth and development of
1971 reproductive organs of the North Pacific phocids. *In* Pinnipeds of the North Pacific, edited by V.A. Arsen'ev and K.I. Panin. Jerusalem, Israel Program for Scientific Translations, IPST Cat. No. 5798:213-41 (Transl. of *Tr. VNIRO*, 68(1968)).

RINGED SEAL

IAN STIRLING & WENDY CALVERT

1 Description

1.1 *Species identification*

1.1.1 *Family:* Phocidae
Species: *Phoca (Pusa) hispida* (Schreber 1775)

1.1.2 *Size*

- Newborn pups: 55-65 cm; 4-5 kg.
- Adults: 85-160 cm (av. 125 cm); 40-90 kg (av. 65 kg).

There is considerable geographical variation in size. Males tend to be slightly larger than females, though there is much seasonal variation in weight, due to loss of blubber during the spring moult: average weight is also thought to be greater in conditions of more stable ice, where pups received longer parental care. Colouring of both sexes is similar, with a dark grey or grey-black background (dorsally) with oval-shaped white ring designs, and light grey ventrally. The white lanugo of the pups is moulted after 3-4 weeks.

1.2 *Stocks*

1.2.1 *Identification*

Although no separate stocks have been identified the species has been divided into six sub-species.

1. *P. h. hispida:* Arctic Ocean and sea-ice of northern Eurasia, Greenland and North America, Labrador & Hudson Bay.
2. *P. h. ochotensis:* Sea of Okhotsk to the northern Kuril Islands and southern tip of Sakhalin.
3. *P. h. krascheninikovi:* Northern Bering Sea, southward with pack ice to St. Michael, Alaska and Bristol Bay.
4. *P. h. botnica:* Baltic Sea, Gulf of Bothnia and Gulf of Finland.
5. *P. h. ladogensis:* Lake Ladoga, USSR.
6. *P. h. saimensis:* Lake Saimaa, Finland.

The forms *P. caspica* and *P. sibirica* are closely related to *P. hispida.*

1.2.2 *Distribution*

See above, 1.2.1 The preferred habitat is the stable inshore ice, which is the best pupping habitat and may also be associated with favourable plankton and fish production. Adult males and females are usually found in this coastal fast-ice, while the subadults concentrate further offshore in the less stable ice. Mass migrations are little known, but there are some seasonal movements in relation to ice distribution, such as along the Greenland coast or in the Beaufort Sea.

1.2.3 *Structure of stocks*

Ringed seals tend to be solitary in distribution but congregate during the moulting period in mid- to late June. In the Gulf of Bothania ringed seals aggregate in the winter, perhaps because of ice-conditions (curry-Lindahl, pers. comm.).

2 Vital Parameters

2.1 *Population size*

2.1.1 *Methods of estimation*

Aerial surveys, ground counts, surveys of occupied and deserted birth lairs, and counts of breathing holes.

2.1.2 *Results*

This is probably the most abundant seal in both the northeast Atlantic and Artic Oceans — estimates are 6-7 million — but it is impossible to know the total accurately because of the wide distribution and the fact that all censuses to date cannot be accurately related to absolute numbers. Density estimates vary with habitat type, (seasonal influx) and geographic area, from 1 to 16 per square nautical mile. Recent estimates for the Caspian and Baikal seals are 520,000 and 50-60,000 respectively.

2.1.3 *Trend in abundance*

Population levels are probably the same as in the 18th and 19th centuries, though this is not well documented. There has been some decrease in the Sea of Okhotsk population, and some large-scale changes have been recently recorded in the Beaufort Chuckchi Seas; long-term fluctuations documented in Greenland.

2.2 *Rates*

2.2.1 *Reproductive*

Age at sexual maturity:

- males 6-8 years, most being fully mature at 7 years
- females 5-8 years, the average age of females at first ovulation is 6 years.

Birth season: late March through to late April, with the peak in mid- to late-March.

Lactation period: 4-6 weeks, varying geographically, possibly related to duration of stable ice.

Mating time: mating occurs in the first month after parturition in the period March to early May, with the peak in mid-April.

Pregnancy rates: estimates range from 80 % to 95 % of all adult females, though the higher estimates were based on ovulation rates rather than the presence of embryos. Recent research has shown that changes in environmental conditions may greatly reduce both ovulation and pregnancy rates.

Gestation: 10.5 to 11 months including a delayed implantation of 3.5 months.

Longevity: 46 years.

2.2.2 *Natural mortality*

Excluding pups, the natural mortality rate is about 9 %. Overall survival for the total population, including pups, is 85 %. Sudden changes in environmental conditions can cause seals to be in poor physical condition and probably increase mortality rates significantly.

2.2.3 *Harvesting*

There are no good data on the total Canadian kill, but the combined Soviet-American kill is estimated at 12-16,000. Reported landings in Greenland 40,000-70,000 annually; total kill may be up to 20 % higher. 3,500 taken annually in White Sea, thought to be under-exploited. Estimates of maximum sustainable yield are about 8 %.

3 **Trophic relationships**

3.1 *Food and feeding*

3.1.1 *Food habits*

Ringed seals have a generalized variable diet, and tend to eat what is available, whether benthic, nektonic, or planktonic, although there is a preference for the latter. From December to February, the diet is mainly fish especially polar cod. During the summer, crustaceans and other invertebrates are more important as food.

3.1.2 *Food base*

To date, there is no reliable estimate of

the biomass of the food base or a quantitative study of trophic relationships.

3.1.3 Requirements and utilization

From 0.8 to 2.4 kg of food at one time have been reported in Caspian seals, but requirements and utilization are as yet unknown.

3.1.4 Changes in food supply

Unknown.

3.2 Competition and predation

The degree of competition with other species is unknown, but recent research shows more ecological overlap with bearded seals than was previously suspected. There is heavy predation by polar bears on young and adults, and by arctic fox on newborn young in birth lairs. Incidental predation by killer whales and walrus has been reported.

4 Relation to man

4.1 Values

4.1.1 Consumptive

The ringed seal is the most important northern seal for native subsistence use; skins, fat and meat are used. The furs and meat are also utilized commercially.

4.1.2 Low-consumptive

Nil.

4.2 Other effects

There is a potential for detrimental effects of human activities such as extensive offshore oil exploration and extraction, inter-island pipeline construction, and shipment of oil with tankers in arctic waters. The effects could be directly on the seals, or indirectly through their food chain. Industrial pollution could become serious in the freshwater-dwelling forms and there is evidence of pollution effects in the Baltic Sea. Hunters in Greenland believe seals avoid areas with heavy boat traffic.

4.3 Management and conservation

The population is not considered overexploited (except in the Baltic), and there are no international agreements and few quotas, except in the U.S. where hunting is by permit only, except for native subsistence use. Local regulations on hunting and boat traffic in Greenland.

5 Threats to stock

Because the population tends to be solitary and widely distributed, there are no threats to the total population, though some local stocks may be over-harvested. The limited stocks of the Caspian and Baikal seals could be quite vulnerable.

6 Research

6.1 Current status

Natural history and population research is being conducted in Canada, Alaska, and USSR; research on censusing methods in Canada, Alaska and Lake Baikal; research on inter-relationships of pack ice species and predation in Canada; research on caloric requirements and physiology in Canada; baseline research on heavy metals and toxic chemicals in Canada and Alaska. Populations studies and analysis of toxic residues in Greenland.

6.2 Future research

— improve techniques for estimating numbers; data on harvest assessment and composition; improve data on female reproductive cycle; detail dispersal and possible migrations; study trophic relationships and food requirements; study influence of environmental factors on production and mortality; study social behaviour; ecological relationships to other phocids.

References

IVASHIN, M.V., L.A. POPOV and A.S. TSAPKO, Morskie
1972 Mlekopitayushchie (Marine Mammals), edited by P.A. Moiseeva. Moscow, Pishchevaia Promyshtlennost. Also issued as: *Transl. Ser. Fish. Res. Board Can.*, (2783) (1973).

JOHNSTON, M.L., *et al.*, Marine mammals. Chapter 33. *In*
1966 Environment of the Cape Thompson region, Alaska, edited by N.J. Wilimovsky and J.N. Wolfe. Oak Ridge, Conn., U.S. Atomic Energy Commission, pp. 877-924.

MCLAREN, I.A., The biology of the ringed seal (*Phoca*
1958 *hispida* Schreber) in the eastern Canadian Arctic. *Bull. Fish. Res. Board Can.*, (118):97 p.

—, The economics of seals in the eastern Canadian
1958a Arctic. *Circ. Fish. Res. Board Can. (Arctic Biol. Stn)*, (1):94 p.

SMITH, T.G., Population dynamics of the ringed seal in
1973 the Canadian eastern Arctic. *Bull. Fish. Res. Board Can.*, (181):55 p.

STIRLING, K.G., R. ARCHIBALD and D. DEMASTER, Dis-
n.d. tribution and abundance of seals in eastern Beaufort Sea. Final report to the Beaufort Department of Environment, Victoria, B.C., 59 p. (mimeo).

LADOGA SEAL

L. Popov

1 Descriptive

1.1 *Species identification*

1.1.1 *Family:* Phocidae
Species: *Phoca (Pusa) hispida ladogensis* (Nordquist 1899)

1.1.2 *Size*

- Newborn pups: 50-60 cm; 4-5 kg.
- Adults: 150 cm; 60-70 kg.

There are four types of coat colour: 47 percent of seals are generally dark brown-black, one-coloured, with light ring-shaped patterns; 29 per cent of seals are dark brown with light vein-like patterns instead of rings; 17 per cent are generally light with a dark belt on the dorsal side, ill-defined rings and brown spots of different sizes.

1.2 *Stocks*

1.2.1 *Identification*
No separate stocks identified.

1.2.2 *Distribution*
Sparsely distributed; denser concentrations in August-September in the northern part of the Lake. Local feeding migrations are characteristic.

2 Vital parameters

2.1 *Population size*

From aerial surveys estimated at 10,000 to 12,000 in winter. During recent years no changes in abundance.

2.2 *Rates*

2.2.1 *Reproductive*
Age at sexual maturity:

- females 4 to 5 years
- males 6 to 7 years.

Birth season: mid-February to mid-March.

Lactation: 5 months.

Mating: March, April.

Moulting: Adults moult generaly on ice by the end of April or the beginning of May. Some individuals finish moulting on land. Most pups lose natal coat by the beginning of March.

Mortality: no data available.

Harvesting (commercial and incidental): 150-200 seals are harvested annually by natives.

3 Trophic relationships

3.1 *Food habits*

Main food item is fish: smelt, ruffe, burbot.

3.2 *Requirements and utilization*

Unknown.

3.3 *Changes in abundance of food supply*

Unknown.

4 Relation to man

4.1 Values

4.1.1 Consumptive

Harvested for fur-bearing animal food. Fur and fat are used by natives.

4.1.2 Low-consumptive

A small number is taken for scientific purposes.

4.2 Effects of human activities other than exploitation

Unknown.

4.3 Management and conservation

Annual limit of 500 seals is set for sealing by natives. No bounties are given for sealing. Sport sealing is prohibited. Areas closed to fishermen and tourists have been designated.

5 Threats to stocks

Unknown.

6 Research

6.1 Current status

Distribution, abundance, general morphology, reproduction and moulting seasons are investigated.

6.2 Recommendations for future research

Investigations on distribution, abundance, ecology during moulting and feeding periods will be continued.

References

PILATOV, I.E., Morskie mlekopitayushchie (Marine 1975 mammals). Part 2. Proceedings of the Sixth All-Union Conference on the Study of Marine Mammals.

SOKOLOV, A.S., Studies on the biology of the Ladoga 1958 seal. *Uch. Zap. Leningr. Gos. Pedagog. Inst.*, 179:97-112.

—, On the feeding of Ladoga seal and advisability of its 1958a harvesting. *Rybn. Khoz. Mosk.*, 10:25-7.

BAIKAL SEAL

L. Popov

1 Description

1.1 Species identification

1.1.1 *Family:* Phocidae
Species: Phoca (Pusa) sibirica (Gmelin 1788)

1.1.2 *Size*

- Newborn pups: 70 cm; 3 kg.
- Adults: 120-140 cm; 80-90 kg.

Back is a uniform dull grey; sides lighter in hue; belly silver; young born in white lanugo.

1.2 Stocks

1.2.1 *Identification*

No separate stocks identified.

1.2.2 *Distribution*

Throughout Lake Baikal (and to a lesser extent, Lake Oron) but concentrating in north during winter and migrating south during summer.

1.2.3 *Structure of stocks*

Sparsely distributed except during the breeding and moulting period when some aggregation occurs; species believed to be polygamous.

2 Vital parameters

2.1 Populations size

Estimated at 40-50,000 seals.

2.2 Rates

2.2.1 *Reproductive*

Age at sexual maturity:

- females, 2-5 years, but most do not breed before 5 or 6 years
- males, about 2 years after females.

Pregnancy rates: about 88 %.
Birth season: Birth of pups born over 10-15 days with peak in middle of March.
Lactation period: 2-2 ½ months.
Mating time: no data
Gestation: about 11 months
Longevity: no data.

2.2.2 *Natural mortality*

Unknown.

2.2.3 *Harvesting*

The limit of seal catch for the last years has been 2-3,000 seals (pups only). Aerial surveys suggested total population of 40-50,000 animals; had been about 5-6,000 from about 1930-1941.

3 Trophic relationships

3.1 Food habits

Principal diet is pelagic oil-fish and cisco but commercial fish estimated to constitute only about 1 % of diet.

3.2 *Requirements and utilization*
Unknown.

3.3 *Changes in abundance in food supply*
Unknown.

3.4 *Competition and predation*
Nil recorded other than man.

4 Relation to Man

4.1 *Values*

4.1.1 *Consumptive*
Mainly for hides; utilization as food not recorded.

4.1.2 *Low-consumptive*
None recorded.

4.2 *Effects of human activities other than exploitation*
Possible detrimental effects of water pollution from pulp and paper mills on seal stocks.

4.3 *Management and conservation*
Harvest regulated (see 2.2.3).

5 Threats to stocks

(see 4.2).

6 Research

6.1 *Current status*
Thanks to regulation measures applied, the abundance of the stock is believed to be increasing (see 2.1).

6.2 *Recommendations for future research*
In future the principal attention will be paid to investigations of the role and significance of Baikal Seal for the biological productivity of the whole Baikal ecosystem.

References

PASTUKHOV, V.D., On autumn and early winter distri-
1961 bution of seals in the Baikal. *Izv. Gos. Nauchno-Issled. Inst. Ozern. Rechn. Rybn. Khoz.*, 2.

—, The methods of quantitative assessment of Baikal
1965 seals. *In* Morskie mlekopitayushchie (Marine mammals), edited by E.N. Pavlovskii *et al.* Moscow, Akademia Nauk USSR, pp. 100-4.

—, New data on the reproduction of Baikal seals. *In*
1968 Morskie mlekopitayushchie (Marine mammals), edited by V.A. Arseniev, B.A. Zenkovich and K.K. Chapskii. Moscow, Nauka, pp. 127-35.

PASTUKHOV, V.D., On some indices of the condition of
1969 Baikal seal populations and harvest. *In* Morskie mlekopitayushchie (Marine mammals), edited by V.A. Arseniev, B.A. Zenkovich and K.K. Chapskii. Moscow, Nauka, pp. 117-26.

—, Birth time and duration of pupping period of Baikal
1975 seal. *In* Morskie mlekopitayushchie (Marine mammals), Sixth All-Union Conference on the Study of Marine Mammals.

CASPIAN SEAL

L. Popov

1 Description

1.1 Species identification

1.1.1 Family: Phocidae
Species: Phoca (Pusa) caspica (Gmelin 1788)

1.1.2 Size

- Newborn pups: 65-79 cm; 5 kg
- Adults: 130-140 cm; 50-60 kg, up to 90 kg when in prime condition

Colouration ashy-grey on back, light grey on sides and belly.

Small dark spots all over body of male, but spots lighter and mainly on back in females. Occasional individuals with reddish snout and head. Pups silvery-grey (after moulting greenish-yellow natal coat), darker above, often with small spots. By autumn pups coloration changes to olive-yellow.

1.2 Stocks

1.2.1 Identification
No separate stocks identified

1.2.2 Distribution
Throughout the Caspian Sea; migrate south after breakup of ice in late May. Location of pupping grounds is determined by distribution of open water in ice fields of north Caspian Sea in late January — early February (breeding season).

1.2.3 Structure of stocks

Sparsely distributed except during the breeding and moulting periods when clumping occurs in the north Caspian Sea; occurrence in pairs suggests possibility of monogamy.

2 Vital parameters

2.1 Population size
Estimated at 500,000-600,000 after some fluctuations, probably resulting from varying levels of harvest.

2.2 Rates

2.2.1 Reproduction
Pregnancy rates not in available literature; females first begin to reproduce at 5 years but most not until 6-7 years old; male sexually mature at 6-7 years; gestation 11 months; longevity 35 years; birth season late January-early February.

2.2.2 Natural mortality rates
Causes and rates of natural mortality are known only for pups during the period of lactation. Natural mortality rates of pups at that time reaches 22 %.

2.2.3 Harvesting rates
Now about 60-65,000 (pups only); has been as high as 164,000 for the years 1933-1940.

3 Trophic Relationships

3.1 *Food habits*

Varied, diet includes small fishes such as bullheads, sprats, sand smelts, herring, roach, carp, pike-perch, shrimp, amphipods, and crayfish.

3.2 *Requirements and utilization*

Unknown.

3.3 *Changes in abundance of food supply*

Unknown.

3.4 *Competition and predation*

Predation by large eagles and wolves.

4 Relation to Man

4.1 *Values*

4.1.1 *Consumptive*

Harvested mainly for hides.

4.1.2 *Low-consumptive*

None recorded.

4.2 *Effects of human activities other than exploitation*

Unknown.

4.3 *Management and conservation*

Annual harvest regulated (see 2.2.3); killing of adult females during the breeding period prohibited since 1966; killing of sexually immature animals and pregnant females prohibited in inshore rookeries since 1976.

5 Threats to stocks

Nil at present based on available data.

6 Research

6.1 *Current status*

Thanks to regulation measures applied, the abundance of the stock is believed to be stabilized.

6.2 *Recommendations for future research*

Cannot be made without complete summary of present state of knowledge and research activities.

References

BADAMSHIN, B.I., Caspian seal stocks and ways of their
1961 rational exploitation (study of the meeting on ecology and harvesting of marine mammals). *Tr. Sov. Ikhtiol. Kom.*, 12:170-9.

TIMOSHENKO, YU.K., Problems of rational exploitation
1967 of Caspian seal stocks. *In* Morskie mlekopitayushchie (Marine Mammals), edited by V.A. Arseniev, B.A. Zenkovich and K.K. Chapskii. Moskva, Nauka, pp. 255-260.

VOROZHTSOV, G.A., *et al.*, The distribution of seals in the
1972 north Caspian Sea. *Tr. Vses. Nauchno-Issled. Inst. Morsk. Rybn. Khoz. Okeanogr.*, 89:30-7.

—, The food habits of seals from the north Caspian Sea.
1972a *Tr. Vses. Nauchno-Issled. Inst. Morsk. Rybn. Khoz. Okeanogr.*, 89:19-29.

HARP SEAL

D. Lavigne

1 Description

1.1 Species identification

1.1.1 Family: Phocidae
Species: *Pagophilus groenlandicus* (Erxleben 1777)

1.1.2 Size

- Newborn pups: 90-105 cm, about 10 kg.
- Adults: 180-200 cm, 100-150 kg.

(much variation due to seasonal and sexual variation in amount of blubber).

1.2 Stocks

1.2.1 Identification

Three stocks reproduce in widely separated areas, located on pack ice in the White Sea, around Jan Mayen Island, and around Newfoundland. The Newfoundland stock is further divided into two groups of which the larger reproduce along the Labrador coast and the smaller in the Gulf of St. Lawrence.

1.2.2 Distribution and migration

During the summer months the animals migrate north as pack ice recedes. Animals from Jan Mayen inhabit the loose pack and ice-free waters along the east coast of Greenland and reach Svalbard, where they mix to some degree with animals of White Sea origin. These summer throughout the northern Barents and Kara Seas north to Svalbard, Franz Josef Land and Severnaya Zemlya. Some of the Newfoundland animals spend the summer along the west coast of Greenland north to about 75° and at least in some years north in the Thule area. The immature animals seem to be especially numerous around Disko Island and in the Umanak district. The Newfoundland animals, particularly immatures, spend the summer on the west coast of Greenland especially about Disko Island and north to Upernavik at 73°N. Adults tend to move rapidly to the cooler waters to the north and west, being abundant in Jones Sound, Lancaster Sound, along the east coast of Baffin Island and in Hudson Strait, extending into Hudson Bay around Southampton Island. An autumn migration, with juveniles lagging behind, brings the animals back to the wintering grounds which lie slightly to the south of whelping sites. Moulting occurs one month after whelping in the same geographical areas as whelping.

1.2.3 Structure of stocks

Aggregate in breeding season in huge herds. Apparently monogamous or promiscuous. No evidence of organised social system.

2 Vital Parameters

2.1 Population Size

2.1.1 Methods of estimation

Direct census of either whelping or moulting adults is possible with conventional photography, but the unknown percentage of adults in the water makes this method incomplete (Sergeant 1975). Census of pups has been achieved by use of ultraviolet photography (Lavigne and Øritsland 1974; Lavigne *et al.* 1976). Capture-recapture tagging of pups, catch-effort analysis (Øritsland 1971), greatest catch of a cohort, a variety of methods of age analysis (Sergeant 1971, 1975; Benjaminsen and Øritsland 1975), cohort analysis and a variety of models (Allen 1975) are other methods used in estimation of populations.

2.1.2 *Results*

The White Sea population is now apparently increasing after a marked decline followed by enhanced protection beginning in 1966. It is now estimated that from 111,000 (Popov 1976) to 175,000 (Benjaminsen and Øritsland 1973), are produced annually. This would correspond to a total population size of 500,000 to 700,000 animals. The Jan Mayen population suffered a long historical decline. Catch per unit effort data show a 70-80 % decline between 1946 and 1965, which had slowed by 1971, probably because of protection of adult females. A quota was introduced in 1971. The average annual catch of 10,800 under a quota of 14,000 in 1971-75 is estimated to be below the equilibrium catch for the present reduced population, estimated in 1971 to be about 25,000 pups or 100,000 older animals. The Newfoundland population has decreased by at least 50 % since 1951. Its present status under subsequent quota management is presently not agreed upon; estimates vary from 700,000 animals other than pups (Lavigne, *et al.* 1976) to 1.5 million (Benjaminsen and Øritsland 1975). The total present population of harp seals is therefore estimated to be between 1.3 and 2.3 million animals (e.g. Dorofeev 1946).

2.2 *Rates*

2.2.1 *Reproductive*

Median age at sexual maturity is about 5 years for females and 6 years for males, with some evidence for density-dependent changes in maturation (Sergeant 1973). The pregnancy rate of adult females is higher than 90 % (Øritsland 1971, Sergeant 1971). Birth seasons: White Sea — late February to early March, Jan Mayen — late March; Newfoundland — early March, earlier in the Gulf of St. Lawrence than off Labrador (Sergeant 1976). The lactation period lasts 8-12 days, ending normally by mating. The gestation period is 11 ½ months, including 4 ½ months delayed implantation. Longevity up to 30 years or more is well documented.

2.2.2 *Mortality*

Newfoundland stock: total annual mortality of adults 8-15 %, according to rate of kill, of which natural mortality believed to be 8-10 % (Allen, 1975). Estimation of an unequivocal rate of natural mortality has not been possible to date.

2.2.3 *Harvesting, commercial and incidental kill*

Quota regulations are reviewed and revised each year. White Sea: quota kill of 30,000 pups by coastal inhabitants in Soviet Union (Popov 1976) plus a quota of 14,000 of all age groups by Norway of which the mean catch is about 10,000. Jan Mayen: 15,000 pups quota to Norway, of which an average of 10,800 taken annually plus small catches by Soviet ships in 1975 and 1976; about 100 additional animals are taken by landsmen in east Greenland. Newfoundland: 120,000 quota for ships of Canada and Norway, equally divided; 30,000 average catch by Canadian (less arctic) landsmen over 3-year period 1972-1974, equal to " allowance "; about 7,000 by landsmen in Canadian arctic and in Greenland, unrestricted. For the 1976 season this quota was reduced to 97,000 divided 52,333 for Canada, and 44,667 for Norway, while the landsmen's allotment of 30,000 remained unchanged. Annual catches under quota regulations from 1971-76 average 166,366.

3 Trophic Relationship

3.1 *Food and Feeding*

3.1.1 Food habits

Harp seals have a wide food spectrum consisting of the larger zooplankton, pelagic fish, benthic crustacea and benthic fish. Food items are taken mainly individually and by suction, small fish being swallowed head first.

3.1.2 Food Base

Euphausiacea constitute the main food of newly-weaned young and are also an important food item in some areas in west Greenland. Capelin, *Mallotus villosus*, is the main food species at all older ages, with polar cod, *Boreogadus saida*, important at higher latitudes. Among other commercial species, some shrimp, *Pandalus borealis*, herring, *Clupea harengus*, and cod, *Cadus morhua*, are taken, none in quantities approaching those taken by man.

3.1.3 Requirements and utilization

Earlier studies on captive animals fed *ad libitum* indicated that young seals eat about 10 % of their body weight each day and adults about 5 % or less. The ecological efficiency value was estimated about 5 %, however. Recent evidence indicates that harp seals can be maintained on a minimum 1.5 % body weight per day (Ronald, per. comm.). Thus to conclude that harp seals are rather inefficient is probably premature. Sufficient data are not presently available to evaluate properly the trophic efficiency of this species. Studies of stomach contents of seals taken at Newfoundland suggest the total weight of foods eaten by harp seals in the northwest Atlantic, based on high estimates of food consumption, for a population size of 1.3 million seals, has been estimated as: all organisms 2×10^6 tonnes, capelin 5×10^5 tonnes; herring 2×10^4 tonnes (Sergeant 1973). These estimates are based on stomach contents data over a 20 year period and food availabilities could have changed. There is now good evidence that these figures overestimate the annual food consumption of the harp seal, and thus overestimate the impact of harp seals on commercial fisheries.

3.1.4 Changes in abundance of food supply

The most insidious threat to the harp seal food supply is the rapid development of the capelin fishing industry. The harvest by man has been increasing dramatically in the last decade and this could have adverse effects on harp seal stocks. The herring stock in the Gulf of St. Lawrence has also been reduced by man.

3.2 *Competition and predation*

Minke whales, *Balaenoptera acutorostrata*, and fin whales, *Balaenoptera physalis*, also feed heavily on capelin. Predation by polar bears, Greenland sharks, *Somniosus microcephalus*, and killer whales, *Orcinus orca*, is low, except possibly by polar bears on pups on breeding grounds. Parasitism and disease also have small significance to harp seal populations. The codworm parasite *Terranova (Porrocaecum, Phocaenema) decipiens* occurs only in small numbers, compared with its incidence in coastal grey seals, *Halichoerus grypus*, and harbour seals *Phoca vitulina.*

4 Relation to Man

4.1 *Values*

4.1.1 Consumptive

Harp seals are hunted primarily for their pelts, both for fur and for leather, and also yield oil which is used primarily for edible fats. Meat is extensively used from the landsmen's catches, and increasingly so from those of the ships. Quota allocation by individual ship (as practiced by Norwegian sealers at Newfoundland) allows planned taking of carcasses. The Canadian landed value of harp seal pelts in 1975 was 2.3 million with an unknown income from the sale of flippers and carcass meat. Norwegian sealing has a total landed value of about 4 million dollars, and exports seal products to a value of about 8 million dollars.

Harp seals are not commonly kept in captivity but major problems in maintenance have been overcome and they can now be successfully maintained in captivity for scientific research.

4.1.2 Low-consumptive

In general, harp seals are not located where they can be enjoyed for recreational use. Some touristic helicopter flights to the whelping ice fields are made but these are relatively few. Much recent public concern over the killing of the seals has been over the method of killing, but also over kill levels. Pups are killed by crushing the skull with a club or bat (Canada) or penetrating the brain with a hakapik (Canada and Norway). Both weapons have specified characteristics. Adults are killed by shooting with ammunition of specified size and muzzle velocity.

4.2 Effect of human activities other than exploitation

Pesticides have been demonstrated in the tissues of harp seals of all stocks but at low levels as compared with some North Atlantic coastal phocids (Holden 1975).

4.3 Management and conservation

Progressive changes in management in the last two decades have been towards reduction of kill of adult females and of moulting adults, by direct prohibition or by reducing the length of the hunting season. Controls by quota have been applied more recently to all populations. These are subdivided between nations and, within nations, between ships. Licensing and control of harp seal hunting are administered by the countries concerned (e.g. Canada, Norway, Russia and Denmark). Agencies involved in conservation are, for the northwest Atlantic, the International Commission for the Northwest Atlantic Fisheries which sets total quota, season, etc. and the Canadian-Norwegian Sealing Commission which allocates quotas. In the Northeast Atlantic the Norwegian-Soviet Sealing Commission sets and allocates quotas. Current quotas in the White Sea appear adequate to allow rebuilding of the stock which is estimated to be increasing at least by 4 % per year.

5 Threats to Stock

Over-exploitation remains the major threat to harp seal stocks, and the major cause of continued declines in population numbers. At present there would appear to be no major indirect threats to this species.

6 Research

Recent evaluation of existing data has emphasized the difficulty of estimating natural mortality for this species. Age samples must be collected annually to ensure continuity in the 25 year data base which already exists. In addition, population models recently developed should be re-evaluated, updated, and perfected and used as a basis for future management decisions.

Aerial surveys of whelping patches using ultra-violet photography and appropriate censusing techniques may soon provide the best data on population size, allowing accurate estimates of pup production. Once this procedure is operational, it should be used to evaluate all three harp seal stocks.

More information is required on food habits of harp seals, throughout the year, in order to assess properly their role in the ecosystem and their impact on commercial species of fish. Such a system's approach to the management of harp seals will require further field and laboratory data on their bioenergetics, including information on digestive efficiences, the energetic cost of migration, etc. It would appear that many remaining questions about harp seals could be answered over the next few years by extensive tagging programs. These include information on mixing of Gulf and Front stocks off eastern Canada, and intermixing of Newfoundland, White Sea, and Jan Mayen stocks, as well as data on mortality, migration etc.

References

ALLEN, R.M., A life table for harp seals in the northwest 1975 Atlantic. *Rapp. P.-V. Réun. CIEM*, 169:303-11.

BENJAMINSEN, T., and T. ØRITSLAND, Vurderinger 1973 vedrørende bestanden av grønlandssel i Østisen og Kvitsjøen. Notat, Fiskeridirektoratets hvaforskningsinstitutti 14 desember 1973, 4 p. (MS).

—, The survival of year-classes and estimates of pro- 1975 duction and sustainable yield of Northwest Atlantic harp seals. *ICNAF Ser. Doc.*, (75/121).

DOROFEEV, S.V., Stocks of Greenland seals and their 1946 utilization. *Rybn. Khoz. Mosk.*

HOLDEN, A.V., The accumulation of oceanic contami- 1975 nants in marine mammals. *Rapp. P.-V. Réun. CIEM*, 169:353-61.

LAVIGNE, D.M., *et al.*, An aerial census of western At- 1976 lantic harp seals (*Pagophilus groenlandicus*) using ultra-violet photography. Paper presented to the Scientific Consultation on the Conservation and Management of Marine Mammals and Their Environment, Bergen, Norway, 31 August-9 September, 1976. Rome, FAO, ACMRR/MM/SC/33:9 p.

LAVIGNE, D.M., and N.A. ØRITSLAND, Ultraviolet pho- 1974 tography: a new application for remote sensing of mammals *Can. J. Zool.*, 52:939-41.

ØRITSLAND, T., The status of Norwegian studies of harp 1971 seals at Newfoundland. *Redbook ICNAF*, 1971(3):185-209.

POPOV, L.A., Status of main ice forms of seals inhabiting 1976 water of the USSR and adjacent to the country marine areas. Paper presented to the Scientific Consultation on the Conservation and Management of Marine Mammals and Their Environment, Bergen, Norway, 31 August-9 September, 1976. Rome, FAO, ACMRR/MM/SC/51:17 p.

SERGEANT, D.E., Calculation of production of harp seals 1971 in the western North Atlantic. *Redbook ICNAF*, 1971(3):157-84.

—, Environment and reproduction in seals. *J. Prerod.* 1973 *Fert.*, Suppl. 19:555-61.

—, Estimating numbers of harp seals. *Rapp. P.-V. Réun.* 1975 *CIEM*, 169: 274-80.

—, History and present status of population of harp and 1976 hooded seals. *Biol. Conserv.*, 10:95-118.

RIBBON SEAL

I. Stirling

1 Description

1.1 Identification

1.1.1 Taxonomic
Family: Phocidae
Species: *Phoca (Histriophoca) fasciata* Zimmerman 1783

1.1.2 Size

- Males and females average 155 cm and 80 kg.
- Pups have white coat at birth, weigh 10 kg and are 80 cm long

Pelage similar in males and females, distinctive dark line over shoulders, along sides and over rump, giving the species its name.

1.2 Stocks

1.2.1 Identification
No separate stocks identified.

1.2.2 Distribution
Occurs to southern limit of drifting pack ice and to a limited degree into the Chukchi Sea. Two populations in Bering Sea and Sea of Okhotsk, relatively little interchange.

1.2.3 Structure of stocks
Solitary.

2 Vital Parameters

2.1 Population size

2.1.1 Methods of estimation
Aerial and shipboard counts.

2.1.2 Results
Estimated total 200-250,000 seals in both populations some variation in U.S. and U.S.S.R. estimates.

2.1.3 Trends
Possibly some decline in numbers because of over-harvesting.

2.2 Rates

2.2.1 Reproductive

- Females mature at 2-4 years
- Males at 3-5 years

Pregnancy rates of 85 % reported by U.S.S.R
Birth season: late March to mid-April
Mating: late April to early May
Gestation: 10½-11 months
Longevity: 22-26 years.

2.2.2 Mortality
44 % in first year, then until 16-18 years — 11.2 % from U.S.S.R. reports.

2.2.3 Harvesting
Since 1961, 8-9,000 taken by U.S.S.R. in Bering Sea; 250 taken annualy by Alaskan residents; figures unavailable from Sea of Okhotsk but may be an over-harvest.

3 Trophic relationships

3.1 Food and feeding

Mainly pelagic and demersal fishes, cephalopods important. Food base, requirements, utilization and changes in abundance of food supply, all unknown.

3.2 Competition and predation

Some predation by polar bears and killer whales, probably not important; interspecific relationships to other pinnipeds unknown.

4 Relation to man

4.1 Values

4.1.1 Consumptive

Hides only; food use limited.

4.1.2 Low-consumptive

None known.

4.2 Effects of human activities other than exploitation

None known

4.3 Management and conservation

In U.S. harvested by permit only except for native subsistence use; probably limited in U.S.S.R. because of limited stocks and restrictions on shipboard taking of seals; U.S.S.R. presently permits taking 3,500 in Sea of Okhotsk and 3,000 in Bering Sea.

5 Threats to stocks

Possibility of over-harvesting in advance of research data.

6 Research

6.1 Current research

An unofficial agreement between U.S.S.R. and U.S. to cooperate on research, natural history work by U.S., U.S.S.R. and Japan, largely on an opportunistic basis.

6.2 Recommendations for future work

Methods of estimating numbers; details of reproductive cycle; details of general biology because is least known of Arctic seals; seasonal distribution and movements.

BEARDED SEAL

I. Stirling & Ralph Archibald

1 Description

1.1 Species identification

1.1.1 Family: Phocidae
Species: *Erignathus barbatus* (Erxleben 1777)

1.1.2 Size

- Newborn: av. 87 cm; 43 kg.
- adults: 225 cm; summer weight to 275 kg.; winter to 340 kg.

Pups are dark at birth with patches of white on the back and dorsal side of the flippers; adult pelage is grey, occasionally with brown on face and neck down to shoulders, which is probably from mud stains gained during feeding; moustachial whiskers are the most characteristic feature, curling in tight spirals at the tips; they have 4 teats.

1.2 Stocks

1.2.1 Identification

North Atlantic and North Pacific populations sometimes named as subspecies *E. b. barbatus* and *E. b. nauticus* respectively; no geographical separation of stocks although some degree of morphological separation exists.

1.2.2 Distribution

Circumpolar in distribution, preferring the moving pack ice over shallow water depths. They are found south to James Bay and the Sea of Okhotsk; also found in the White Sea with occasional reports from Hokkaido, Scotland, Norway, and the Gulf of St. Lawrence.

1.2.3 Structure of Stocks

Solitary in distribution except for small aggregations during the breeding season. Densities are higher in favoured areas. Found predominantly in moving pack-ice areas over shallow water, but recent studies have shown bearded seals use self-maintained holes in areas of fast-ice several hundred miles from nearest pack; probably non-migratory in most areas though distribution may change with ice movement.

2 Vital parameters

2.1 Population size

2.1.1 Methods of estimation

Aerial surveys and shipboard counts.

2.1.2 Results

Soviets estimate 450,000 seals in East Siberia, Chukchi, Bering, Okhotsk and Japan Seas; Alaska Department of Fish and Game estimates 300,000; no Canadian or Norwegian estimates available; world population probably in excess of 500,000:

2.1.3 Trend in abundance

No data available from most areas; a possible decline in the Barents Sea because of over-harvest.

2.2 Rates

2.2.1 Reproductive

Age at sexual maturity:

- female, 5-6 years
- male, 6-7 years.

Pregnancy rates: Alaska reports 85 % U.S.S.R. reports 75 %. Birth season, mid April to late May, varying with latitude.

Lactation period: 12-18 days.

Mating time: May

Gestation: 10½-11 months (delay of development 2½-3 months).

2.2.2 Natural mortality

Unknown.

2.2.3 Harvesting

U.S. and U.S.S.R., 8000-10,000; Norway, 2000-3000; Canada not recorded. There is much loss in native hunting because of sinking.

3 Trophic relationships

3.1 Food habits

3.1.1 Diet

The bearded seal feeds almost exclusively on bottom invertebrates and the more sedentary fishes.

3.1.2 Food base

Crustaceans and mollusks are most common with polychaetes and fishes important locally.

3.1.3 Requirements und utilization

Unknown.

3.1.4 Changes in abundance of food supply

Unknown.

3.2 Competition and predation

Heavy seasonal predation on some local populations by polar bears; some incidental predation by killer whales.

4 Relation to man

4.1 Values

4.1.1 Consumptive

The skins and blubber have native subsistence use.

Bearded seals are also marketed for industrial leather, food and oil.

4.1.2 Low-consumptive

Nil.

4.2 Effects of human activities other than exploitation

There is potential for detrimental effects from extensive offshore oil exploration and production and from proposed inter-island pipeline construction and shipment of oil with tankers in the arctic waters. The effects could be on the seals themselves or on their food chain.

4.3 Management and Conservation

There are no quotas or seasons in Canada. In the U.S. collecting is only by permit from the Marine Mammal Commission, except for native use. Harvest is prohibited in the White and Barents Sea.

5 Threats to stock

There is a possible over-harvesting in restricted areas. The total population is not presently threatened.

6 Research

6.1 Current status

Norway is studying the age structure and reproductive rates. Alaska is continuing natural history studies in conjunction with other ice breeding species. There are no specific studies in Canada but data are being collected in conjunction with studies on other species.

6.2 *Recommendations for future research*

Require information on the reproductive cycle and the degree of natural variations in annual productivity; data also required on estimating numbers of animals and determining the ecological relationships to other phocids.

References

BENJAMINSEN, T., Age determination and the growth and
1973 age distribution from cementum layers of bearded seals at Svalbard. *Fiskeridir. Skr. (Ser. Havunders.)*, 16:159-70.

BURNS, J.J., The Pacific bearded seal. Federal Aid
1967 Wildlife Restoration Project (W-6-R) △ (W-14-R). *Annu. Proj. Segm. Rep. Alaska Dep. Fish. Game,* (8).

CHAPSKII, (ed.), Issledovaniia morskie mlekopitayush-
1971 chie (Research on marine mammals). *Tr. Atl. Nauchno-Issled. Inst. Rybn. Khoz. Okeanogr.,* (39). Issued also as: *Transl. Ser. Fish. Res. Board Can.*, (3185) (1974).

IVASHIN, M.V., L.A. POPOV and A.S. TSAPKO, Morskie
1972 mlekopitayushchie (Marine mammals), edited by P.A. Moieseev. Moscow, Pishchevaia Promyshlennost. Issued also as: *Transl. Ser. Fish. Res. Board Can.*, (2783) (1973).

MANNING, T.H., Variations in the skull of the bearded
1974 seal. *Biol. Pap. Alaska Univ.*, (16).

McLAREN, I.A., Some aspects of growth and reproduc-
1958 tion of the bearded seal, *Erignathus barbatus* (Erxleben). *J. Fish. Res. Board Can.*, 15(2):219-27.

HOODED SEAL

D.E. SERGEANT

1 Description

1.1 Species identification

1.1.1 Family: Phocidae
Species: *Cystophora cristata* (Erxleben 1777)

1.1.2 Sizes

- Newborn pups: 1 m; 10-15 kg.
- Adult males: 2.5 m; 400 kg.
- Adult females: 2.2 m, 350 kg.

1.2 Stocks

1.2.1 Identification

Tagging results are few to date, but the balance of evidence suggests only small interchange between stocks whelping east and west of Greenland. (The eastern stock is the larger one). The whelping group so far identified in only 3 seasons in Davis Strait (Sergeant, 1974) may be inconsistent in appearance and be part of the Newfoundland group.

1.2.2 Distribution

Whelping groups occur around Jan Mayen Island and off Newfoundland including the Gulf of St. Lawrence, but only in negligible numbers near the White Sea. In some years at least, whelping groups form in Davis Strait (Sergeant, 1974). Concentrations of hooded seals are found in June and July in the Davis Strait and on the east coast of Greenland, and off the west coast of Greenland as far north as Cape York and Lancaster Sound. At the end of the summer they disperse and are apparently solitary in habits until the whelping period the following March.

The main moulting area is found east of Greenland. Many tags placed on pups at Jan Mayen have been recovered later in Denmark Strait. One tag from Newfoundland was recovered close to the moulting area at S.E. Greenland, but there is not yet enough evidence to say to what extent Newfoundland animals join Jan Mayen animals to moult here. It is possible that some moulting occurs in the Davis Strait area and moulters are regularly seen off north-west Greenland.

1.2.3 Structure of stocks

Scattered concentrations at the whelping ice fields are made up of "families", i.e. a female pup with one attending and sometimes several competing males. Moulting groups on the pack ice south east of Greenland and between Jan Mayen and Svalbard in summer are similarly concentrated and consist of animals aged 1 (more commonly 2) years and upwards. Because adult females actively defend pups, and because of their value many are taken in hunting at the whelping patches. Males are often taken at the same time as they aggresively defend against hunters.

2 Vital Parameters

2.1 Population size

2.1.1 Methods of estimation

Direct photographic survey has been attempted. It is difficult primarily because of the scattered nature of many whelping animals and the ridging of the ice which hides many pups. Aerial surveys of moulting animals are also difficult to interpret since the number of animals in the water at the time of the survey is difficult to estimate.

Age class strengths and analysis of them in relation to pup catch have been used to estimate production and permissible catch.

***2.1.2** Results*

Catches show that the Jan Mayen population is larger than the Newfoundland population. The present quotas for the two areas are 30,000 and 15,000 respectively.

Jan Mayen — Catch statistics and year-class abundance derived from age samples indicate that pup production may have been as high as 120,000 per year around 1955. Catch per ship, corrected for an increasing hunting efficiency of the ships, suggests that the availability of hooded seals was reduced by about 40 per cent during the years from 1955 to 1970. Production probably was reduced correspondingly, to perhaps 70,000 pups per year by 1970.

The protection of moulting hooded seals in the Denmark Strait since 1961, the quota of 30,000 introduced in 1971 and the postponment of the opening date of the hunting season from March 20 to March 23 in 1972, have reduced the mortality of adult seals and increased the survival of females to maturity. A conservative assessment suggests that 1970 adult mortality was about 20 per cent per year, survival of females to productive maturity at age five was 60 per cent and that annual production may be assumed to be 70,000 pups. From these figures and an average fertility of 95 per cent the equilibrium catch has been estimated to be 21,000 pups per year. With an additional catch of 30 per cent adults allowed for in the assessed mortality rate, the total allowable catch of hooded seals of the Jan Mayen stock, therefore, should be in the order of 27,000 animals per year.

During the four years which have passed since the quotas were introduced, catches have remained an average 14 per cent below the quota and four per cent below the established sustainable yield. This narrow margin allows for errors in the basic assumption made in the estimates and possibly also for a future slow recovery of the stock. The effects of the quota regulations are presently being assessed using recent age samples.

Newfoundland — Catches during the years since 1945 show large variations between the minimum of 950 seals taken in 1957 and the largest catch of 27,357 seals taken in 1966. The average catch at Newfoundland during the period 1964-1974 is just above 8,000 hooded seals per year. In spite of these variations, the catches show an increasing trend through this period, and even with corrections for increasing ship's efficiency, the catches per ship give no indication of a reduced availability of hooded seals at Newfoundland. However, hooded seals are hunted together with harp seals, and the apparent increase may partly have been caused by the decreasing stock, and thus availability, of harp seals and later by the quota limitation for harp seals, with the result that effort has gradually been diverted to the hunting of hooded seals. The breeding group recently discovered in the Davis Strait also may have contributed to the increase in catches at Newfoundland. Increased catches in Greenland since 1960 indicate increasing availability and cannot be related to decreasing effort in harp seal hunting.

Regression of the survival of year-classes as estimated from recent age samples, in relation to catches of pups in respective years, indicates that production in the period 1966-1970 exceeded 30,000 pups per year. From this estimate, and the age specific pregnancy and mortality rates, the sustainable catch is estimated at 16,000 pups plus 30 per cent adults, or a total of about 23,000 hooded seals per year at Newfoundland. An alternative regression of the same data using 5 year old females gives an estimate of production of 26,000 pups, with a more cautious estimate of yield. It should be stressed, however, that more data are required in order to carry out an adequate assessment of hooded seals in the western Atlantic.

2.2 *Rates*

2.2.1 *Reproduction*

Median age of female sexual maturity is 3 years and median age at pupping is 4; i.e., there is a high probability of conception at first ovulation. Per cent pregnancy of adults is also very high (95%). The whelping season occurs the second half of March in all populations. Lactation period lasts 10 days, and is followed by mating. The gestation period is 11.7 months, including a delay in implantation lasting more than 4 months.

2.2.2 *Mortality*

Total annual mortality rates of fully-recruited adults are estimated at Newfoundland to be 20-22 percent for females, 25-30 per cent for males (Øritsland and Benjaminsen, 1975). Similar estimates for moulters in Denmark Strait of 20 per cent for both sexes.

2.2.3 *Harvesting Rates and Commercial Kill*

The present quotas are 30,000 animals for the Jan Mayen stock and 15,000 for Newfoundland. These quotas include both pups and adult animals.

3 Trophic Relationships

3.1 *Food*

3.1.1 *Food Habits*

Food organisms include squid, *Gonatus fabricii*, and redfish, *Sebastes marinus* and Greenland halibut, *Reinhardtius hippoglossoides*. Capelin, *Mallotus villosus*, and polar cod, *Boreogadus saida*, and amphipods may also be taken by pups.

3.1.2

There are no data on metabolic rates and few on rates of food consumption. However relatively low stock size combined with a wide food spectrum and their migratory habits, implies that no large effect on any commercial fish species can be expected.

3.2 *Competition and predation*

Hooded seals generally occur in deeper water, and are deeper divers than harp seals. They are also larger than harp seals and may tend to consume larger food organisms. Some predation by polar bears, *Ursus maritimus*, at whelping areas, and by Greenland sharks at moulting areas is known to occur. Heartworm, *Dipetalonema spirocauda*, has also been reported as a cause of death, but its prevalence is not well known.

4

4.1 *Value*

4.1.1 *Consumptive values*

Hooded seals, especially the young (bluebacks), have pelts of high commercial value, and the blubber is also utilized as a source of oil. The value of catch is therefore disproportionate to numbers in the combined fishery of harp and hooded seals. Thus, the hooded seal contributes about 40 per cent of the total Norwegian land value of seal pelts or an estimated Kr 8 million ($ 1.2 million) annually.

4.1.2 *Low consumptive values*

As for Harp seals, WP 22.

4.1.3 *Management and Conservation*

Control of hunting first began by phasing out and eliminating the hunting of moulting seals, and by regulating the starting date for hunting at the whelping patches. Because of the very rapid cycle the fixing of an exact opening date has very important consequences on total catch and sex composition of adults taken. The catch of hooded seals now comprises about 30 per cent adults, sometimes more, of which 60-70 per cent are females. Delay in the starting date for hunting reduces the catch of adult female seals, but the period of catch is so short that further delay is resisted by industry. Quota control has been applied to both catch areas in recent years as noted above.

5 Threats to Stock

Overhunting, especially at Jan Mayen, is the major threat to hooded seal stocks. At Newfoundland, catch per unit effort data suggests increasing availability over the last 30 years. This could be due to the existence of a Davis Strait herd and subsequent recruitment from this herd to Newfoundland. It could also reflect increased hunting activity directed at hooded seals as the availability of harp seals declined.

The continuing exploitation of adult hooded seals, especially adult females must be viewed as the most serious threat to hooded seal stocks at the present time.

Research

For the Newfoundland stock, at least, there are insufficient data adequately to evaluate the present status of the herd. There is an obvious need to obtain further documentation on the Davis Strait whelping herd and its relationship to other hooded seals whelping in the western Atlantic off the east coast of Canada.

Age frequency samples should be obtained annually to ensure the continuity of the data base available for analysis. Improved methods of population assessment and further evaluation of the present level of hunting mortality must be forthcoming. Basic data on morphometrics, food consumption, migration, and intermixing of stocks are also required. Some of these data could be obtained through increased tagging programmes.

References

ØRITSLAND, T., Sexual maturity and reproductive per-
1975 formance of female hooded seals at Newfoundland. *Res. Bull. ICNAF*, (11):37-42.

ØRITSLAND, T., and T. BENJAMINSEN, Additional data on
1975 the sex ratio, age composition and mortality of Newfoundland hooded seals, with an estimate of pup production and sustainable yield. *ICNAF Ser. Pap.*, (3626)/22 p.

SERGEANT, D.E., A rediscovered whelping population of
1974 hooded seals *Cystophora cristata* Erxleben and their possible relation to other populations. *Polarforschung*, 44:1-7.

Anon., Ressrsoversikt for 1975. A Sjøpattedyr. *Fisken*
1975 *Havet*, 1975 (Saernr): 104-29.

GREY SEAL

W.N. Bonner

1 Description

1.1 Species identification

1.1.1 Taxonomic. Family: Phocidae
Species: Halichoerus grypus (Fabricius 1791)

1.1.2 Size

- Newborn pups 87-105 cm; 14.5 kg.
- Adult males 195-230 cm; (av. 207.3 cm) 170-310 kg.; (av. 233 kg.)
- Adult females 165-195 cm; (av. 179.6 cm)

There is a marked sexual dimorphism in coat-pattern, size and appearance. Apart from generally darker tone on back which shades into lighter belly, there are two tones, a lighter and a darker. In males the darker tone is more extensive forming a continuous dark background with light patches; in females the lighter tone is continuous with dark spots. Colour varies from almost black in some bulls to silver grey or cream in light females. Pups born in white lanugo moulted after 2-3 weeks.

1.2 Stocks

1.1.1 Identification

Three stocks (western Atlantic, eastern Atlantic and Baltic) can be distinguished by geographical isolation and differences in breeding season (see section 2.2.1).

1.2.2 Distribution

The grey seal is normally an inhabitant of rocky shores and is found on both sides of the Atlantic and in the Baltic Sea. In the western Atlantic the main breeding colonies are at the Magdalene Islands (Deadman Island), Amet Island in Northumberland Strait, Sable Island, Point Michaud on the east coast of Cape Breton Island and on the fast-ice along the west Cape Breton shore from the Strait of Canso to Inverness (Mansfield, 1963). During the summer the seals disperse around the Gulf of St. Lawrence and the coasts of Newfoundland, Labrador and the Maritime Provinces. The limits of distribution are from Hebron in Labrador to Nantucket Island (where a very few breed) in the south.

In the Northeast Atlantic grey seals breed around the coast of Iceland, particularly in the west (Hook 1961; Arnlaugsson 1973); on the Faroe Islands (Smith 1966); on the Norwegian coast from Møre and northwards to North Cape (Øynes 1964). Small numbers breed on the Murman coast near the mouth of the White Sea (Karpovich, Kokhanov and Tatarinkova, 1967).

The great majority breed around the British coasts, chiefly on the western side. The largest breeding groups are found in the Hebrides, North Rona, Orkney and the Farne Islands, with smaller groups at Cornwall and Scilly Isles, the Welsh coast, Isle of Man and the Shetland Isles. There is a very small breeding group on a sandbank, Scroby Sands, off the east Norfolk coast (Bonner 1972; 1976). Small breeding groups are found round the coast of Ireland, particularly in the west and southwest (Lockley 1966). A very small breeding group is found in Brittany (Roux

1957; Didier in Bonner 1972).

The limits of distribution in the eastern Atlantic appear to be the Murman coast in the north and Brittany, or exceptionally Spain (Luis de Blas 1964) in the south.

A distinct population of ice-breeding grey seals occurs in the Baltic, from Oland and the Gulf of Danzig in the south to the Gulf of Bothnia in the north (Hook and Johnels 1972; Bonner 1973).

1.2.3 Structure of stocks

Except for the ice-breeding form in Canada and the Baltic, grey seals aggregate at the breeding season and disperse afterwards. There is no evidence of migratory movement. Usually (but not at Farne Islands) breeding and feeding grounds distinct. Generally highly polygynous, but approaches monogyny in low-density situations, as on ice.

2 Vital parameters

2.1 Population size

2.1.1 Methods of estimation

White pups conspicuous on land. Direct counts from land, boat or aircraft possible. Interpretation of aerial photographs extensively used in U.K. (Vaughan 1971).

2.1.2 Results

	(Thousands)	
Canada	22	(Mansfield, pers. comm.)
Iceland and Faroes	3-6	(Hook 1961; Smith 1966; Arnlaugsson 1973)
U.K.	53-54	(Bonner 1976)
Ireland	2	(Smith 1966)
Norway	2-3	(Øynes 1964, Summers, Bonner and van Haaften, in press)
U.S.S.R.	1-2	(Karpovich, Kokhanov and Tatarinkova, 1967 adjusted)
Baltic	5	
	88-94	

2.1.3 Trends in abundance

The grey seal has shown a remarkable increase in numbers in the last 25 years at its two major population centres in the U.K. and Canada. This increase has been of the order of 9 % annually for some colonies (Summers, Bonner and van Haaften, in press; Bonner 1975). In the Baltic numbers have decreased markedly over the last 50 years and the trend continues (Hook and Johnels 1972; Joensen, Søndergaard and Hansen, 1976).

2.2 Rates

2.2.1 Reproductive

Age at sexual maturity:

- female 4-7 years (Hewer 1964) (but up to 9 in some crowded colonies, Platt, Prime and Whittames, 1974)
- males probably similar, but not socially mature until at least age 10.

Birth season: western Atlantic; January-February; eastern Atlantic; September-January.

(Most in September-*October*; Farne Islands, *November*-December). Some spring pups (March-May) born in west of England and Wales (Backhouse and Hewer 1957) but not recorded elsewhere.

Baltic: February-March

(The now extinct breeding colony of grey seals at Arnholt produced pups in January-February, Bynch 1801 in Møhl 1970).

Mating time: within a week of end of lactation

Gestation: 11.5 months (delay of implantation 3 months)

Longevity: *female* 46 years (Bonner 1971); *male* 26 years (Platt, Prime and Whittames, 1974) (43 years in captivity).

2.2.2 Natural mortality

No data for males. Platt, Prime & Whittames, 1974, found values between 50% and 75% for females of age classes 10-16, assuming pregnancy rates of 80% and 90% for seals from the Farne Islands.

2.2.3 Harvesting, commercial and incidental kill

U.K.:	1 000-1 500/year (nearly all pups)
Iceland:	500 pups/year
Faroe Islands:	no data
Canada:	no data
Baltic:	no data

No data on incidental kill, though a small number (less than 100?) of seals known to be drowned each year in salmon nets.

Trophic relationship

3.1 Food and feeding

3.1.1 Food habits

Like *Phoca vitulina*, grey seals are generalised coastal feeders, eating most of those fish which are locally abundant. They congregate in estuaries where there are salmon runs.

3.1.2 Food base

Eat a wide variety of fish, with smaller quantities of cephalopods and crustaceans. Gadids, salmonids, pleuronectids and clupeids were most abundant in Scottish grey seal stomach. (Rae 1968; Bonner 1972). Mansfield (1963) found that in Canada adult seals fed chiefly on skates, flounders, cod, hake and herring, and occasionally on salmon, smelt, haddock, sea-bass, dogfish, squid and crustaceans. Söderberg (1972; 1975) found the food in the Baltic was mainly herring, cod, salmon and sea trout.

3.1.3 Requirements and utilization

No firm data, but perhaps between 5 and 7.5 kg/day. 10 kg of salmon has been found in one stomach.

3.1.4 Changes in abundance of food supply

No data.

3.2 Competition and predation

Perhaps some competition with *Phoca vitulina* where they occur together. Killer whales only known predator on adults but unlikely to have significant effect in any populations.

4 Relation to man

4.1 Values

4.1.1 Consumptive

Skins of pups provide a low-quality fur. Adult skins used for leather and blubber processed for oil.

4.1.2 Non-consumptive

Grey seals are a tourist attraction in some places but the remoteness of most of their colonies limits this.

4.2 Effects of human activities other than exploitation

Probably few; disturbance by human activities may cause seals to abandon breeding sites. Oil extraction off Scottish coast and oil spills anywhere may affect seals.

4.3 Management and conservation

Grey seals are the major definitive host of the cod-worm, *Terranova decipiens*, the larvae of which infest food-fishes, chiefly cod. Area of large seal concentrations show a correlation with high incidence of wormy cod. For this reason, and because of the direct damage to fisheries via catch and net-damage, grey seals are generally regarded as harmful to fisheries. Stock control for the benefit of fisheries is practised in Scotland, but this take of seals is mainly of pups and the catch is not more than the MSY level. Similar control in Canada. No control or management in Iceland or Faroes. Elsewhere grey seals are mostly protected though fishermen may be allowed to kill seals in vicinity of nets.

5 Threats to stock

Not known.

6 Research

6.1 *Current state*

Intensive population and behavioural research in U.K. and Canada. Relation to fisheries investigated in U.K., Canada and Sweden. Minor research effort from U.S.A., Iceland, Norway, U.S.S.R. and France.

6.2 *Recommendations for future research*

All aspects of grey seal biology at the major population in the Faroe Islands need investigation. Population estimates and to a less extent, behavioural observation, needed from Iceland, U.S.S.R., Ireland and Baltic.

References

ARNLAUGSSON, T., Selir vid Island. Rannsoknastofnun
1973 fiskidnadarins. 25 p. (mimeo).

BACKHOUSE, K.M., and H.R. HEWER, A note on spring
1957 pupping in the grey seal. *Proc. Zool. Soc. Lond.*, 128:593-4.

BONNER, W.N., An aged grey seal (*Halichoerus grypus*).
1971 *J. Zool.*, 164:261-2.

—, The grey seal and common seal in European waters.
1972 *Oceanogr. Mar. Biol.*, 10:461-507.

—, status of grey seals in the Baltic. *IUCN Suppl. Pap.*,
1973 (39):164-74.

—, Population increase of grey seals at the Farne Is-
1975 lands, northeast England. *Rapp. P.-V. Réun. CIEM*, 169-366-70.

—, The stocks of grey seals (*Halichoerus grypus*) and
1976 common seals (*Phoca vitulina*) in Great Britain. *Publ. Ser. Natl. Environ. Res. Counc. (C)*, (16).

HEVER, H.R., The determination of age, sexual matur-
1964 ity, longevity and a lifetable in the grey seal (*Halichoerus grypus*). *Proc. Zool. Soc. Lond.*, 142:593-624.

HOOK, O., Notes on the status of seals in Iceland, Ju-
1961 ne-July, 1959. *Proc. Zool. Soc. Lond.*, 137:628-30.

HOOK, O., and A.G. JOHNELS, The breeding and distri-
1972 bution of the grey seal *(Halichoerus grypus* Fab.) in the Baltic Sea with observations on other seals of the area. *Proc. R. Soc. Lond. (B. Biol. Sci.)*, 182:37-58.

JOENSEN, A.M., N.O. SØNDERGAARD and E.B. HANSEN,
1976 Occurrence of seals and seal hunting in Denmark. *Dan. Rev. Game Biol.*, 10(1).

KARPOVICH, V.N., V.D. KOKHANOV and I.P. TATARINKO-
1967 VA, The grey seal in the Murman coast. *In* Research on marine mammals, edited by K.K. Chapskii and M.Y. Yakovenko. *Tr. Polyar. Nauchno-Issled. Proektn. Inst. Morsk. Rybn. Khoz. Okeanogr.*, 21:117-225.

LOCKLEY, R.M., The distribution of grey and common
1966 seals on the coasts of Ireland. *Ir. Nat. J.*, 15:136-43.

LUIS DE BLAS, S.M., Una nueva foca de la especie *Hali-*
1964 *choerus grypus* (Fabricius) capturada en Santona. *Bol. R. Soc. Esp. Hist. Nat. (Biol.)*, 62:233-4.

MANSFIELD, A.W., Seals of arctic and eastern Canada.
1963 *Bull. Fish. Res. Board Can.*, (137):30 p.

MØHL, U., Fangstdyrene ved de dansk strand - den
1970 zoologiske baggrund for harpunere. *Aarb. Jysk Arkaeol. Selsk.*, 1970:297-329.

ØYNES, P., Sel pa norskekysten fra Finmark til Møre.
1964 *Fisk. Gang*, (48):694-707.

PLATT, N.E., J.H. PRIME, and S.R. WHITTAMES, The age
1974 of the grey seal at the Farne Islands. ICES C.M. 1974/N:3, 7 p. (mimeo).

RAE, B.B., The food of seals in Scottish waters. *Mar.*
1968 *Res.*, 1968(2):23 p.

ROUX, F., Sur la présence de phoques à l'Ile d'Ouessant.
1957 *Penn Bed*, 11:13-8.

SMITH, E.A., A review of the world's grey seal popula-
1966 tion. *J. Zool., Lond.*, 150:463-89.

SÖDERBERG, S., Sälens födoval och skadegörelse pa lax-
1972 fisket i Östersjön Svenska Ostkustfisk renas Celtralförbund, 60 p. (mimeo).

—, Feeding habits and commercial damage of seals in
1975 the Baltic. *In* Proceedings of the Symposium, The Seal in the Baltic. National Swedish Environmental Protection Board, pp. 66-75.

SUMMERS, C.F., W.N. BONNER and J. VAN HAAFTEN, Changes in the seal population of the North Sea. *Rapp. P.-V. Réun. CIEM*, (in press).

VAUGHAN, R.W., Aerial survey in seals research. *In* The
1971 application of aerial photography to the work of the Nature Conservancy Council, edited by R. Goodier. Edinburgh, The Nature Conservancy Council, pp. 88-98.

MEDITERRANEAN MONK SEAL

J. Boulva

1 Description

1.1 Species identification

1.1.1 Family: Phocidae
Species: Monachus monachus Hermann, 1779)

1.1.2 Size

- Newborn pups: 87-120 cm, av. 98.8 cm; 17-26 kg.
- Adult males: 194-290 cm, av. 240.6 cm; 260 kg.
- Adult females: 210-380 cm, av. 264.6 cm; 300-302 kg.

Most authors do not specify total or nose-tail length. There appear to be only slight variations in the colour of the pelage. Generally the animal is dark brown with often a light yellowish-white ventral patch, which gave the species its former name, *M. albiventer*. The hair is very short, about 0.5 cm long in the adult, while in the pup it is soft and woolly, 1.0-1.5 cm in length. The dental formula of the adult is i 2/2, c 1/1, m 5/5, while the milk dentition is given as 2/2, 1/1, 3/3. The female has four teats.

1.2 Stocks

1.2.1 Identification

Although this species is sparsely scattered with an apparent discontinuous range, there have been no subspecific population described.

1.2.2 Distribution

Past records suggest that this species used to be widely distributed in the Black Sea, Mediterranean Sea, and along the coast of northwest Africa. At present, it still occurs in coastal areas or islands with cliffs having caves at sea level. Its preference for life in caves often with underwater entrance might be a result of increasing disturbance by man (Bareham and Furredu 1975). Areas where the species still occurs are: Madeira Islands, Canary Islands, other small Atlantic ridge islands, the former Spanish Sahara, northern Mauritania near Cap Blanc, the Atlantic and Mediterranean coasts of Morocco, Algeria mostly from the western border to Alger, Northern Tunisia, Lybia, Lebanon, Cyprus, Turkey, Bulgaria, Greece mainly on the islands of the Aegean Sea, Cyprus, and on some of the islands of the western Mediterranean: some Yugoslavia islands in the Adriatic (Gamulin-Brida, Kameranovic and Mikulic, 1965); Montecristo, Egadi and Sardinia in Italy; la Grita in Tunisia; Mallorca and Alboran in Spain.

The species is most likely extinct along the mainland coasts of Yugoslavia, Italy, southern France, southern Spain, the United Arab Republic of Egypt, Israel, the U.S.S.R. and Romania. No information is available from Albania and Syria.

This seal appears to be sedentary and no extensive migration has been reported. However, one individual sighted at sea 30 km off Cape Bojador in the former Spanish Sahara, and numerous sightings of seals as far as 15 km off shore Cap Blanc, Mauritania suggest these seals may move away from the coast to feed. The southern limit of the Mediterranean monk seal is about the latitude of Cap Blanc (Monod 1923) and coincides with the 20°C winter isotherm of the sea temperature (Bundker 1945). However isolated animals have been reported as far south as Senegal (Maigret and Trotignon, 1975).

1.2.3 Structure of stocks

Because of the scarcity of animals and their characteristic of inhabiting remote inaccessible areas, very little is known of the social structure of this species. One cave in Sardinia surveyed from December 1970 to January 1972 is being used by six animals, two males and four females, one of them a pup born in the fall of 1970 (Bareham and Fureddu 1975).

2 Vital parameters

2.1 Population size

2.1.1 Methods of estimation

Aerial and boat surveys are impractical because of the vast range, relative scarcity and secretive habits of this species. Censusing has been conducted by personal communication with local inhabitants and by publicly distributed questionnaires.

2.1.2 Results

The following estimates of number of monk seals are given for various geographical areas.

Albania	no information
Algeria	100
Balearic Islands (Spain)	5-10
Bulgaria	several pairs
Canary Islands	a few
Cape Verde Islands	a few
Corsica (France)	possibly a few
Cyprus	a few
Flores Island (Azores)	a few
Greece	150
Italy (except Sardinia and Sicily)	3
Lebanon	12
Libya	20-30
Madeira's Islands	20-30
Morocco	25)30
Santa Maria Island (Azores)	a few
Sardinia (Italy)	10
Senegal	possibly a few
Sicily (Islands of Egadi)	5
Spanish Sahara including Cap Blanc	55-100
Tunisia	5-10
Turkey	50-60
Yugoslavia	5-6

The total population is estimated at about 500-600.

2.1.3 Trends in abundance

Information available for the last decades suggest a rapid rate of decline in numbers. In Corsica, *Monachus* was reported from 17 localities in 1955, 12 in 1965 and at most four in 1973. At the island of La Galite off northern Tunisia, there were at least 30 seals in 1950 while only 3 remained in 1974 in spite of legal protection. Most disturbing is an apparent recent decline in numbers of animals combined with a high death rate at the colony located in the former Spanish Sahara, 15-20 km northwest of Nouadhibou, Mauritania. This colony is at present the largest known for this species and has up to now been considered the least endangered because of its remoteness. This is the same colony where Cousteau and Dumas (1953) estimated 200 monk seals in 1948, but this appears to have been an exageration as the table below giving counts of seals suggests:

Date	Numbers	References
21- 7-1923	2	Monod 1923
26-12-1945	2	Morales-Agacino 1950
1948	21	Postel 1950
1948	60	Cousteau and Dumas
28- 2-1959	200	1953
	57	Boulva 1975

Date	Number	References
19-10-1968	8	Wijngaarden 1969
25-10-1968	6	Wijngaarden 1969
7-1969	46	Maigret and Trotignon 1975
7- 7-1973	50	Boulva 1975
9- 9-1973	30-35	Boulva 1975
7-1974	25	Maigret and Trotignon 1975
6-1975	15	Maigret and Trotignon 1975

This colony appears to have numbered at most about 60 seals during the last 30 years. Maigret and Trotignon (1975) have surveyed it since 1970. No dead animals were found until July 1974 when two were discovered. During the first half of 1975, nine dead monk seals were counted, including one pup still attended by its mother. Two showed signs of injury, possibly by ship propellers. Empty shells from firearms were also discovered near the cave inhabited by the seals. The site used to be protected by Spanish regulations, but the political status of this area has become uncertain at the time of writing.

2.2 Rates

2.2.1 Reproductive

Age at sexual maturity: reported to be at 4 years of age (Maxwell 1967) but adequate data are lacking.

Birth season: newborn pups have been found at different times during the year, but more often in summer and early fall.

Observations suggest that whelping is asynchronous in this species and may take place year round.

Mating time: unknown.

Pregnancy rate: no data. In Sardinia, frequent abortions have been noted (Bareham and Furredu 1975). Inbreeding or internal contamination by pollutants such as DDT or heavy metals are possible explanations.

Gestation: believed to be 11 months (Troitzky 1953).

Weaning: at 6 to 7 weeks of age.

Longevity: no data.

2.2.2 Natural mortality; no data

2.2.3 Harvesting, commercial and incidental kill

These animals are protected throughout most of their range and are not being harvested. However the incidental kill appears to be important. Drowning of the seals when caught in fishing nets and attempts by the fishermen to eliminate it by shooting are important mortality factors. These seals are often a nuisance to fishermen, taking fish from their nets and damaging them.

3 Trophic relationship

3.1 Food and feeding

3.1.1 Food habits

The Mediterranean monk seals are shallow water feeders. They are reported to be more active at night (Bareham and Furredu 1975) even though they are often seen feeding during the day.

3.1.2 Food base

Eel, carp, whiting, sardine, bonito, octopus, lobster, *Dentex, Labra*, whitefish, *Mullus surmuletus, Boops boops, Mugil cephalus*, other flat fish and other fish species. Green algae have been reported from the stomach.

3.1.3 Requirements and utilization

No data for wild animals. Gavard (1927) reports that a captive female about 200 cm long and weighing 120 kg was eating daily 1/10 of her weight in fish.

3.1.4 Changes in abundance of food supply

No data for the Black Sea and the Mediterranean Sea. Maigret and Trotignon (1975) think that intense fishing off the coast of southern Spanish Sahara may be having an adverse effect by depleting fish stocks on which the seals are feeding.

3.2 Competition and predation

This species is the only pinniped in the Mediterranean and competition with species other than man are not likely. Predation does not seem to be a cause of significant mortality.

4 Relations to man

4.1 Values

4.1.1 Consumptive

Because of their scarcity and protection, these animals are not being harvested.

4.1.2 Low consumptive

The Mediterranean monk seal is considered an endangered species. Because of its shyness and remoteness of habitat it is unlikely to represent an extensive recreational potential except possibly in protected areas. It is an animal likely nearing extinction and would be a sad reflection on our society should we allow it to disappear.

4.2 Effects of activities other than exploitation

Many human factors seem to have led to the decrease in this species' abundance. A major cause would appear to be increased human population in areas of breeding habitat. These animals are shy and it seems that they cannot coexist in areas with people. Many seals are killed incidentally in fishermen's nets and traps. Also some others are shot by fishermen. The effects of toxicants and pollutants on these animals are not known. The Mediterranean is, however, becoming increasingly polluted.

4.3 Management and conservation

Very little has been, and is being, done in this respect. Most countries where the species occurs have adopted protective legislation but only in a few areas such as Bulgaria, certain islands of Greece, Madeira, Sardinia and Yugoslavia does this protection seem to be effective; elsewhere there is little or no enforcement.

The creation of parks and natural reserves in areas formerly occupied by the species, such as the Parc Naturel Régional in western Corsica, raises the question of reintroduction of this seal in suitable sites. Recolonisation of such sites by wandering animals is possible on the long term but unlikely on the short term. For example, the species may disappear altogether before a sufficient number of males and females have a chance to reach by their own means reserves created in the northern part of the western Mediterranean.

The possibility of human intervention should be examined.

Regularly some animals are captured and kept in isolated pools or zoos. At present, there are 4 known captive Mediterranean monk seals: 2 at the Zoo de Cansado in Nouadhibou, Mauritania, and 2 in Lisbon, Portugal. All captive animals in Turkey mentioned by Mursaloglu in 1964 are now dead.

It should be the role of an international organisation to purchase these animals and to operate a properly equipped pool in an attempt to build up a captive breeding herd such as exists for the common seal, *Phoca vitulina* in the Netherlands. This long term effort would insure: 1) the survival of the species; 2) a supply of animals with little fear of man which could be used for reintroduction in protected areas or to supply other zoos and aquaria. When released, it would be possible to keep the animals in a restricted zone by offering the food on a daily basis; 3) a proper way of studying the various parameters of this species' life history.

At least for the first years of the experiment, the animals should not be in contact with visitors (use of one-way glass).

Without the creation of a captive breeding herd formed from animals which would die without human intervention (sick or injured seals, abandoned pups), there appears to remain little chance of saving this species.

5 Threats to stocks

The major threat to this species comes in the form of increased human activity in the breeding area. This takes the form of increased pollution, population expansion and increased recreational exploitation throughout the species range.

6 Research

6.1 Current status

Monitoring of the distribution and numbers throughout the range of the species is continuing by means of a network of correspondents under the coordination of IUCN. A study of the still important Algerian population has been initiated at the Université d'Oran.

6.2 Recommendations for future research

An effort should be made to improve our knowledge of the abundance of these seals in areas for which only vague information is available (see section 2.1.2). A feasibility study should be initiated to examine the possibility of creating a research center associated to an existing zoo or aquarium preferably in a Mediterranean country, where a captive breeding herd would be kept and studied. Even though much needed, studies of wild animals should be restricted and under the supervision of scientists with experience in research on Pinnipeds. Field work should be non-disturbing to surviving colonies, and knowldege of the present distribution should be confined to a small group of specialists to prevent harassment by tourists.

References

BAREHAM, J.R., and A. FUREDDU, Observations on the
1975 use of grottos by Mediterranean monk seals (*Monachus monachus*). *J. Zool., Lond.*, 175:291-8.

BOULVA, J., Survey of the Mediterranean monk seal,
1975 *Monachus monachus*, in the western Mediterranean and eastern Atlantic. Report to the International Fund for Animal Welfare and to the International Union for the Conservation of Nature. Jan. 1975, 16 p. (MS).

BUDKER, P., Pinnipèdes et siréniens d'Afrique. *Notes*
1945 *Afr. Inst. Fr. Afr. Noire*, 27:4-6.

COUSTEAU, J.Y., and F. DUMAS, The silent world. Lon-
1953 don, 148 p.

GAMULIN-BRIDA, H., M. KAMERANOVIC and Z. MIKULIC,
1965 Sur la distribution du phoque moine dans l'Adriatique. *Rapp. P.-V. Réun. CIEM*, 18-257-60.

GAVARD, J., Observations sur le phoque moine,
1927 *Monachus albiventer* Bodd., faites au laboratoire de Castiglione (Algérie). *Bull. Stn. Exp. Aquicult. Pêche Castiglione*, (2):175-211.

HERMANN, J., Beschreibung der Munchs-Robbe. *Bes-*
1779 *chaf. Berlin Ges. Naturf. Freunde*, 48:456-509.

KING, J.E., The monk seals (genus *Monachus*). *Bull.*
1956 *Brit. Mus. (Nat. Hist.) Zool.*, 3:201-56.

—, Seals of the world. London, British Museum (Natu-
1966 ral History), 154 p.

MAIGRET, J., and J. TROTIGNON, Le phoque moine
1975 *Monachus monachus* (Hermann 1779) sur les côtes méridionales du Sahara. (Unpubl. MS).

MAXWELL, G., Seals of the world. London, Constable.
1967

MONOD, T., Note sur la présence du *Monachus albiven-*
123 *ter* Bodd. sur la côte saharienne. *Bull. Mus. Natl. Hist. Nat., Paris*, 29:555-7.

MORALES-AGACINO, E., Notes sur les phoques moines
1950 (*Monachus monachus Herm.*) du littoral espagnol. *Mammalia, Paris*, 14:1-16.

MURSALOGLU, B., Occurrence of the monk seal on the
1964 Turkish coasts. *J. Mammal.*, 45:316-7.

POSTEL, E., Un phoque tropical: le phoque moine. *Nat-*
1950 *ure, Paris*, (3187):341-7.

RONALD, K., The Mediterranean monk seal *Monachus*
1973 *monachus. IUCN Publ. (New Ser.) Suppl. Pap.*, (39):30-41.

RONALD, K., and P. HEALEY, Present status of the
1974 Mediterranean monk seal. *Migrat. Ser. UFAW-IUCN, Lond.*, (100)(MS).

TROITZKY, A., Contribution à l'étude des pinnipèdes à
1953 propos de deux phoques de la Méditerranée ramenés de croisière par S.A.S. le PRINCE RAINIER III de MONACO. *Bull. Inst. Océanogr. Monaco*, (1032):46 p.

WIJNGAARDEN, A. VAN, The monk seal colony at la
1969 Guera, Rio d'Oro. *IUCN Bull.*, 2(10):77.

CARIBBEAN MONK SEAL

J. Boulva

(The following information has been taken mainly from King (1956) and Rice (1973) who have summarized most of the knowledge available for this species).

1 Description

1.1 Species identification

1.1.1 *Family:* Phocidae
Species: Monachus tropicalis (Gray, 1850)

1.1.2 *Size*

Nose-tail lengths are available for 4 adult females (220, 216, 211 and 198 cm), 1 male (226 cm) and one full term foetus (85 cm); a 160 kg adult female, 211 cm in total length, is the only weight record for this species. Females are reported to be slightly smaller than males.

Adults are grayish-brown or grizzled on the back, ochreous-yellow to yellowish-white ventrally. Females seem to have much less of the yellow or white on the ventral surface. Hairs lie close to the body and are extremely short, the longest, those of the sides, being about 1 cm long. The female has four teats. The dental formula of the adult is: i 2/2, c 1/1, m 5/5.

1.2 Stocks

1.2.1 *Identification*

There has been no description of subspecific populations.

1.2.2 *Distribution*

The species is now considered extinct, the last recorded colony being noted in 1952 on the Serranilla Bank about halfway between northern Nicaragua and Jamaica (Lewis in Rice 1973). There have been unconfirmed sightings off Yucatan in the late 1960's and early 1970's (Rice 1973 and Diana Magor, pers. comm.).

The Caribbean monk seal probably hauled out and bred regularly mainly on uninhabited offshore islets and atolls. Its northernmost limit appears to have been the Bahama Islands and southern Florida, and to the south, Isla de Providencia (13.5 n, 81.5 W) off eastern Nicaragua.

Past distribution included the bahama islands, the Dry Tortugas islands and Key in Florida, Texas, Arrecifes Triangulos and Alacran north of Yucatan (Mexico), Cuba, Jamaica, Pedro Cays south of Jamaica, the island of Alta Vela about 240 km south of Haiti, Guadeloupe and Isla de Pinos.

2 Vital Parameters

2.1 Population size

2.1.1 *Methods of estimation*

Aerial surveys were flown in 1950 over reefs north of Yucatan and in 1969 off the

Chincorro Reef, eastern Yucatan. Circulars in English and Spanish offering a $500 reward for information on recent sightings of the species have been distributed throughout the Caribbean (IUCN 1973).

2.1.2 Results

No seals were seen during the surveys or reported following the distribution of the circulars.

2.1.3 Past abundance

The species appears to have been once abundant. Reports mention the capture of 100 seals in one night on the Bahama Islands in the early 18th century. In January 1911, about 200 seals were killed on Arrecife Triangulos; 4 were seen there in 1948 and none in 1950. Around 1967, 20 were seen sleeping on a beach off Guadeloupe.

2.2 Rates

2.2.1 Reproductive

Age at sexual maturity: unknown.

Birth season: reported to be in December on Arrecife Triangulos (Ward 1887).

Pregnancy rate: of the 41 seals closely examined by Ward (1887) in December 1886 on Arrecife Triangulos, there were 5 females with near-term foetuses, and one female with a pup. This suggests a birth rate of 0.15 (6/41) which would mean that the female Caribbean monk seal rarely bears a pup two years in succession (Rice 1973).

No data are available for the length of gestation, duration of nursing, longevity and natural mortality rates.

2.2.2 Harvesting

These seals were harvested mainly for their oil. The following numbers of seals have been reported killed: 8 on the island of Alta Vela in 1494, 14 on the Dry Tortugas, Florida, on 21 June 1513, 100 per night on the Bahamas early in the 18th century, about 200 on Arrecife Triangulos in January 1911. It thus seems that the species has been heavily exploited by man.

3 Trophic relationship

Only in one report (Ward 1887) is there mention of stomachs being examined for contents and only some fluid was found. Sharks were considered likely predators of these seals (Rice 1973).

4 Relation to man

4.1 Values

Rice (1973) suggests that the main factor responsible for the reduction or extinction of the Caribbean monk seal is the large, rapidly growing and mostly indigent human population within the seal's range. Many of these people make their living from the sea by fighting or catching turtles, and would probably kill any seal that they encountered.

4.2 Effects of human activities other than exploitation

Tourists and yachtsmen are reported to be increasingly invading the seal's habitat.

4.3 Conservation

No effective conservation measures have ever been applied to this species. It is legally protected in Jamaica (Lewis 1948). Attempts have been made to keep the species in captivity. However, of the 18 animals involved, none bred or survived for more than 5½ years.

5 Threats to stock

The Caribbean monk seal, if not already extinct, is certainly nearly so. Even if a few animals still survive, it appears unlikely that successful reproduction can take place either because adults of opposite sexes are too scattered to meet or because secluded, undisturbed beaches on which to bear and rear a pup are becoming very difficult to find.

6 Research

6.1 Current status

Research has been limited to occasional aerial surveys such as those over the islands off northern Yucatan in 1950, and over the Chincorro Reef, eastern Yucatan, in 1969, when no seals were found. A survey by means of circulars also gave no results.

6.2 Future research

There is a remote possibility that the species may survive in some isolated area. A widespread aerial survey during the whelping season in December might allow the discovery of unknown colonies. Should seals be found they should be protected as described by Rice (1973).

References

GRAY, J.E., Catalogue of the specimens of Mammalia in
1850 the collection of the British Museum. Pt. 2. Seals. London, British Museum (Natural History), 48 p.

IUCN, Working Meeting on Threatened and Depleted
1973 Seals of the World. Report on the Meeting *IUCN Publ. (New Ser.) Suppl. Pap.*, (39): 12-26.

KING, J.E., The monk seals (genus *Monachus*). *Bull.*
1956 *Brit. Mus. (Nat. Hist.) (Zool.)*, 3:201-56.

LEWIS, C.B., The west Indian seal. *Nat. Hist. Notes Nat.*
1948 *Hist. Soc. Jamaica*, 34:169-72.

RICE, D.W., Caribbean monk seal (*Monachus tropica-*
1973 *lis*). *IUCN Publ. (New Ser.) Suppl. Pap.*, (39):98-112.

WARD, H.L., Notes on the life history of *Monachus tro-*
1887 *picalis*, the west Indian seal. *Am. Nat.*, 21:257-64.

HAWAIIAN MONK SEAL

C. Brenton

1 Description

1.1 Species identification

1.1.1 Taxonomic
Family: Phocidae
Species: Monachus schauinslandi (Matschie 1905)

1.1.2 Size
- Newborn pups: 100 cm; 16-17 kg.
- Adult males: to 210 cm; to 173 kg.
- Adult females: to 230 cm; to 273 kg.

1.2 Stocks

1.2.1 Identifiation
No subspecific or geographically isolated populations have been identified.

1.2.2 Distribution
This species breeds on French Frigate Shoals, Lisianski Island, Laysen Island, Pearl and Hermes Reef and Kure Atoll. These animals are not known to have a migratory pattern but movement between islands is noted.

1.2.3 Structure of stocks
Little is known about the social structure of this species. Copulation has never been observed but is presumed to take place in the water. Monk seals do not congregate in large numbers on the breeding grounds but rather are found in scattered numbers along beaches and haul-outs providing easy access to and from water.

2 Vital Parameters

2.1 Population size

2.1.1 Methods of estimates
Both aerial and surface counts are used.

2.1.2 Results
Surveys in 1956-57 and 1957-58 showed a total of 1,013 and 1,208 seals respectively. More recent estimates (1972) would indicate a slight decrease in numbers with a population of at least 700 animals and possibly to about 1,000.

2.2 Rates

2.2.1 Reproduction
Age of sexual maturity:
- not known; possibly 3 years

Birth season: December to July with peak in April-May
Lactation: about 6 weeks
Mating season: not known
Gestation period: not known.
Pregnancy rate: in a two-year study 56 of the "mature" females bred over the two years. 34 % of these breeding females bred in both seasons, 32 % only in the first year and 34 % only in the second year.
Longevity: not known; a male has been aged at 20 years and a female at 11 years.

2.2.2 Natural mortality rates
Shark attack is an obvious cause of mortality. Although no mortality figures are

available 12 % of the seals observed in 1969 showed evidence of shark attack.

On islands occupied by humans pup mortality has been recorded at 19-39 %.

2.2.3 Harvesting rates

These animals are completely protected by U.S. federal law. A few permits to take specimens have been issued.

3 Trophic relationships

3.1 Food and feeding

Very little known. Spewings included the remains of eels, cephalopods and reef and bottom fish. No data on requirements, utilization or changes in abundance of food supply.

3.2 Competition and predation

At present no competition problems are seen except with man for habitat. As mentioned above sharks are apparent important predators on monk seals.

4 Relation to man

4.1 Values

4.1.1 Consumptive

These animals are totally protected and are so few in number and widely scattered that consumptive use is unlikely.

4.1.2 Low-consumptive

These animals have been vacating areas of human population and disturbance and therefore represent a limited recreational resource.

4.2 Effects of human activities other than exploitation

Human disturbance has caused a sharp decrease in the number of animals in certain areas. An increase in pup mortality appears to be the cause. There is also competition between seals and man for areas used as seal pupping sites.

4.3 Management and conservation

This species is protected by U.S. federal law. The majority of the breeding sites are located within the Hawaiian Islands National Wildlife Refuge (HINWR). In this area visits by people are discouraged or prohibited.

5 Threats to stocks

The major threat appears to be human disturbance.

6 Research

6.1 Current status

At present a pup tagging and recovery programme is being conducted by the HINW Refuge Manager. Counts are also being made in the HINWR in spring and late summer.

6.2 Recommendations for future research

Continued monitoring of existing small populations.

SOUTHERN ELEPHANT SEAL

R.M. Laws

1 Description

1.1 Species identification

1.1.1 Family: Phocidae
Species: Mirounga leonina (Linnaeus, 1758)

1.1.2 Size

- Newborn:

127 cm, 46 kg. (South Orkney Is.)
127 cm, 40 kg. (Macquarie Is.)

- Adult males:

4.5 m, 4000 kg. (South Georgia)
4.2 m, 3000 kg. (Macquarie Is.)

- Adult females:

2.8 m, 900 kg. (South Georgia)
2.6 m, 400 kg. (Macquarie Is.)

(Laws, 1953a, 1960; Bryden, 1972; Carrick, Csardas and Ingham, 1962).

This species derives its name from the large size (it is the largest of all pinnipeds) and the proboscis of adult males. There is a striking sexual dimorphism, a male dominance hierarchy and polygynous breeding behaviour. Pups are born with a stiff black lanugo and at South Orkney Is. increase to up to 200 kg at about 23 days of age at which point they are deserted by the female; they moult until 6 weeks of age into a blue-grey coat lighter centrally. Adults are dark grey, lighter ventrally, weathering to shades of brown (Laws 1953a).

1.2 Stocks

1.2.1 Identification

There are three main breeding stocks, centred on South Georgia (including South America, Falkland Islands, Scotia arc), about 300,000; Kerguelen and Heard Island, about 200,000; and Macquarie Island (and New Zealand subantarctic islands), about 100,000 (Laws 1960). No interchange between stocks has been demonstrated and the different growth rates and sizes attained by South Georgia and Macquarie stocks point to their discreteness. Reproductive parameters also differ (Carrick, Csardas and Ingham, 1962; Bryden 1972).

1.2.2 Distribution

Nothing is known but tagged or branded animals have been recovered up to 1,500 mi from their breeding grounds (Dickinson 1967; Ingham 1957, 1967).

2 Vital parameters

2.1 Population size

2.1.1 Methods of estimation

Counts of weaned pups on the beaches are raised by a factor (3.5) estimated from the age structure of the population (Law 1960).

2.1.1 Results

Of uncertain accuracy and relate to 1950-1960 period. Total numbers then estimated at 600,000. With cessation of commercial sealing at South Georgia in 1964 numbers now probably higher.

2.1.3 Trends in abundance

After near extermination by sealers in the nineteenth century elephant seal stocks increased with protection since 1910. At South Georgia a rationally managed industry, for adult males, continued until 1964; since then this population may have increased and its sex and age structure will have changed. Most other populations are now thought to be more or less stable (Laws 1953, 1960, 1973).

2.2 Rates

2.2.1 Reproductive (Laws 1956, Carrick, Csardas and Ingham, 1962)

Sexual maturity:

- female 2-3 years (South Georgia); 4-7 years (Macquarie)
- male 4 years (South Georgia), 5-6 years (Macquarie)
- male (harem holding) 7 years (South Georgia) 10 years (Macquarie Is.)

Birth season: September-November

Lacatation period: 23 days

Mating: 19 days post-partum

Gestation: 50 weeks, including 12 weeks delayed implantation

Longevity: c. 20 years maximum for both sexes.

2.2.2 Natural mortality

Natural mortality rates (South Georgia estimate, Laws 1960)

female: 0-1 year, 40 %; 1-2 years, 20 %; 2-10 years, 13 %; increasing to 100 % at 20 years

male: 0-1 year, 57 %; 1-2 years, 30 %; 2-10 years, 17 %; increasing to 100 % at 20 years.

2.2.3 Harvesting

No stocks currently harvested but formerly at South Georgia the sealing industry took 6,000 adult bulls annually to 1964; this represents 6 % of annual total estimated pup production (Laws 1960).

3 Trophic relationships

3.1 Food and feeding

3.1.1 &
3.1.2 Food base and habits

Elephant seals have not been sampled pelagically and fast for long periods when on land. Fish and squid remains have been identified in stomachs. Possibly feed on fish in inshore waters and squid and fish oceanically. Inferred to be deep diving from type of visual pigment (Laws 1956, 1977a; Lythgoe and Dartnall 1970; Øritsland 1977).

3.1.3 Requirements and utilization

Probably about 6 % of body weight per day for 9-10 months (2-3 months fasting) (Laws 1977a).

3.1.4 Changes in abundance of food supply

Not known. At South Georgia and Kerguelen Is. large catches of fish (to 360,000 tons) may have had adverse effects in recent years (Laws 1973).

3.2 Competition and predation

Very little is known. Nearest pinniped competitor seems to be the Ross seal, but geographical separation is complete. Other possible competitors — albatrosses (?), some fish, sperm whale (Laws 1977, 1977a). Killer whale only known predator on adults and leopard seal on young, but unlikely to have significant effects.

4 Relation to man

4.1 Values

4.1.1 Consumptive

None at present Future potential, 20,000-30,000 tons biomass annually on sustainable basis (Laws 1960). This species was harvested primarily for its blubber oil, the blubber oil being similar to high grade whale oil in value. Hides were occasionally taken and could substitute for walrus hide for buffing castings, etc. Meat has not usually been taken but should be in any future industry (Laws 1953).

4.1.2 Low-consumptive

The species is found far from areas populated by man and therefore represents little recreational potential. Antarctic tourism is increasing but the species' breeding season is too early to provide a wildlife spectacle.

4.2 Effects of human activities other than exploitation

Probably none of significance to species.

4.3 Management and conservation

Protected by national legislation. Industry at South Georgia, which ended in 1964, based on take of adult males during breeding season when oil yield maximal. Island divided into four sealing areas, one of which unhunted annually in rotation and several seal reserves where no hunting occurred. Management practices revised in 1952. Limited open season imposed October-November. Catch quota of 6,000 limited to adult males over 3.5 m long. Lower canine tooth from 5 % sample of catch for age determination. Government sealing inspector undertook analysis of catch. Mean age of catch increased from 6.6 years to stabilize at 7.7 years (Laws 1953. 1960).

5 Threats to stock

Apart from possible effects of commercial fishing activities at South Georgia and Iles Kerguelen, no threats to the stocks of this species have been identified.

6 Research

6.1 Current status

At Macquarie Is. routine resightings of branded animals for population analysis (Ingham 1967). At South Georgia a project has just started which is concerned with breeding behaviour and social organization for comparison of currently unexploited herd with situation in the 1950's when exploitation was maximal (British Antarctic Survey).

6.2 Future research

The southern elephant seal is one of the better known species from studies at South Georgia and Macquarie Island. Further information is needed on trends in abundance, possible changes in social structure during the breeding season (harem size, sex ratios) since sealing ended, and on age structure and mortality rates.

The pelagic phase is virtually unknown but the practical difficulties of studying the species at sea are extreme. Qualitative and quantitative information on food and trophic relationships is lacking, and energetics data virtually non-existent. Age-specific pregnancy rates are unknown and can only be determined from pelagic samples.

In this species valuable comparisons have been made between exploited and unexploited stocks. The opportunity now exists to make this comparison for one stock (at South Georgia) formerly exploited, up to 1964, and since unexploited. There exists a unique opportunity to compare abundance, reproductive, behavioural and other population parameters.

References

BRYDEN, M.M., 1972 Growth and development of marine mammals. *In* Functional anatomy of marine mammals, edited by R.J. Harrison. London, Academic Press, vol. 1:1-79.

CARRICK, R., S.E. CSORDAS and S.E. INGHAM, 1962 Studies on the southern elephant seal, *Mirounga leonina* (L.). 4. Breeding and development. *CSIRO Wildl. Res.*, 7(2):161-97.

DICKINSON, A.B., 1967 Tagging elephant seals for life-history studies. *Polar Rec.*, 13:443-6.

INGHAM, S.E., Elephant seals on the Antarctic Conti-
1957 nent. *Nature, Lond.*, 180:1215-6.

—, Branding elephant seals for life-history studies.
1967 *Polar Rec.*, 13:447-9.

LAWS, R.M., The elephant seal industry at South Geor-
1953 gia. *Polar Rec.*, 6:746-54.

—, The elephant seal (*Mirounga leonina* Linn.). 1.
1953a Growth and age. *Sci. Rep. Falkland Isl. Dep. Surv.*, (8):1-62.

—, The elephant seal (*Mirounga leonina* Linn.). 2. Ge-
1956 neral, social and reproductive behaviour. *Sci. Rep. Falkland Isl. Dep. Surv.*, (13):1-88.

LAWS, R.M., The elephant seal (*Mirounga leonina*
1956a Linn.). 3. The physiology of reproduction. *Sci. Rep. Falkland Isl. Dep. Surv.*, (15):1-66.

—, The southern elephant seal (*Mirounga leonina* Linn.)
1960 at South Georgia. *Norsk Hvalfangsttid.*, 49(10): 466-76; (11): 520-42.

—, The current status of seals in the Southern Hemis-
1973 phere. *IUCN Resour. Publ. (New Ser.) Suppl. Pap.* (39):144-61.

—, The significance of vertebrates in the Antarctic ma-
1967 rine ecosystem. *In* Adaptations within Antarctic ecosystems, edited by G.A. Llano. Third Symposium on Antarctic Biology. Scientific Committe for Antarctic Research. Houston, Texas. Gulf Publishing Co. for Smithsonian Institution.

—, Seals and whales of the Southern Ocean. *Philos.*
1977a *Trans. R. Soc. Lond. (B)*, 110:81-96.

LYTHGOE, J.N., and H.J.A. DARTNALL, A "deep sea rho-
1970 dopsin" in a mammal. *Nature, Lond.*, 227-955-6.

ØRITSLAND, T., Food consumption of seals in Antarctic
1977 pack ice. *In* Adaptations within Antarctic ecosystems, edited by G.A. Llano. Third Symposium on Antarctic Biology. Scientific Committee for Antarctic Research. Houston, Texas, Gulf Publishing Co. for Smithsonian Institution.

NORTHERN ELEPHANT SEAL

B.J. Le Boeuf

1 Description

1.1 Species identification

1.1.1 Family: Phocidae
Species: Mirounga angustirostris (Gill 1866)

1.1.2 Size

- Newborn pups: males 1.53 m, 36.0 kg.; females 1.47 m, 31.5 kg
- Weaned pups (4 weeks old) 158 kg
- Adult males 4.5 m, 1800-2700 kg
- Adult females 3.6 m, 900 kg

Males can be distinguished from females by their long noses and rugose, corrugated neck shields; both features become more pronounced with age. There is no sexual dimorphism in coat pattern. Pups moult from their black natal pelage to a silver coat at 5 to 6 weeks of age. Juveniles and some adult females moult annually in the spring; breeding-age males moult in summer. The process takes about a month in adults.

1.2 Stocks

1.2.1 Identification
No separate stocks have been identified.

1.2.2 Distribution
The breeding range is restricted to offshore islands from central Baja California, Mexico, in the south to central California, U.S.A., in the north; or from Isla Cedros, Mexico to Point Reyes, California. Ten rookeries are distinguished; from south to north these are: Isla Cedros, Islas San Benito, Isla de Guadalupe, Los Coronados, San Nicolas Island, Santa Barbara Island, San Miguel Island, Ano Nuevo Island, Southeast Farallon Island and Point Reyes Peninsula. The largest breeding aggregations are found at Isla de Guadalupe, Islas San Benito and San Miguel Island. The Northern colonies have been founded recently from immigrants to the south. Individuals are seen as far north as southeastern Alaska and as far as 240 km from shore. There is some mixing between individuals from all colonies. Thus, there is considered to be but one population.

Elephant seals can be found on rookeries at all times of year but the distribution varies with sex and age.

1.2.3 Movements and Migration
There is no migration en masse. Widespread dispersion in the northward direction occurs as soon as weaned pups desert their place of birth at around three months of age.

2 Vital parameters

2.1 Population size

2.1.1 Methods of estimation
Aerial, ship and land censuses. Extrapolation from known characteristics of the annual cycle.

2.1.2 Results

The present population is estimated to number 45,000.

2.1.3 Trend in abundance

The population has been increasing in number since its nadir in 1884-1892, when the entire population may have consisted of as few as 8 individuals, and probably no more than 100 (Townsend 1912; Bonnell and Selander 1974). Numbers have increased logarithmically since that time (Bartholomew and Hubbs 1960) and continue to rise, particularly in northern colonies (Le Boeuf, Ainley and Lewis 1974).

2.2 Rates

2.2.1 Reproductive

Age at sexual maturity:

- females give birth for the first time at 3-5 years of age
- males undergo puberty at 4-5 years of age but social maturity (and domination of breeding) does not occur until age 9 or 10

Longevity: approximately 14 years for both sexes

Birth season: December, January and February

Mating time: 19 days after parturition; January, February and the first part of March

Gestation: 11.3 months (delay of implantation is about 3 months) if they are like southern seals.

Fecundity: aproximately 95 % of all females present on rookeries during the breeding season give birth. Females give birth annually from the time they first give birth until they die.

Reproductive behaviour of males and females is described in Le Boeuf and Peterson (1969a), Le Boeuf (1974), Le Boeuf, Whiting and Gantt (1972), Le Boeuf (1974) and Cox & Le Boeuf (1976).

2.2.2 Natural mortality

Pups - from birth to weaning at 28 days of age (absolute measure):
Ano Nuevo Island: 1968 to 1976 — 15 to 26 % (Le Boeuf & Briggs 1976)
Southeast Farallon: 1972 to 1975 — O to 73 % (Le Boeuf, Ainley and Lewis, 1974).

Los Coronados (estimate based on 2 censuses): 1974 and 1975 — Slightly more males die than female pups. Bartholomew (1952) estimated pup mortality at 5 to 10 % on Isla de Guadalupe and Odell (1974) estimated pup mortality at less than 3.5 per cent on San Nicolas Island. Considering the method of estimation, these figures are probably low.

Stillborns make up less than 19 % of the pup mortality rate.

Cause of death: injury and starvation due to intrasexual competition of adult males and females (Le Boeuf & Briggs 1976).

Adult males: in one sample, 85 to 97 % mortality before reaching age 8 (Le Boeuf 1974).

Annual mortality of males at Ano Nuevo island, 1968 to 1973, was 50 % for fully grown adults 46 % for males that were not quite full grown and 42 % for males of pubertal age (Le Boeuf 1974).

Adult females: annual mortality rate is considerably lower than in males. No reliable figure available at present.

Cause of adult deaths: unknown. Perhaps shark and killer whale predation, known to occur but not known to what extent.

2.2.3 Harvesting

No killing for commercial profit. Some seals are killed by fishermen; this number appears to be small.

2.2.4 Trend in abundance (Historical)

Elephant seals were abundant along the coasts of Baja California and California before commercial exploitation (for oil extracted from the blubber) began around the year 1800. Exploitation was intense and indiscriminate of age and sex. Populations were noticeably low by the 1840's, and it was no longer economically profitable to pursue them by the 1860's. Then the museum representatives seeking rare specimens almost succeeded in finishing them off. They were considered extinct by 1884. In 1892, Townsend (1912) saw 8 elephant seals on the most remote beach on Isla de Guadalupe; the eminent naturalist shot 7 of them for specimens. There were probably fewer than 100 elephant seals in existence at the time (Bonnell and Selander 1974). With time they recovered their former breeding range and numbers. All animals living today are descendants of the remnant band that occupied Isla de Guadalupe in 1892. The present population appears to be genetically depauperate, a situation which may cause problems for the species should the environment of the abundance of its prey change drastically (Bonnell and Selander 1974).

3 Trophic relationship

3.1 Food and feeding

3.1.1 Food habits

Feeds nearshore and offshore at depths of 100 fathoms. Known feeding place is off the coast of Seattle, Washington and the southern tip of British Columbia. Species include bottom and mudwater fishes, skates, rays, ratfish, small sharks, squid, Pacific Hake (Huey 1930; Morejohn and Baltz 1970).

3.1.2 Requirements and utilization

No data.

3.1.3 Destruction of food supply

No data.

3.2 Competition and Predation

Inhabits same rookeries as *Zalophus, Eumetopias, Phoca* and *Callorhinus* but breeds at time of year when others are mostly at sea. Generally peaceful coexistence with other species on land. Tolerates man except at close range. Adults are dangerous. Preyed on by killer whales and large sharks throughout its range.

4 Relation to Man

4.1 Values

4.1.1 Consumptive

Blubber can be processed for oil.

4.1.2 Low-consumptive

The animal has considerable appeal to the general public as evidenced by the great number of tourists that view them annually on the California mainland at Ano Nuevo Point.

4.2 Effects of human activities other than exploitation

Their rookeries can be disturbed by human activities such as exploration for oil, or tours being led through their rookeries during the breeding season.

4.3 Management and conservation

Protected in U.S.A. and Mexico.

5 Threats to stock

None known at present.

6 Research

6.1 Current research

The northern elephant seal is being subjected to intensive study from the point of view of population dynamics and behaviour; physiological studies are just beginning.

6.1.1 Population dynamics

Population dynamics data have been gathered on all colonies (periodic on some and intensive on others) in the breeding range since 1968 by Le Boeuf and collaborators. Over 10,000 animals, mostly pups, have been tagged to facilitate analysis of movements, recruitment, development and mortality. Monitoring of tagged animals has been most thorough and systematic on Ano Nuevo Island and southeast Farallon Island. Additional censuses were made on San Miguel Island by the California Fish and Game and the National Marine Fisheries Service. On Ano Nuevo Island, a nine-year study of pup mortality and the annual mortality rate of adult males has been performed, the growth and development of the colony has been documented, the annual cycle in numbers has been established, immigration and emigration rates are known, as well as where individuals are coming from and going to. The age at which females first give birth and the loss of pups as a function of the age of the mother is known. The manner in which a new colony is formed has been observed and studied. A model for estimating the number of females that breed on a rookery, based on one or a few censuses, has been constructed.

The above work has been supported by the National Science Foundation. In 1975, the Bureau of Land Management awarded Le Boeuf and collaborators a one-year contract to study the number, distribution and movements of all pinnipeds, including the northern elephant seal, in the southern California bight. This information, based on aerial, ground and sea surveys, will enhance our knowledge of the population dynamics of this species. Very little of this information has been published to date (but see Le Boeuf, Ainley and Lewis 1974 and Le Boeuf, Countryman and Hubbs 1975).

6.1.2 Behaviour

Various aspects of behaviour have been and are being studied. These studies include:

1) male-male competition and reproductive success (Le Boeuf and Peterson, 1969a; Le Boeuf 1974);
2) the nutritional relationship between mother and pup (Le Boeuf, Whiting and Gantt 1972);
3) reproductive strategies of females (Cox and Le Boeuf 1976);
4) dialect formation in male vocalizations (Le Boeuf and Peterson 1969b; Le Boeuf and Petrinovich 1974);
5) the causes of pup mortality (Le Boeuf and Briggs 1976);
6) the development of swimming, diving and social behaviour in the newly weaned pup;
7) the role of aggression in female elephant seals (Christenson and Le Boeuf in press);
8) food studies based on stomach content analysis.

6.1.3 Physiology

Physiological studies are just getting underway. They include:

1) the loss of genetic variability due to going through a population bottleneck (measured by blood protein analysis) (Bonnell and Selander 1974);
2) ketamine immobilization of elephant seals (Briggs, Hendrickson and Le Boeuf 1975);
3) milk analysis;
4) water balance studies;
5) DDT and heavy metal studies;
6) estimation of maximum age at death from analysis of annuli in teeth.

6.2 Recommendations for future research

The fantastic logarithmic growth of some colonies in the population should continue to be studied particularly in light of the reduced genetic variability present in the species. The ease of studying the northern elephant seal makes it an ideal animal to study under natural conditions. It is possible to gather sufficient data on population dynamics to make it a model for future studies on closely related animals. Because individuals can be marked and followed on a daily as well as annual basis, and known genetic relationships can be established, this animal is excellent for testing predictions from sociobiological theory. Additional physiological studies should be encouraged. There is a gap in this area because the animal has long been on the endangered species list. The greatest hiatus in our knowledge concerns feeding behaviour at sea. We need to know where they feed, on what, how much and how.

References

BARTHOLOMEW, G.A., Reproductive and social behaviour of the northern elephant seal. *Univ. Calif. Publ. Zool.*, (47)369-471.
1952

BARTHOLOMEW, G.A., and C.L. HUBBS, Population growth and seasonal movements of the northern elephant seal, *Mirounga angustirostris. Mammalia*, 24:313-24.
1960

BONNELL, M.L., and R.K. SELANDER, Elephant seals: genetic variations and near extinction. *Science, Wash.*, 184:908-9.
1974

BRIGGS, G.D., R.V. HENDRICKSON and B.J. LE BOEUF, Ketamine immobilization of northern elephant seals. *J. Am. Vet. Med. Assoc.*, 167:546-8.
1975

CHRISTENSON, T.E., and B.J. LE BOEUF, Aggression in female elephant seals. *Behaviour.*
1976

COX, C., and B.J. LE BOEUF, Female incitation of male competition: a mechanism in sexual selection. *Am. Nat.*
1976

HUEY, L.M., Capture of an elephant seal off San Diego, California, with notes on stomach contents. *J. Mammal.*, 11:229-31.
1930

LE BOEUF, B.J., Male-male competition and reproductive success in elephant seals. *Am. Zool.*, 14:163-76.
1974

LE BOEUF, B.J., and K.T. BRIGGS, The cost of living in a seal harem. *Mammalia, Paris*, (in press).

LE BOEUF, B.J., and R.S. PETERSON, Social status and mating activity in elephant seals. *Science, Wash.*, 163:91-3.
1969

—, Dialects in elephant seals. *Science, Wash.*, 166:1654-6.
1969a

LE BOEUF, B.J., and L.F. PETRINOVICH, Dialects of northern elephant seals, *Mirounga angustirostris*: origin and reliability. *Anim. Behav.*, 22:656-63.
1974

LE BOEUF, B.J., D.G. AINLEY and T.J. LEWIS, Elephant seals on the Fallarones: population structure of an incipient breeding colony. *J. Mammal.*, 55:370-85.
1974

LE BOEUF, B.J., D.A. COUNTRYMAN and C.L. HUBBS, Records of elephant seals, *Mirounga angustirostris*, on Los Coronados Islands, Baja California, Mexico, with recent analysis of the breeding population. *Trans. San Diego Hist. Soc. Nat. Hist.*, 18(1):1-8.
1975

LE BOEUF, B.J., R.J. WHITING and R.F. GANTT, Perinatal behaviour of northern elephant seal females and their young. *Behaviour*, 43:121-56.
1972

MOREJOHN, G.V., and D.M. BALTZ, Contents of the stomach of an elephant seal. *J. Mammal.*, 51:173-4.
1970

ODELL, D.K., Studies on the biology of the California sea lion and northern elephant seal on San Nicolas Island, California. *J. Mammal.*, 55:81-98.
1974

TOWNSEND, C.H., The northern elephant seal, *Macrorhinus angustirostris* Gill. *Zoologica, N.Y.*, 1:159-73.
1912

CRABEATER SEAL

R.M. Laws

1 Description

1.1 Species identification

1.1.1 *Family:* Phocidae
Species: *Lobodon carcinophagus* (Hombron & Jacquinot 1842)

1.1.2 *Size*

- New born pups: 120 cm; 20 kg (Bertram 1940; Laws 1958, Øritsland 1970a)
- Adults: male to 257 cm (224 kg); female to 262 cm (227 kg) (Scheffer 1958)

Pups born with light gray lanugo. Weaning inferred at approximately one month. Growth rapid with young attaining near adult size after four months (Laws 1958). Adult coat relatively uniform in color mostly light gray but some specimens quite dark. Moulted young dark gray to quite dark with black mottling. Open-mouthed displays characterisitic when disturbed. Skins frequently showing major scars presumably resulting from killer whale or leopard seal attacks (Bertram 1940; Hofman *et al.* 1977).

1.2 Stocks

1.2.1 *Identification*

Although the species occurs over a wide range, no separate stocks have been identified.

1.2.2 *Distribution*

The species occurs throughout the Antarctic pack ice wherever it can gain free access for haulout. It is found in greatest abundance at the periphery of the pack in heavily broken ice, particularly small cake type ice. The distribution of the species is in large measure determined by the seasonal ice limits of the Antarctic pack. During the late austral summer the species is distributed adjacent to the continent, in association with six residual ice areas thought possibly to be population centres.

Distribution during the austral winter is principally along the outer pack at approximately the Antarctic convergence. Studies of the population genetics of the crabeater seal reveal no specific genetic sub-populations (Erickson *et al.* 1971). While the species is largely non-gregarious, pods numbering up to 28 or more individuals are occasionally observed. Area segregation of young and adult and breeding and non-breeding groups are evident (Gilbert & Erickson 1977). The crabeater seal is not believed to be migratory although major shifts of large numbers have been observed from time to time (Bertram 1940). The principal movement of the animals is associated with the annual melting and refreezing of the Antarctic pack ice. Consequently, the movements of the species are more passive than active.

2 Vital parameters

2.1 Population size

2.1.1 *Methods of estimation*

Systematic censuses covering an approximate 2/3rds of the Antarctic pack ice have been performed over the course of the past decade. These surveys were conducted over transects along which seals were counted from icebreakers and helicopters operating off icebreakers. Limited counts have also been made for the Ross Sea by aerial photography (Gilbert & Erickson 1977).

2.1.2 Results

The minimal population of crabeater seals is currently (1972) estimated to be 15 million comprising about half the total world population of all species of pinnipeds. Actual populations probably exceed this value inasmuch as the censuses taken to date did not sample seals in the water or in several large areas of pack ice (Gilbert & Erickson 1977). By area, minimal estimates for the area which have been censused are 9 to 11 million for the Weddell Sea, 1.3 million for the Amundsen and Bellinghausen Seas, 650,000 for the Oates and George V Coasts, and 600,000 for the Adelie, Clairie and Banzare Coasts (Gilbert & Erickson 1977).

2.1.3 Population trend

Stocks unexploited and possibly now in greater abundance than before decline of baleen whale stocks. The age at puberty appears to have advanced at least in one stock (Laws 1977).

2.2 Rates

2.2.1 Reproductive

Age at sexual maturity:

- 2-6 yr (Øritsland 1970 & 1970a: Laws 1977)

Birth season: September-October (Bertram 1940; Øritsland 1970a)

Lactation period: not known

Mating time: unknown, presumed 2-3 weeks after parturition

Gestation: 11 months including delay of implantation of 2-3 months (Harrison, Matthews and Siniff, 1973)

Longevity: 33 yr (Laws, unpublished).

2.2.2 Natural mortality

Annual mortality about 20 % total population (Erickson, unpublished) c. 14.5 % annually from 8 years onwards (Laws 1977).

Cause: predation by leopard seals, and killer whales believed most significant; occasional mass deaths resulting from disease of undetermined type occasionally noted.

2.2.3 Harvesting

No commercial harvest.

3 Trophic relationships

3.1 Food and feeding

3.1.1 Food habits

3.1.2 Food base

The staple food of the crabeater seal is krill, mostly *Euphausia superba* (Øritsland 1977)

3.1.3 Requirements and utilization

Unknown, but estimated at 7 % of body weight per day for 335 days (one month fasting) (Øritsland 1977).

3.1.4 Changes in abundance of food supply

Aereal and seasonal changes are unknown but it has been postulated that availability of krill has increased as the baleen whale stocks have declined (Laws 1977).

3.2 Competition and predation

Potential competition for food exists between the crabeater seal, the leopard seal (an opportunistic predator), baleen whales, the Adelie penguin and other seabirds and fish. The extent of this competition is believed minimal on the assumption that the leopard seal would probably not prey heavily on krill when it is in low abundance and by virtue of the fact that the number of penguins and other sea birds is low in the outer pack ice zone (Erickson unpublished). The markedly reduced state of the baleen whales and the fact that they feed principally outside the pack ice suggests that competition for food at present may be low. The pack ice seals are currently estimated to consume about 1½ times as much food as the large whales (Laws 1977a). The degree of competition with fishes is unknown (Laws 1977).

The principle mortality factor bearing on crabeater seals appears to be the leopard seal and killer whale. That such predation is quite intense is evident from the high percentage of crabeater seals bearing slash scars. The great majority of these scars appear to be caused by leopard seal attacks (Hofman *et al.* 1977).

4 Relation to man

4.1 Values

4.1.1 Consumptive

A few thousand individuals have been taken in small scale pilot pelagic sealing expeditions in 1892/93 and 1964 (Laws 1973; Øritsland 1970a). Currently very small numbers are taken for dog food (Laws & Christie 1976). This situation is not expected to change drastically in the near future but future exploitation of the stocks seems inevitable.

4.1.2 Low-consumptive

Low-consumptive use of the crabeater seal will be limited except for aesthetic appreciation of the species by tourists from cruise ships, and in films. As the most abundant seal in the world and one least affected by man there is a unique research potential.

4.2 Effects of human activities other than exploitation

Indirect human effects on crabeater seals are possible contaminants and human disturbance. The advent of pelagic oil exploration and development would possibly have significant impact. Accumulation of toxic residue might also affect the animals directly or through their food chains.

A further potential indirect impact adversely affecting the crabeater seal is the possible development of an industry based on krill when man might become a direct competitor for the staple food.

4.3 Management and conservation

The creabeater seal is potentially one of the most valuable of the world's seals by virtue of its great abundance. Management of the stocks could be quite precise since selective harvests should be possible as the species can be easily approached. Further, the Convention for the Conservation of Antarctic Seals provides in its Annex the legal vehicle for the implementation of rational harvest regulations (Great Britain Foreign and Commonwealth Office, London 1972). It is not yet in force. Possible drawbacks to conservation and management are the limited number of signatory nations and the present lack of provisions for international inspection and enforcement.

5 Threats to stocks

See 4.2 above.

6 Research

6.1 Current status

Relatively little major research has been performed of Antarctic seals in the pack ice and in the main this has concerned population census. These efforts have yielded information making possible minimal estimates of pack ice populations in the Weddell Sea, the Amundsen-Bellingshausen Seas, the Ross Sea and the Wilkes Land Coast areas. Additional research has concerned analysis of the population genetics of the pack ice seals, the niche association of the several species in the pack and the development of some basic life history information based on age determinations and specimen analyses. Investigations in the pack ice are severely limited by the unavailability of icebreakers in support of the work.

6.2 Recommendations for future research

Knowledge of the pack ice seals, namely the crabeater, leopard and Ross seals is exceedingly meager. The research recommended as a priority is to complete and extend the baseline inventory of the populations. This effort will require two or three summers utilizing icebreakers and supporting helicopters. The surveys should then be extended to reassess the areas formerly censused with a view to (1) evaluating trends in abundance and (2) narrowing the confidence limits of the estimates. These efforts should, ideally, be followed up by area reassessments at 5 to 10 year intervals. Specific and detailed assessments should be obtained before and after active exploitation of any particular stock.

An attempt should also be made in these assessments to differentiate separate unit stocks and to characterize population structure of the several stocks.

A second research activity requiring early attention is a programme of studies designed to provide basic life history data on Antarctic pack ice seals. Specific studies are required of the reproductive biology of the several species and the identification of possible unit stocks particularly as bearing on recruitment rates.

Ideally, life history studies would best be accompanied by a major marking programme. These studies would provide information on population structure, breeding biology, movements, etc. Unfortunately, they would be very difficult to execute owing to logistic difficulties and the fact that pack ice studies must at least for the foreseeable future be limited to the summer season. Despite this it is recommended that an effort be mounted to attempt the initiation of local marking studies. Possibilities would include marking efforts in the vicinity of permanent scientific shore stations. Major marking efforts might also be attempted in the Ross Sea, or Bransfield Strait, and adjacent areas where, once again perennial activities continue. This would provide a number of known aged specimens by areas.

References

BERTRAM, C.C.L., The biology of the Weddell and crabeater seals: with a study of the comparative biology of the Pinnipedia. *Sci. Rep. Brit. Graham. Land. Exped. 1934-37*, 1:139 p.
1940

ERICKSON, A.W., *et al.*, Distributional ecology of Antarctic seals. *In* Symposium on Antarctic Ice and Water Masses, Tokyo 1970, edited by G.E.R. Deacon. Cambridge, SCAR, pp. 55-76.
1971

GILBERT, J.R., and A.W. ERICKSON, Status of seals in pack ice of the Pacific sector of the Southern Ocean. *In* Adaptations within Antarctic ecosystems, edited by G.A. Llano. Third Symposium on Antarctic Biology. Scientific Committee for Antarctic Research. Houston, Texas, Gulf Publishing Co. for Smithsonian Institution.
1977

GREAT BRITAIN, Foreign and Commonwealth Report of the Conference on the Conservation of Antarctic Seals. London, HMSO, 136 p.
1972

HARRISON, R.J., L.H. MATTHEWS and J.M. ROBERTS, Reproduction in some Pinnipedia. *Trans. Zool. Soc. Lond.*, 27(5):437-541.
1952

HOFMAN, R.J., *et al.*, Leopard seal movement and behavior at Palmer Station, Antarctica. *In* Adaptations within Antarctic ecosystems, edited by G.A. Llano. Third Symposium on Antarctic Biology. Scientific Committee for Antarctic Research. Houston, Texas, Gulf Publishing Co. for Smithsonian Institution.
1977

LAWS, R.M., Growth rates and ages of crabeater seals, *Lobodon carcinophagus* Jacquinot and Pucheran. *Proc. Zool. Soc. Lond.*, 130(2):275-88.
1958

—, The current status of seals in the Southern Hemis-
1973 phere. *IUCN Publ. (New Ser.) Suppl. Pap.*, 39:144-61.

—, The significance of vertebrates in the Antarctic ma-
1977 rine ecosystem. *In* Adaptations within Antarctic Ecosystems, edited by G.A. Llano. Third Symposium on Antarctic Biology. Scientific Committee for Antarctic Research. Houston, Texas, Gulf Publishing Co. for Smithsonian Institution.

—, Seals and whales of the Southern Ocean. *Philos.*
1977a *Trans. R. Soc. Lond. (B)*, 110:81-96.

LAWS, R.M., and E.C. CHRISTIE, Seals and birds killed or
1976 captured in the Antarctic Treaty area, 1970-73. *Polar Rec.*, 18:318-20.

ØRITSLAND, T., Biology and population dynamics of
1970 Antarctic seals. *In* Antarctic ecology, edited by M.W. Holdgate. London, Academic Press, vol. 1:361-6.

—, Sealing and seal research in the south-west Atlantic
1970a pack ice, September-October 1964. *In* Antarctic ecology, edited by M.W. Holdgate. London, Academic Press, vol. 1:367-76.

—, Food consumption of seals in the Antarctic pack ice.
1977 *In* Adaptations within Antarctic ecosystems, edited by G.A. Llano. Third Symposium on Antarctic Biology. Scientific Committee for Antarctic Research. Houston, Texas, Gulf Publishing Co. for Smithsonian Institution.

SCHEFFER, V.B., Seals, sea lions and walruses: a review
1958 of the Pinnipedia. Stanford, California, Stanford University Press, 179 p.

ROSS SEAL

R.M. Laws & R.J. Hofman

1 Description

1.1 Species identification

1.1.1 Taxonomic

Family: Phocidae
Species: *Ommatophoca rossi* (Gray 1884)

1.1.2 Size

- Newborn pups: uncertain 105-120 cm; 27 kg.
- Adult males: 168-208 (av. 199) cm; 129-216 (av. 173) kg.
- Adult females: 196-326 (av. 213) cm; 159-204 (av. 186) kg.

Ross seals are in the same size range as crabeater seals. Females tend to be somewhat larger than males. However, there are insufficient data to determine if this apparent sexual dimorphism is real. The large eye orbits, minute teeth, and tendency to lift the head and inflate the throat in a "singing posture", are the most distinguishing field characteristics (see photographs and descriptions in Ray 1970; Erickson and Hofman 1974). The pelage is dark gray to chestnut dorsally, with contrasting silvery-white ventrally. Anteriorly, the light and dark merge about the eyes to give the appearance of a mask. Frequently there may be dark stripes from the chin to the chest and along the sides of the neck. Most adults have small scars about the neck and shoulders which Wilson (1907) atrributed to intraspecific aggression.

1.2 Stocks

1.2.1 Identification

There is no evidence for or against the existence of separate stocks.

1.2.2 Distribution

The Ross seal seems to be restricted to the heavy, consolidated ice pack of the Southern Oceans. The only sighting north of 55° South was made at Heard Island in September 1953 (Ingham 1960). Fewer than 50 sightings were reported prior to 1945, but increased use of ice breakers in the antarctic ice pack have resulted in more frequent sightings in recent years (summarised in Hoffman, Erickson & Siniff, 1973). Occurrence seems to be related to the density of the ice pack (King 1964; Erickson *et al.* 1972; Gilbert 1974; Gilbert & Erickson 1977) and individuals may be concentrated in pockets of local abundance (Ray 1970). The patchy distribution of sightings may be related to the non-uniform distribution of preferred ice types, food, or both.

1.2.2 Structure of stocks

Most sightings have been of solitary individuals (Erickson & Hofman 1974; Gilbert & Erickson 1977).

2 Vital Parameters

2.1 Population size

2.1.1 Methods of estimation

Most sightings have been opportunistic. Gilbert (1974) and Gilbert & Erickson (1977) discuss census methodology and report the results of systematic ice breaker and helicopter surveys in the Pacific sector of the Southern Ocean.

2.1.2 Results

Ross seals comprise about one to two percent of the total antarctic pinniped population (Øritsland 1970; Hoffman, Erickson & Siniff, 1973; Gilbert 1974; Gilbert & Erickson, 1977). Scheffer (1958) postulated a total population of 20,000-50,000, but Hoffman Erickson & Siniff (1973) and Gilbert & Erickson (1977) feel that this is a gross under-estimate inasmuch as past census efforts failed to penetrate the consolidated ice pack which is preferred Ross seal habitat. Gilbert and Erickson estimated 37,462 Ross seals in the Amundsen and Bellingshausen Seas; 63,964 in the ice pack off the Oates and George the V coast; and used additional data from Erickson *et al.* (1971) to arrive at a total population estimate of 220,000.

2.1.3 Trends in abundance

Not known, but most likely stationary.

2.2 Rates

2.2.1 Reproductive

Age at sexual maturity: uncertain, but Øritsland (1970) estimates, on the basis of 12 specimens, that females and males achieve sexual maturity at 3-4 years and 2-7 years, respectively.

Birth season: uncertain, but most likely in November-December (Øritsland 1970).

Mating time: unknown

Gestation: unknown

Longevity: unknown, but at least 12 years (Øritsland 1970a).

2.2.2 Natural mortality

Unknown.

2.2.3 Harvesting

Unexploited except for opportunistic collection for research purposes.

3 Trophic relationships

3.1 Food and feeding

3.1.1 Food habits

Cephalopods are thought to be the primary food item (Hamilton 1901; Wilson 1907; Brown 1913; Solyanik 1965), and King (1969) suggests that Ross seals feed on cephalopods of a larger size than do other seals.

3.1.2 Food base

Øritsland (1977) gives the proportions of food items as: squid, 47 %; fish 34 %; other invertebrates 19 %.

3.1.3 Requirements and utilization

Unknown.

3.1.4 Changes in abundance of food supply

Unknown.

3.2 Competition and predation

Habitat preference and food habits suggest that there may be little or no competition with other species of seals or whales. Predation by killer whales or leopard seals seems unlikely because of the species' habitat preference.

4 Relations to man

4.1 Values

4.1.1 Consumptive

No commercial exploitation at present; future exploitation is rather unlikely because of the preference for habitat which is inaccessible except by ice breaker or aircraft.

4.1.2 Low-consumptive

Tourism is unlikely because of the inaccessible nature of the preferred habitat. It might be anticipated, however, that small numbers will be taken for public display or research purposes.

4.2 Effects of human activities other than exploitation

Direct effects are unlikely, however, pollution of the antarctic marine environment could result in the build-up of toxic residues due to contamination of species lower in the food chain.

4.3 Management and conservation

Because of its seeming scarcity, the Ross seal is totally protected under the Convention for the Conservation of Antarctic Seals. Small numbers may be taken, under permit, for scientific purposes.

5 Threats to stocks

None known.

6 Research

6.1 Current status

Opportunistic observations only.

6.2 Recommendations for future research

Ross seals should be included in a general study of the Antarctic pack ice ecosystem. The most important research requirement is to determine trophic relationships and to establish baseline population parameters (density, age at first reproduction, birth rates and death rates) that can be used to identify and monitor changes in the populations.

References

BARRETT-HAMILTON, G.E.H., Zoologie: seals. *Result.* 1901 *Voyage S.Y. Belgica 1897-99 Exped. Antarct. Belge*, 1901:1-20.

—, Mammalia. *In* Report on the collections of natural 1902 history made in the Antarctic regions during the voyage of the SOUTHERN CROSS. London, British Museum (Natural History), 66 p.

BONNER, W.N., and R.M. LAWS, Seals and sealing. *In* 1964 Antarctic Research: a review of British scientific achievement in Antarctica, edited by R. Priestley, R.J. Adie and G. de Q. Robin. London, Butterworths, pp. 163-90.

BROWN, R.N.R., The seals of the Weddel Sea: notes on 1913 their distribution. *Rep. Sci. Result. Scott. Natl. Antarct. Exped.*, 4(13):185-98.

CHARCOT, J., The voyages of the WHY NOT? in the 1911 Antarctic. *In* The journal of the second French South Polar Expedition, 1908-1910, translated by P. Walsh. New York, Hodder and Stoughton, 315 p.

EKLUND, C.R., Population studies of Antarctic seals and 1964 birds. *In* Biologie antarctique, Premier Symposium organisé par SCAR, Paris, 1962, edited by R. Carrick, M. Holdgate and J. Prevost. Paris, Hermann, pp. 415-9.

EKLUND, C.R., and E.L. ATWOOD, A population study of 1962 Antarctic seals. *J. Mammal.*, 43:229-38.

ERICKSON, A.W., and R.J. HOFMAN, Antarctic seals. *An-* 1974 *tarct. Map Folio Ser.*, (18):4-13.

ERICKSON, A.W., D.R. CLINE and R.J. HOFMAN, Popu- 1969 lation study of seals in the Weddell Sea. *Antarct. J.U.S.*, 4:99-100.

ERICKSON, A.W., J.R. GILBERT and J. OTIS, Census of 1973 pelagic seals off the Oates and George V coast, Antarctica. *Antarct. J.U.S.*, 8(4):191-4.

ERICKSON, A.W., *et al.*, Seal survey in the South Shet- 1970 land and South Orkney Islands. *Antarct. J.U.S.*, 4:130-1.

—, Distributional ecology of Antarctic seals. *In* Pro- 1971 ceedings of the Symposium on Antarctic Ice and Water Masses, Tokyo, Japan, 19 September, 1970, edited by G. Deacon. Cambridge, SCAR, pp. 55-75.

—, Populations of seals, whales and birds in the Bel-
1972 lingshausen and Amundsen seas. *Antarct. J. U.S.*, 7(4):70-2.

GILBERT, J.R., The biology and distribution of seals in
1974 the Antarctic pack ice. Ph. D. Thesis. University of Idaho, Moscow, Idaho.

GILBERT, J.R., and A.W. ERICKSON, Distribution and
1977 abundance of seals in pack ice of the Pacific sector of the Southern Ocean. *In* Adaptations within Antarctic ecosystems, edited by G.A. Llano. Third Symposium on Antarctic Biology. Scientific Committee for Antarctic Research. Houston, Texas, Gulf Publishing Co. for Smithsonian Institution.

GLESS, E.E., and E.A. HICHK, Entomological studies at
1968 Hallet Station. *Antarct. J. U.S.*, 3:123.

GREY, J.E., The zoology of the voyage of H.M.S. ERE-
1844 BUS and TERROR, 1839-43: 1. Mammalia. 1. The seals of the Southern Hemisphere. London, E.W. Jansen.

HOFMAN, R.J., and A.W. ERICKSON, Antarctic seals. *An-*
1974 *tarct. Map Folio Ser.*, (18):4-13.

HOFFMAN, R.J., A.W. ERICKSON and D.B. SINIFF. The
1973 Ross seal (*ommatophoca rossi*). *IUCN Publ. (New Ser.) Suppl. Pap.*, (39):129-39.

INGHAM, S.E., The status of seals (Pinnipedia) at Aus-
1960 tralian Antarctic stations. *Mammalia, Paris*, 24:422-30.

KENYON, K.W., Antarctic seal observations, February
1967 1967. Sandpoint Nav. Sta., Seattle, Washington, USFWS, 17 p. (unpubl. rep.).

KING, J.E., Seals of the world. London, British Museum
1964 (Natural History), 154 p.

—, The Ross and other Antarctic seals. *Trans. Aust.*
1968 *Mus.*, 15(1).

—, Some aspects of the anatomy of the Ross seal, *Om-*
1969 *matophoca rossi. Sci. Rep. Brit. Antarct. Surv.*, (63):1-54.

LA GRANGE, J.J., Notes on the birds and mammals on
1962 Marion Island and Antarctic (SANAE). *J.S. Afr. Biol. Soc.*, 3:27-84.

LAWS, R.M., The seals of the Falkland Islands and De-
1953 pendencies. *Oryx*, 2:87-97.

MARR, J.W.S., The South Orkney Islands. *Discovery*
1935 *Rep.*, 10:283-382.

MAWSON, D., The home and the blizzard. Philadelphia,
1915 Lippincott, 305 p.

MEDVEDEV, L.P., and V.A. BORONIN, Seal observations
1968 during the 12th voyage of the OB. *Inf. Byull. Sov. Antarkt. Exped. 1955-8*, (68):64-6.

MOSSMAN, R.C., The South Orkneys in 1907. *Scott.*
1908 *Geogr. Mag.*, 24:348-55.

NOBLE, J., Illustrated official handbook of the Cape
1893 and South Africa. London, Edward Stanford, 568 p.

ØRITSLAND, T., Biology and population dynamics of
1970 Antarctic seals. *In* Antarctic ecology, edited by M.W. Holdgate. London, Academic Press, vol. 1:361-6.

—, Sealing and seal research in the south-west Atlantic
1970a pack ice, Sept.-Oct. 1964. *In* Antarctic ecology, edited by M.W. Holdgate. London, Academic Press, vol. 1:367-76.

—, Food consumption of seals in the Antarctic pack ice.
1977 *In* Adaptations within Antarctic ecosystems, edited by G.A. Llano. Washington, Smithsonian Institution, PP. 749-68.

PERKINS, J.E., Biology at Little America III, the west
1945 base of the United States Antarctic Service Expedition, 1939-1941. *Proc. Am. Philos. Soc.*, 89:270-84.

POHLE, H., Die Pinnipedier der Deutschen Sudpo-
1927 lar-Expedition 1901-1903.
In Deutsche Sudpolar-Expedition 1901-1903, edited by E. von Drygalski. Berlin, W. de Gruyter, vol. 19:449-62.

POLKEY, W., and W.N. BONNER, The pelage of the Ross
1966 seal. *Bull. Brit. Antarct. Surv.*, (8): 93-6.

RAY, C., Population ecology of Antarctic seals. *In* An-
1970 tarctic ecology, edited by M.W. Holdgate. London, Academic Press, vol. 1:393-44.

SCHEFFER, V.B., Seals, sea lions and walruses: a review
1958 of the Pinnipedia. Stanford, California, Stanford University Press, 179 p.

SHACKELTON, E., The heart of the Antarctic. Philadel-
1909 phia, Lippincott, vol. 1:365 p., vol. 2:451 p.

SINIFF, D.B., and D.R. CLINE, Population dynamics of
1968 Antarctic seals (IWSOE-1968). *Antarct. J.U.S.*, 3:86-7.

SINIFF, D.B., D.R. CLINE and A.W. ERICKSON, Popula-
1970 tion densities of seals in the Weddell Sea, Antarctica, in 1969. *In* Antarctic ecology, edited by M.W. Holdgate. London, Academic Press, vol. 1:377-94.

SOLYANIK, G.A., Some information on Antarctic seals.
1964 *Inf. Byull. Sov. Antarkt. Exped. 1955-8*, (47)-54-9. Issued also as: *Transl. Am. Geophys. Union*, 5(3):179-82 (1965).

WILSON, E.A., Mammalia (whales and seals). *In* Natio-
1907 nal Antarctic Expedition, 1901-1904. Vol. 2. Natural history. London, British Museum (Natural History), 66 p.

WILTON, D.W., J.H.H. PIRIE and R.N.R. BROWN, Zoo-
1908 logical log. *Rep. Sci. Results Scott. Natl. Antarct. Exped.*, 4(1):103 p.

ZENKOVICH, B.A., Sea mammals as observed by the
1962 round-the world expedition of the Academy of Sciences of the U.S.S.R. in 1957-58. *Norsk Hvalfangsttid.*, 51:193-210.

LEOPARD SEAL

R.J. Hofman

1 Description

1.1 Species identification

1.1.1 Taxonomic
Family: Phocidae
Spelcies: *Hydrurga leptonyx* (de Blainville, 1820)

1.1.2 Size

- Newborn pups: uncertain, probably 150-160 cm; 35 kg.
- Adult males: 250-320 (av. 279) cm; 200-455 (av. 324) kg.
- Adult females. 241-338 (av. 291) cm; 225-591 (av. 367) kg.

Free ranging leopard seals are readily differentiated from other antarctic phocids on the basis of their long, streamlined body, massive, reptile-like head, and long, tapered fore flippers. The ventral surface is distinctly lighter than the dorsum and may be mottled or spotted. Females tend to be somewhat larger than males, but the difference is not sufficient to be used as a field characteristic for judging sex. When disturbed, the head usually will be lifted in an alert posture; at close quarters, the well-developed dentition is distinctive. (See photographs in Ray 1970; Erickson & Hofman 1974).

1.2 Stocks

1.2.1 Identification
There is no evidence, at this time, to suggest that there is more than a single stock.

1.2.2 Distribution
The leopard seal, like the crabeater seal, is more or less uniformly distributed througout the unconsolidated ice pack surrounding the Antarctic continent (see the distribution map in Erickson & Hofman 1974). Stragglers have been sighted on most of the southern continents (Kemp & Nelson 1931; Marr 1935; Hamilton 1939; Berchervaise 1962; Bonner & Laws 1964).

1.3 Migration and movements

Most leopard seal sightings in the antarctic pack ice are of solitary individuals (Eklund & Atwood 1962; Ray 1970; Siniff 1970; Erickson *et al.* 1971; Gilbert 1974; and Gilbert & Erickson 1977). However, non-breeding aggregations are regularly seen on some of the sub-Antarctic islands, presumably as a result of winter migration toward the northern parts of the range (Turbott 1952; Gwynn 1953; Brown 1957; Csordas 1963; and King 1964). Hofman *et al.* 1977 report a summer influx into the area near Palmer Station on the Antarctic Peninsula.

At Macquarie Island, leopard seals come ashore between June and December, but most of these seem to be young females (Turbott 1952). Further south, at Heard Island, all sex and age classes are present throughout the year and include pregnant females in winter (Csordas 1963). Analysis of body length data from different geographical areas suggests that leopard seals may be segregated by age (Laws 1957; Hofman *et al.* 1977).

2 Vital Parameters

2.1 *Population size*

2.1.1 *Methods of estimation*

Approximately two thirds of the antarctic ice pack has been surveyed over the past fifteen years (Eklund & Atwood 1962; Zenkovich 1962; Stirling 1969; Aguayo 1970; Ray 1970; Siniff, Cline and Erickson 1970; Erickson *et al.* 1971; Gilbert 1974; and Gilbert and Erickson 1977). Methodology for using icebreakers and helicopeters to carry out strip censuses in the pack ice is discussed in Siniff, Cline & Ericson 1970; Gilbert 1974; and Gilbert & Erickson 1977.

2.1.2 *Results*

Scheffer (1958) estimated the total population to be between 200,000 and 300,000. Gilbert and Erickson (1977) estimate a pack ice population of 220,000. Inasmuch as this species is reasonably abundant on the subantarctic islands and in ice free areas along the antarctic coast, the total population may be more nearly in the range of 500,000.

2.1.3 *Trends in abundance*

Leopard seal stocks are unexploited and probably are at the carrying capacity of the habitat. The carrying capacity, however, may be greater than in former times because of major reductions in the antarctic populations of baleen whales; i.e., leopard seals feed both on krill and crabeater seals and an increase in either prey species may have been followed by a concurrent increase in leopard seals (see the relevant discussion on krill and crabeater seals in Laws, 1977).

2.2 *Rates*

2.2.1 *Reproductive*

Age at sexual maturity: uncertain, estimated to be 3-7 years for females and 2-6 years for males (Øritsland 1970a).

Birth season: November-December (D.B. Siniff, personal communication).

Mating time and gestation period: uncertain; most authors assume that copulation occurs soon after whelping and that there is a delayed implantation (Øritsland 1970); Harrison (1960) indicates that breeding occurs in the period January-March, and that there is no delay in implantation.

Longevity: 26 + (Øritsland 1970a).

2.2.2 *Natural Mortality*

Uncertain, but Øritsland (1970a) estimates 25 % mortality during the first year, 8 % per year from age 1 through 10, and about 5 % per year in older age groups.

2.2.3 *Harvesting*

There is no commercial or incidental kill. Laws (1973) reports that 108 were taken, mainly for dog food, between the years 1964 and 1969. Øritsland (1970a) reports that 84 leopard seals were taken during the 1964 exploratory sealing expedition in the *MV Polarhav.*

3 Trophic relationship

3.1 *Food and feeding*

3.1.1 *Food habits and food base*

The leopard seal seems to be an opportunistic predator, best known for its predatory association with the Adelie penguin (Kemp & Nelson 1931; Csordas 1963; Penney & Lowry 1967; Muller-Schwarze & Muller-Schwarze 1975). Brown (1957) and El-Sayed (1971) postulated that leopard seals feed on krill, and this hypothesis has been substantiated (Hofman *et al.*, 1977). Other seals also are known to be components of the leopard seal's diet (Mawson 1915; Hamilton 1939; Rankin 1951; Erickson & Hofman 1974). Gilbert (1974) reports that leopard seals and crabeater seals are found in association in the ice pack and suggests that this association may indicate a common food resource (krill) or alternatively, leopard seals prey on crabeater seals. Marlow

(1967) suggested, and Hofman *et al.* (1977) concur, that leopard seals, rather than killer whales, may be responsible for much of the scarring found on crabeater seals. Laws (in press) indicates that virtually all adult crabeater seals are scarred, and intuitively it seems more likely that a juvenile crabeater seal would be able to escape from a leopard seal rather than a killer whale. D.B. Siniff (personal communication), on the basis of recent investigations, hypothesizes that leopard seals whelp slightly later than crabeater seals to take advantage of the seasonal availability of vulnerable prey; i.e., the whelping period of the leopard seal is adaptive in that it falls in a period when vulnerable prey (juvenile crabeater seals) are most abundant. There may be an age-related dietary transition, (Hofman *et al.*, 1977). Krill, for example, may be more important for juvenile animals that, because of their relatively small size and limited experience, are unable to take larger prey species.

3.1.2 Requirements and utilization

No firm data; however, 18 kg of crabeater seal were removed from the stomach of a large female leopard seal collected in the Weddell Sea ice pack in January 1969 (Erickson & Hofman 1974). Assuming an average weight of 300 kg and a population of 220,000, the total weight of leopard seals is about 66,000 metric tons (Laws, 1977) and annual consumption of prey species might be expected to be in the order of 1-2 million metric tons.

3.1.3 Changes in abundance of food supply

The importance of krill in the diet of leopard seals is unknown. It is possible, however, that leopard seals compete to a certain extent with other krill predators, including crabeater seals, baleen whales, penguins, flying bird and fish. If, as hypothesized, juvenile crabeater seals are an important dietary component of leopard seals, recovery of the baleen whale stocks or an expanding krill fishery could have direct or indirect effects on antarctic leopard seal populations. Killer whales and man are the only known predators, thus it seems unlikely that predation is important in regulating numbers of leopard seals.

4 Relations to man

4.1 Values

4.1.1 Consumptive

At present, there is no commercial exploitation. An antarctic sealing industry, if one develops, would most likely be dependent primarily on crabeater seals; leopard seals, however, probably would be taken opportunistically in any seal fishery. Some small numbers (probably fewer than 1,000 per year) will be taken for research purposes.

4.1.2 Low-consumptive

At present, the only low-consumptive value is to tourists aboard cruise ships. In the future, there may be some demand for public display animals.

4.2 Effects of human activities other than exploitation

As suggested earlier, an antarctic krill fishery could have direct and/or indirect effects on the leopard seal populations. The advent of off-shore oil exploration and development conceivably could have a negative impact. Toxic residue build-ups might also affect the animals directly or through their food chains.

4.3 Management and conservation

The Convention for the Conservation of Antarctic Seals has adequate provisions to insure the development of sound management practices if an antarctic seal industry should develop. However, there is insufficient knowledge of trophic and other ecological relationships in the pack ice ecosystem, thus there is no way to assess the possible effects of a krill fishery or other indirect human activities. Inasmuch as krill is a keystone species in the antarctic food web, it is imperative that management be based on an ecosystem, rather than a single species, perspective.

5 Threats to stock

Uncontrolled exploitation of the various living or mineral resources of the area could have adverse effects on leopard seals.

6 Research

6.1 Current research

Opportunistic observations by investigators carrying out other studies; at present there appear to be no studies directed primarily at leopard seals.

6.2 Recommendations for future research

Studies directed specifically at leopard seals should be designed to ascertain population size, distributions, movements, age-sex structure, trophic relationships, reproductive parameters and natural mortality rates. The ultimate objective would be to provide sufficient quantitative data to construct models that would reliably predict the effects of natural or man-induced perturbations. Inasmuch as financial and logistic resources are limited, it is unlikely that comprehensive studies will be undertaken in the absence of commercial exploitation. Therefore, pilot studies should be initiated to develop methodology and to identify parameters that would be most useful for monitoring populations' trends. As an example, it might be cost-effective to invest in a satellite tracking system to study and monitor daily and seasonal movements of a representative sample of radio-tagged seals.

References

AGUAYO, A., Census of Pinnipedia in the South Shet-
1970 land Islands. *In* Antarctic ecology, edited by W.M. Holdgate. London, Academic Press, vol. 1:395-7.

BECGERVAUSE, J., The leopard is not for branding. *Vict.*
1962 *Nat.*, 79(8):237-43.

BONNER, W.N., and R.M. LAWS, Seals and sealing. *In*
1964 Antarctic research, edited by R. Priestley, R.J. Adie and G. de Q. Robin. London Butterworths, pp. 163-90.

BROWN, K.G., The leopard seal at Heard Island,
1957 1951-1954. *Aust. Natl. Antarct. Res. Exped. Interim Rep.*, (16):1-34.

CLINE, D.R., D.B. SINIFF and A.W. ERICKSON, Immob-
1969 ilizing and collecting blood from antarctic seals. *J. Wildl. Manage.*, 33(1):138-44.

CSORDAS, S.E., Leopard seals on Macquarie Island. *Vict.*
1963 *Nat.*, 79(12):358-62.

EL-SAYED, S.Z., Biological aspects of the pack ice eco-
1971 system. *In* Symposium on Antarctic ice and water masses, edited by G. Deacon. Cambridge, England, SCAR, pp. 35-54.

EKLUND, C.R., and E.L. ATWOOD, a population study of
1962 antarctic seals. *J. Mammal.*, 43:229-38.

ERICKSON, A.W., and R.J. HOFMAN, Antarctic seals. *An-*
1974 *tarct. Map Folio Ser.*, 18:4-13.

ERICKSON, A.W., D.R. Cline and R.J. Hofman, Popula-
1969 tion study of seals in the Weddell Sea. *Antarct. J.U.S.*, 4:99-100.

ERICKSON, A.W., *et al.*, Seal survey in the South Shet-
1970 land and South Orkney Islands. *Antarct. J.U.S.*, 5(4):130-1.

—, Distributional ecology of antarctic seals. *In* Sympo-
1971 sium on Antarctic ice and water masses, edited by G. Deacon. Cambridge, England, SCAR, pp. 55-76.

GILBERT, J.R., The biology and distribution of seals in
1974 Antarctic pack ice. Ph. D. Thesis, University of Idaho, Moscow.

GILBERT, J.R., and A.W. ERICKSON, Distributions and
1977 abundance of seals in pack ice of the Pacific sector of the Southern Ocean. *In* Adaptations within Antarctic ecosystems, edited by G. Llano. Washington, D.C., Smithsonian Institution, pp. 703-40.

GWYNN, A.M., The status of the leopard seal at Heard
1963 Island and Macquarie Island, 1948-1950. *Aust. Natl. Antarct. Res. Exped. Interim. Rep.*, 3:1-33.

HAMILTON, J.E., The leopard seal, *Hydrurga leptonyx*
1939 (De Blainville). *Discovery Rep.*, (18):239-64.

HARRISON, R.J., Reproduction and reproductive organs.
1969 *In* The biology of marine mammals, edited by H.T. Andersen. New York, Academic Press, pp. 253-348.

HOFMAN, R.J., Distribution patterns and population
1975 structure of antarctic seals. Ph. D. Thesis, University of Minnesota, St. Paul.

—, The leopard seal (*Hydrurga leptonyx*) at Palmer
1977 Station, Antarctica. *In* Adaptations in Antarctic ecosystems, edited by G. Llano. Washington, D.C., Smithsonian Institution, pp. 769-82.

KEMP, S., and A.L. NELSON, The south Sandwich Is-
1931 lands. *Discovery Rep.*, (3): 133-97.

KING, J.E., Seals of the world. London, British Museum
1964 (Natural History), 154 p.

LAWS, R.M., On the growth rates of the leopard seal,
1957 *Hydrurga leptonyx* (De Blainville). *Säugetierkd. Mitt.*, 5:49-55.

—, The current status of seals in the Southern Hemis-
1973 phere. *IUCN Publ. New Ser. (Suppl. Pap.)*, (39):144-61.

—, The significance of vertebrates in the Antarctic ma-
1977 rine ecosystem. *In* Adaptations in Antarctic ecosystems, edited by G. Llano. Washington, D.C., Smithsonian Institution, PP. 411-38.

LEVICK, G.M., Natural history of the Adelie penguin. *In*
1915 The British Antarctic Terra Nova Expedition, 1910. Zoology. London, vol. 1:55-83.

MARLOW, B.J., Mating behaviour in leopard seal, *Hyd-*
1967 *rurga leptonyx* (Mammalia: Phocidae), in captivity. *Aust. J. Zool.*, 15:1-5.

MARR, J.W.S., The south Orkney Islands. *Discovery*
1935 *Rep.*, (10):283-382.

MAWSON, D., The home of the blizzard. Philadelphia,
1915 Lippincott.

MULLER-SCHWARZE, D., Behaviour of antarctic penguins
1971 and seals. *Publ. Am. Assoc. Adv. Sci.*, (93):259-76.

MULLER-SCHWARZE, D., and C. MULLER-SCHWARZE, Re-
1975 lations between leopard seals and Adelie penguins. *Rapp. P.-V. Réun. CIEM*, 169:394-404.

ØRITSLAND, T., Biology and population dynamics of
1970 antarctic seals. *In* Antarctic ecology, edited by M.W. Holdgate. London, Academic Press, vol. 1:361-6.

—, Sealing and sealing research in the south-west At-
1970a lantic pack ice, September-October, 1964. *In* Antarctic ecology, edited by M.W. Holdgate. London, Academic Press, vol. 1:367-76.

PENNY, R.L., and G. LOWRY, Leopard seal predation on
1967 Adelie penguins. *Ecology*, 48:878-82.

RANKIN, N., Antarctic Isle. London, Collins.
1951

RAY, C., Population ecology of antarctic seals. *In* An-
1970 tarctic ecology, edited by M.W. Holdgate. London, Academic Press, vol. 1:398-414.

SCHEFFER, V., Seals, sea lions and walruses; a review of
1958 the Pinnipedia. Stanford, California, Stanford University Press, 179 p.

SINIFF, D.B., D.R. CLINE and A.W. ERICKSON, Popula-
1970 tion densities of seals in the Weddell Sea, Antarctica, in 1968. *In* Antarctic ecology, edited by M.W. Holdgate. London, Academic Press, vol. 1:377-94.

STIRLING, I., Distribution and abundance of the Weddell
1969 seal in the western Ross Sea, Antarctica. *N.Z.J. Mar. Freshwat. Res.*, 3:191-200.

TURBOTT, E.G., Seals of the Southern Ocean. *In* The
1952 Antarctic today, edited by F.A. Simpson. Wellington, New Zealand Antarctic Society, pp. 195-215.

WILSON, E.A., Mammalia. (Whales and seals). *in* Na-
1907 tional Antarctic Expedition 1901-1904. London, British Museum (Natural History), vol. 2:66 p.

ZENKOVITCH, B.A., Sea mammals as observed by the
1972 round-the-world expedition of the Academy of Sciences of the U.S.S.R. in 1957/58. *Norsk Hvalfangsttid.*, 51(5):193-210.

WEDDELL SEAL

D.P. De Master

1 Description

1.1 *Species identification*

1.1.1 *Taxonomy*

Family: Phocidae
Species: *Leptonychotes weddelli* (Lesson, 1826)

1.1.2 *Size*

- Newborn pups: 120 cm, 22-25 kg.
- Adults: 210-329 cm, 318-550 kg.

Pups are born in September through early November depending on the latitude. They have a grey to dark lanugo. Pupping usually occurs in fast ice areas along coast lines or ice shelves where annual tide cracks or other openings in the ice make egress to the surface predictable and where snow accumulation creates sufficient depression of the surface ice relative to the water level to facilitate the haul out of the young of the year. Growth of pups is rapid with weaning occurring around six weeks of age, when pups weigh approximately 125 kg. By this time, moulting of the lanugo is complete. The adult coat is dark dorsally and mottled laterally and ventrally, where white predominates. This species can be easily approached when on the surface of the sea ice.

1.2 *Stocks*

1.2.1 *Identification*

The species is distributed in somewhat discrete breeding units around the Antarctic Continent. The areas of occupancy are close to the continent and concentrated in fast ice regions. Little is known about stock identification but it appears as though there is little exchange between breeding populations.

1.2.2 *Distribution and migration*

The species has a circumpolar range and inhabits the fast ice areas of the Antarctic Continent. South Georgia is usually considered the northern-most breeding population. Individual sightings have been made at the following location: Islas de Lobos, Uruguay; Patagonia; Falkland Islands; Islas Juan Fernandez; Wellington, New Zealand; Auckland, New Zealand; Auckland Islands; and Macquarie Island; South Australia; Heard Island; and Kerguelen Island. The species is not known to be migratory but is thought to follow the fast ice at it moves from season to season.

1.2.3 *Structure of stocks*

The Weddell seal is found in colonies ranging to many hundreds in size. However, colony grouping appears more a response to limited areas of suitable habitat than to gregariousness on the part of the species. This is manifest by the relatively even spacing between animals in colonies. Area segregation of young and adult, and of breeding and non-breeding groups is evident. The species appears to be seasonally territorial.

2 Vital Parameters

2.1 *Population size*

2.1.1 Method of estimation

Censuses have been carried out by counting from ships passing through pack ice as well as from ship-supported helicopters. Strip census methods are usually used and the animals which occur in a strip of predetermined width are tallied. For the McMurdo Sound population mark-recapture methods have been applied based on the theory developed by Seber and Jolly.

2.1.2 Results

Estimates of the Weddell have been unsatisfactory since most are derived from pack ice counts which do not include the most desired habitat. These counts suggest a minimum of 750,000. This figure would probably be adjusted upward substantially if counts of inshore regions were available.

2.1.3 Trends in abundance

There is no information about population trends from the Weddell Sea; however, data are available on the trends of the McMurdo Sound population. This population was taken to a low level in the 1950's because of harvest for dog food. It has since recovered and seems to be relatively stable at around 2,500.

2.2 Rates

2.2.1 Reproductive

Sexual maturity is reached at 3 to 6 years. However, males probably to not become socially mature until 7 or 8. Data on pregnancy rates indicate that 80 % of adult females are pregnant at the time of implantation, and 70 % of adult females produce pups in any given year. The lactation period is 5 to 6 weeks. The exact time of mating is uncertain but appears to be shortly before or shortly after weaning. The gestation period is about 11 months with about 2 months delay before implantation. The longevity is at least 25 years.

2.2.2 Natural survival

Estimated annual survival rates for adult males is between .50 and .70 and for adult females between .82 and .87.

2.2.3 Harvesting

This species has not been harvested commercially. The only significant harvest has occurred close to Antarctic facilities where they have been used for dog food. This effort has diminished recently.

3 Trophic Relationships

3.1 Food and feeding

The food of the adult Weddell seal consists primarily of fish. The distribution of subadults is not known and, therefore, their food habitats are unknown. At McMurdo Station in December, Weddell seals have been found to feed primarily on *Dissostichus mawsoni*. One study suggests that at this time, the average daily weight of the seal's catch is about 150 pounds (88 kg). A study conducted primarily in February suggests that at this time seals are feeding on smaller fish, primarily *Trematomus* sp. and *Pleuragramma antarcticum*.

3.2 Competition and predation

Intraspecific competition occurs during the pupping season for space in the colony. The males establish "territories" under the ice which are defended vigorously as evidenced by the fact that territorial males usually are wounded rather severely by the end of the breeding season. Intraspecific competition also occurs among females for space in the colony but little outward fighting occurs. The primary evidence of competition among females is spacing. There is probably little predation on the Weddell because of its fast ice habitat, however, reaction to the presence of killer whales has been observed and Weddell seals have been found in the stomach contents of leopard seals. It appears also, that younger age classes may be forced to the pack ice areas where they may be subject to considerable exposure to killer whale predation.

4 Relation to Man

4.1 *Values*

4.1.1 *Consumptive values*

The major consumptive value has been for dog food and on rare occasions for human use.

4.1.2 *Low-consumptive use*

At the present time there is little low-consumptive use although at times this species does provide certain tourist value near Antarctic bases. The species is also an ideal research subject.

4.2 *Effects of Human activities other than exploitation*

Little is known about the direct effects from human activities but it has been suggested that continued human activity in the vicinity of pupping colonies will cause abandonment of pupping site. The species demonstrates little fear of man but continued handling for scientific purposes does influence behaviour during subsequent encounters.

4.3 *Management and conservation*

The Weddell seal is very vulnerable to harvest where it congregates for pupping and breeding. Regulations which govern take should have provisions to insure that irreversible population damage does not occur at these sites.

5 Threat to Stocks

There are no known immediate threats to Weddell seal stocks. Future threats probably include harvest by man and environmental damage caused by man's activities such as those in support of mineral exploitation.

6 Recommendations for Research

The locations of colonies is poorly known and work is needed to correct this deficiency. Aerial photography would be helpful for such documentation. The life history of the McMurdo Sound Weddell population is relatively well known and the important factors limiting population size are becoming available. Work is needed to document how and/or if factors change over time for the McMurdo population and comparisons should be made between the McMurdo and other populations. It is probable that the population regulatory processes vary between areas and populations.

References

AGUAYO, L., A., Census of Pinnipedia in the South
1970 Shetland Islands. *In* Antarctic ecology, edited by M.W. Holdgate. London, Academic Press, vol. 1:395-7.

ANGOT, M., Observations sur les mammifères marins de
1954 l'Archipel de Kerguelen. *Mammalia, Paris,* 18:1-111.

ARSENIEV, V.A., Observations on the seals of the An-
1957 tarctic. *Byull. Mosk. O.-Va. Ispyt. Prir. (Otd. Biol.),* (62): 39-44 (in Russian).

—, Observations on seals during the voyage of the OB in
1958 1956-57. *Inf. Byull. Sov. Antarkt. Exped. 1955-8,* (3):148.

BERTRAM, G.C.L., The biology of the Weddell and cra-
1940 beater seals, with a study of the comparative behaviour of the Pinnipedia. *Sci. Rep. Brit. Graham Land Exped. 1934-37,* (1):139 p.

BEVERLY-BURTON, M., Helminths from the Weddell seal,
1971 *Leptonychotes weddelli.* Lesson 1826, in the Antarctic. *Can. J. Zool.,* 49(1):75-83.

BONNER, W.N., and R.M. LAWS, Seals and sealing. *In*
1964 Antarctic research: a review of British scientific achievement in Antarctica, edited by R. Priestley, R.J. Adie and G. de Q. Robin. London Butterworths, pp. 163-90.

BROWN, R.M.R., The seals of the Weddell Sea; notes on

1913 their distribution. *Rep. Sci. Results Scott. Natl. Antarct. Exped.*, 4(13):185-98.

BRYDEN, M.M., and R.A. TEDMAN, Studies of lactation
1974 in Weddell seals. *Antarct. J.U.S.*, 9(14):105-6.

CALHAEM, I., and D.A. CHRISTOFFEL, Some observations
1969 of the feeding habits of a Weddell seal, and measurements of its prey, *Dissostichus mawsoni*, at McMurdo Sound, Antarctica. *N.Z.J. Mar. Freshwat. Res.*, 3(2):181-90.

CLINE, D.R., D.B. SINIFF and A.W. ERICKSON, Immob-
1969 ilizing and collecting blood from Antarctic seals. *J. Wildl. Manage.*, 33:138-44.

—, Underwater copulation of the Weddell seal. *J.*
1971 *Mammal.*, 52:216-8.

DEARBORN, J.H., Food of Weddell seals at McMurdo
1965 Sound, Antarctica. *J. Mammal.*, 46:37-43.

DE VRIES, A., and D.E. WOHLSCHLAG, Diving depths
1968 of the Weddell seal. *Science, Wash.*, 145(3629):292.

EKLUND, C.R., and E.L. ATWOOD, A population study of
1962 Antarctic seals. *J. Mammal.*, 43:229-38.

ERICKSON, A.W., D.R. CLINE and R.J. HOFMAN, Popu-
1969 lation study of seals in the Weddell Sea. *Antarct. J.U.S.*, 4:99-100.

ERICKSON, A.W., *et al.*, Seal survey in the South Shet-
1970 land and South Orkney Islands. *Antarct. J.U.S.*, 5(4):130-1.

—, Distributional ecology of Antarctic seals. *In* Sym-
1971 posium on Antarctic Ice and Water Masses, edited by G. Deacon. Cambridge, SCAR, pp. 55-7.

FENWICK, G.D., Breeding biology and population dy-
1973 namics of the Weddell seal, *Leptonychotes weddelli*: a review. *Mauri Ora*, 1:29-36.

HOLDGATE, M.W., P.J. TILBROOK and R.W. VAUGHAN,
1969 The biology of Bouvetøya. *Bull. Brit. Antarct. Surv.*, (15):1-7.

INGHAM, S.E., The status of seals (Pinnipedia) at Aus-
1960 tralian Antarctic stations. *Mammalia, Paris*, 24:422-30.

KAUFMAN, G.W., D.B. SINIFF and R. REICHLE, Colony
1975 behaviour of Weddell seals, *Leptonychotes weddelli*, at Hutton Cliffs, Antarctica. *Rapp. P.-V. Réun. CIEM*, 169:228-46.

KOOYMAN, G.L., Techniques used in measuring diving
1965 capacities of Weddell seals. *Polar Rec.*, 12:391-4.

—, Maximum diving capacities of the Weddell seal,
1966 *Leptonychotes weddelli. Science, Wash.*, 151-1553-4.

—, Polar adaptation of the Weddell seal. *Antarct.*
1966a *J.U.S.*, 1:219.

—, An analysis of some behavioural and physiological
1968 characteristics related to diving in the Weddell seal. *Antarct. Res. Ser.*, (2):227-61.

—, The Weddell seal. *Sci. Am.*, 221:101-6.
1969

—, Respiratory adaptations in marine mammals. *Con-*
1973 *trib. Scripps Inst. Oceanogr.*, (43):312-9.

KUECHLE, L.B., J.R. TESTER and D.B. SINIFF, Population
1969 studies of Weddell seals at McMurdo Station. *Antarct. J.U.S.*, 4(4).

LINDSEY, A.A., The Weddell seal in the Bay of Whales,
1937 Antarctica. *J. Mammal.*, 18:127-44.

LUGG, D.J., Annual cycle of the Weddell seal in the
1966 Vestfold Hills, Antarctica. *J. Mammal.*, 47:317-32.

MACKINTOSH, N.A., Estimates of local seal populations
1967 in the Antarctic, 1930/37. *Norsk Hvalfangst-tid.*, 56:57-64.

MANSFIELD, A., The breeding behaviour and reproduc-
1958 tive cycle of the Weddell seal: the Weddell seal population of the South Orkney Islands. *Sci. Rep. Falkland Isl. Depend. Surv.*, (18): 41 p.

MATTHEWS, L.H., The natural history of the elephant
1929 seal, with notes on other seals found at South Georgia. *Discovery Rep.*, 1:233-55.

ØRITSLAND, T., Biology and population dynamics of
1970 Antarctic seals. *In* Antarctic ecology, edited by M.W. Holdgate. London, Academic Press, vol. 1:361-6.

—, Sealing and seal research in the south-west Atlantic
1970a pack ice, Sept.-Oct. 1964. *In* Antarctic ecology, edited by M.W. Holdgate. London, Academic Press, vol. 1:367-76.

PREVOST, J., Observations complémentaires sur les pin-
1964 nipèdes de l'Archipel de Pointe Geologie. *Mammalia, Paris*, 28:351-8.

RAY, C., Social behaviour and acoustics of the Weddell
1967 seal. *Antarct. J.U.S.*, 2:105-6.

—, Population ecology of Antarctic seals. *In* Antarctic
1970 ecology, edited by M.W. Holdgate. London, Academic Press, vol. 1: 398-414.

RAY, C., and M.S.R. SMITH, Thermoregulation of the
1968 pup and adult Weddell seal, *Leptonychotes weddelli* (Lesson). *Antarct. Zool.*, 53:33-46.

SCHEVILL, W.E., and W.A. Watkins, Underwater play-
1967 back of their own sounds to *Leptonychotes* (Weddell seals). *J. Mammal.*, 49(2):287-95.

SEAL, U.S., *et al.*, Blood chemistry and protein poly-
1971 morphisms in three species of Antarctic seals (*Lobodon carcinophagus, Leptonychotes weddelli* and *Mirounga leonina*). *Antarct. Res. Ser.*, 18:181-92.

SHAUGHNESSY, P.D., Transferrin polymorphism and po-
1969 pulation structure of the Weddell seal *Leptonychotes weddelli* (Lesson). *Aust. J. Biol. Sci.*, 22:1581-4.

SINIFF, D.B., and D.R. CLINE, Population dynamics of
1968 Antarctic seals (IWSOE-1968). *Antarct. J.U.S.*, 3:86-7.

SINIFF, D.B., D.R. CLINE and A.W. ERICKSON, Popula-
1970 tion densities of seals in the Weddell Sea, Antarctica, in 1968. *In* Antarctic ecology, edited by M.W. Holdgate. London, Academic Press, vol. 1:377-94.

SINIFF, D.B., J.R. TESTER and V.B. KEUCHLE, Some ob-
1971 servations on the activity patterns of Weddell seals as recorded by telemetry. *Antarct. Res. Ser.*, 18:173-80.

SINIFF, D.B., *et al.*, Population dynamics of McMurdo
1974 Sound's Weddell seals. *Antarct. J.U.S.*, 9(4):104-5.

SMITH, E.A., and R.W. BURTON, Weddell seals of Signy
1970 Island. *In* Antarctic ecology, edited by M.W. Holdgate. London, Academic Press, vol. 1:415-28.

SMITH, M.S.R., Seasonal movements of the Weddell seal
1965 in McMurdo Sound, Antarctica. *J. Wildl. Manage.*, 29:464-70.

—, Injuries as an indicator of social behaviour in the
1966 Weddell seal (*Leptonychotes weddelli*). *Mammalia, Paris*, 30:241-6.

STIRLING, I., Populations studies on the Weddell seal.
1967 *Tuatara*, 15:133-41.

—, Ecology of the Weddell seal in McMurdo Sound,
1969 Antarctica. *Ecology*, 50:573-86.

—, Distribution and abundance of the Weddell seal in
1969a the western Ross Sea, Antarctica. *N.Z.J. Mar. Freshwat. Res.*, 3:191-200.

—, Birth of a Weddell seal pup. *J. Mammal.*,
1969b 50(1):151-6.

—, Tooth wear as a mortality factor in the Weddel seal,
1969c *Leptonychotes weddelli. J. Mammal.*, 50(2):559-65.

—, *Leptonychotes weddelli. Mammal. Spec. Monogr.*
1971 *Am. Mammal. Soc.*, (6):105.

—, Population dynamics of the Weddell seal (*Lepteny-*
1971a *chotes weddelli*) in McMurdo Sound, Antarctica, 1966-1968. *Antarct. Res. Ser.*, 18-141-62.

—, Population aspects of Weddell seal harvesting at
1971b McMurdo Sound, Antarctica. *Polar Rec.*, 15(98):653-67.

—, Variation in sex ratio of newborn Weddell seals
1971c during the pupping season. *J. Mammal.*, 52(4): 842-4.

—, Regulation of numbers of an apparently isolated
1971d population of Weddell seals. *J. Mammal.*, 52:87-91.

ANNEX B APPENDIX VII OF THE REPORT OF THE

FAO ADVISORY COMMITTEE ON MARINE RESOURCES RESEARCH WORKING PARTY ON MARINE MAMMALS

REPORT ON SIRENIANS

PREFACE

This report summarizes present knowledge of the state of the four living species of the order Sirenia, relevant aspects of their general biology and ecology, man's effects on them and his attempts to manage and conserve them.

The report, based originally on the report of *Ad hoc* Group II (Small Cetaceans and Sirenia) of the Working Party on Marine Mammals of FAO's Advisory Committee on Marine Resources Research (ACMRR), was prepared during the Scientific Consultation on the Conservation and Management of Marine Mammals and their Environment (Bergen, Norway, 31 August - 9 September 1976).

The draft was prepared by Dr. G.E. Heinsohn, Convenor of the Working Group on Sirenians which met during the Bergen Consultation, and was revised by the Working Group, with the participation of C. Barnett, G.C.L. Bertram, H.W. Campbell, D.P. Domning, D.O. Hill, M. Hill, B.E.T. Hudson, S. Jones, D.M. Magor, F. Mongul, D.K. Odell, S.L. Peterson, C.K. Ricardo Bertram, P. Wray and T. Wyatt; information useful in this revision was also contributed during the Consultation by P. Dohrn, M. Nishiwaki, G.C. Ray and V.B. Scheffer.

Subsequent editing was carried out by the FAO Secretariat in order that the final report conforms to the organization used in the Proceedings of the Consultation. An abridged version of the report was considered by the plenary meeting of the Bergen Consultation and constitutes section 6 of the Proceedings of the Consultation. At a subsequent meeting (Svanøy, 11-14 September 1976) the Working Party on Marine Mammals considered that the full version should be published separately in view on the one hand of its scientific value and on the other, in view of its exceptional length and the special nature of the sirenians and of programmes for their conservation as compared with the other marine mammals.

The report as presented here does not include the section on research, which originally constituted its final section. This material has more appropriately been incorporated into the research proposals prepared by the Working Party and it is published as section 3.4 of FAO Fisheries Technical Paper FIRS/T 177.

1. PURPOSE

This report is designed to summarize the present state of knowledge of the 4 living species of the order Sirenia (the West African manatee (*Trichechus senegalensis*), the Caribbean manatee (*T. manatus*), the Amazonian manatee (*T. inunguis*) and the dugong (*Dugong dugon*).

It examines relevant aspects of their general biology and ecology, the effects on them of contemporary human civilization and man's attempts to manage and conserve these species.

2. IDENTITY, DISTRIBUTION, LIFE HISTORY AND STATE

The Order Sirenia is comprised of the only completely acquatic herbivorous mammals. The Order includes four living species in two Genera and two Families. These are the three species of manatee in the Family Trichechidae — the West African manatee (*Trichechus senegalensis*), the Caribbean manatee (*T. manatus*) and the Amazonian manatee (*T. inunguis*) — and the dugong (*Dugong dugon*) in the Family Dugongidae. A second recent species of this latter family. Steller's sea cow (*Hydrodamalis gigas*) is thought to have been exterminated over most of its North Pacific range by prehistoric man and was apparently hunted to extinction within about thirty years following its discovery by western explorers in 1741 in the Bering Sea (Bertram and Bertram, 1973) — the last animals are thought to have persisted near the uninhabited Commander Islands until 1768 (Domning, 1972). Reports of Steller's sea cow's continued survival should not be dismissed without investigation.

Despite its small number of extant species, the Order has an extensive fossil record. Sirenians are placed in a Superorder of herbivorous subungulates, the Paenungulata, which includes the modern Proboscidea (elephants) and Hyracoidea (hyraxes or conies), plus several extinct mammalian orders (Romer, 1966; Simpson, 1945). They appear to have evolved from terrestrial paenungulates during or before the early Eocene (Reinhart, 1959). The taxonomy of all species of manatees needs further study. Geographical and subspecific variation in both dugongs and manatees should be examined. It is important that the remains of dead sirenian specimens be collected for use in further taxonomic studies. Material already preserved in public collections should be re-examined. Tagging of sirenians to determine the extent of movements and the collection of blood and tissue samples for biochemical, electrophoretic and karyotypic study is also required. Karyotypes are already available for the Caribbean manatee (White, Harkness, Isaacks and Duffield, 1976) and the Amazonian manatee (Loughman, Frye and Herald, 1970). The use of particular "races" of manatees or dugongs may become important in programmes of captive breeding.

Except for Steller's sea cow, all sirenians, both fossil and living, have been confined to tropical and subtropical waters, with living species being sensitive to low temperatures (Domning, in press; Campbell and Powell, 1976). A thorough account of available information on the distribution of recent sirenians has been given by Bertram and Bertram (1973); summarized distributions of the four living species are also given in the *Red Data Book* (IUCN, 1976). All species are shallow water, near-shore animals. This is a result of their dependence on aquatic angiosperms and, to a limited extent, on other attached plants growing in the littoral and sublittoral zones. The dugong is believed to be exclusively marine. The Amazonian manatee occurs only in freshwater, while the other two manatee species range in freshwater, brackish water and the sea. All of the living sirenians have been seriously reduced in numbers by overexploitation for meat, oil and other products. The *Red Data Book* (IUCN, 1976) summarizes conservation measures that have so far been taken. It lists the dugong and the Caribbean and West African manatees as *Vulnerable*, and the Amazonian manatee as *Endangered*. This appraisal was not agreed with in part, as the West African Manatee should, it is felt, also be listed as *Endangered*. Husar (1975, in press, Unpubl. MS) also reports on the conservation of the Sirenians.

2.1 Dugong

Dugongs occur in the shallow coastal waters of the Indian and western Pacific Oceans from Madagascar and Mozambique, north along the East African coast to the northermost reaches of the Red Sea; east along the south coast of Asia, including India and Sri Lanka, to Malaysia; north along the Asian coast to the Ryukyu Islands; east through Indonesia, the Philippines, the Palau and Yap Islands, Guam, Papua New Guinea, the Solomon Islands, the New Hebrides and New Caledonia; and south to the western, northern and eastern coasts of Australia (Bertram and Bertram, 1973; Husar, 1975). There are unconfirmed reports from Kyushu Island and the Republic of Korea (Hirasaka, 1934).

Recent aerial surveys indicate that dugongs migrate, although they may also occur as local residents (Heinsohn and Wake, 1976). During calm weather, dugongs move from protected into exposed waters (*G. Heinsohn, personal communication*). Biomass figures are not available for total populations. However, using a weight length curve and an estimated mean weight (200 kg), the biomass of captured dugongs can be estimated (Spain and Heinsohn, 1975). In the Townsville area, eighty-two dugongs, comprising most of a local population, were caught in shark nets in one year (Heinsohn, 1972) and the total biomass was estimated to be approximately 16 400 kg. Little information is available on factors limiting distribution. While the species requires sheltered bays with seagrass beds, animals may occur at considerable distances (twenty-three km) from shore (*Heinsohn, Spain and Anderson, personal communication*). Very little information is available on natality, recruitment and mortality. A single calf is born and accompanies the female for more than a year. Dugons appear to take two years to reach sexual maturity and growth is rapid (Heinsohn, 1972). Although the calving interval is not known directly, ratios of calves to adults (Heinsohn, Spain and Anderson, 1976) suggest that one calf is born every three years. Mitchell (1976) suggests that dugongs can attain an age of just under sixty or just under thirty years and that they reach sexual maturity at about ten or five years of age, depending on interpretation of dental growth ring data. Dugongs occur singly and in groups of two to more than 100 (Bertram and Bertram, 1973; Heinsohn, 1972; Heinsohn and Spain, 1974; Heinsohn, Spain and Anderson, 1976; Heinsohn, 1976a).

Neither absolute population sizes nor densities are known for any dugong population, although some qualitative estimates have been made. Bertram and Bertram (1973) give an account of the present world-wide status of dugongs in qualitative terms; they consider the species to be rare over most of its range and to be approaching extinction in some regions. Large populations of dugongs are still found in Australian waters (Bertram and Bertram, 1973; Heinsohn, 1972; Heinsohn and Spain, 1974; Heinsohn, Spain and Anderson, 1976; Heinsohn and Wake, 1976; Ligon, 1976a) and the species remains abundant along some coastal areas of Papua New Guinea (Hudson, 1976; Ligon and Hudson, 1976).

Additional notes not reported by Bertram and Bertram (1973) on the state of dugongs follow:

Red Sea. Several dugongs have been collected in recent years in the Gulf of Aqaba (Por, 1972; Lipkin, 1976); and analysis of stomach contents and other data from six specimens has been published by Lipkin (1976). An additional specimen has recently been reported from the Red Sea (Ilani, 1976).

Kenya. Only eight dugongs were sighted during a recent aerial survey (Ligon, 1976b).

India. Some dugongs occur in the Gulf of Cutch (S. Jones, personal communication). Additional information is available in Jones (1967, 1976).

Bangladesh. Dugongs may occur here (Aminul Haque, 1976).

Malaysia. Dugongs occur on both sides of the Malay Peninsula and around Phuket and Surat Thani (M. Nishiwaki, personal communication).

Viet Nam. One dugong was captured in 1960 (Tranngocloi, 1962). Dugong populations are still present, especially in the area of the Mekong Delta (M. Nishiwaki, personal communication).

Philippine Islands and Indonesia. Perhaps 1 000 dugongs occur around Palawan; larger numbers occur in the area of Halmahera and West Irian, extending to the Palau Islands. The species is scarce in the Celebes Sea and around the island of Borneo (M. Nishiwaki, personal communication).

New Caledonia and the New Hebrides. Recent information indicates that dugongs are present in these areas in moderate numbers (estimated crudely at 1 000 or more animals) but are reduced from past levels of abundance. Local hunting continues despite some protection; however, no intense commercial utilization is presently occurring (R. Martini, personal communication).

Ryukyu Islands. About ten dugongs have been captured over the last thirty years, the most recent being within the last two or three years. The animals are mostly found in the Okinawa-Sakishima area but also occur as far north as Amami O-shima (M. Nishiwaki, personal communication).

Additional surveys of the present state of this species over its entire range are needed. Population counts can be made from aircraft. Hughes and Oxley-Oxland (1971) counted a total of twenty-seven dugongs in two hours flying time in northern Mozambique. In 1974, extensive aerial surveys were begun along stretches of the Queensland coast in Australia, and an individual herd of more than sixty-seven dugongs was observed north of Cooktown (Heinsohn, Spain and Anderson, 1976). Subsequently, single herds of 100 or more dugongs were observed in Shalwater Bay (Heinsohn, 1976a), In Moreton Bay and off Cape York, (Heinsohn, personal communication). Total numbers of dugongs per kilometre of coast varied from 0.7 along an isolated stretch of the Cape York Peninsula north of Cooktown, to 0.3 along a length of coast near Townsville inhabited by man (Heinsohn, Spain and Anderson, 1976). In March and April 1975, an aerial survey of about 3 400 km of coast from the northwestern border of Queensland around Cape York and south to Gympie, recorded 604 dugongs (Ligon, 1976a). A similar survey was conducted in Papua New Guinea, with 130 dugongs recorded in the Daru and Warrior Reefs area (Ligon and Hudson, 1976). Another aerial survey has been conducted along the Kenya coast (Ligon, 1976b).

The greatest decline of dugongs has occurred in regions that have high populations of indigenous fishermen. The main cause of the species' decline has been uncontrolled hunting principally for local consumption, the main products being meat and oil. Increased efficiency of hunting techniques through the use of, for example, power boats and monofilament nets, has greatly accelerated this decline. Accidental netting is also a major threat to dugongs (Heinsohn, Marsh and Spain, 1976). Accidental deaths in nets used in some tropical fisheries, for example, in Sri Lanka, Kenya and Australia (Bertram and Bertram, 1973; Heinsohn, Marsh and Spain, 1976), and in shark nets set to reduce shark numbers near swimming beaches in Queensland have been important (Heinsohn, 1972, Heinsohn, Marsh and Spain, 1976; Heinsohn and Spain, 1974).

2.2 West African Manatee

The West African manatee formerly occurred in coastal lagoons and rivers of western Africa from Senegal in the North, to the Cuanza River in northern Angola in the south. It mainly occurs in the Senegal, Niger and Benue river system and below the cataracts in the lower Zaire (Bertram and Bertram, 1973; Meester and Sitzer, 1971). Data on movements, population biomasses and factors limiting production are not available. Hunting pressure appears to limit distribution (Poche, 1973; Bouveignes, 1952). Beal (1939) reported social groups consisting of an adult pair, a half-grown calf and a young calf. Cadenat (1957) noted a cruising group of fifteen animals in marine waters.

Numerical data on the state of the West African manatee are unavailable. The species is rare and appears to be declining throughout its range (Allsopp, 1974; Poche, 1973; Robinson, 1971; Sikes, 1974). According to the IUCN *Red Data Book* (1976), informed local opinions are that numbers in most areas are small and that the species is already locally extinct in some areas. The species is totally protected by law in many of the countries in which it is found, but enforcement is generally lacking. Uncontrolled hunting is considered to be the main cause of its decline. Although the West African manatee has never been subjected to large-scale commercial hunting, it has been heavily exploited by subsistence hunters who use the meat for their own consumption or for local sale. Incidental netting and drowning in commercial fishing operations has been documented (Bertram and Bertram, 1973; Cadenat, 1957), but the extent and effects of such mortality are unknown.

2.3 Caribbean Manatee

The Caribbean manatee occurs in coastal waters, lagoons and rivers from North Carolina to southern Texas in the United States, in the Bahamas and Greater Antilles to southern Mexico, and along the Caribbean and Atlantic coasts of Central and South America to central Brazil (Bertram and Bertram, 1973; Campbell and Powell, 1976).

Population biomasses and factors limiting production are unknown. Seasonal movements occur in the northern part of the species range (Hartman, 1971; Campbell and Powell, 1976). Factors such as environmental temperatures, food distribution and abundance, availability of freshwater (Hartman, 1971) and human disturbances including man-made structures such as dams, canals and thermal power plants, may affect manatee distribution. Hartman (1971) documented basic behaviour patterns and social groupings; new data indicate that social groupings of various sizes and cohesions are more frequent than previously believed, and shed doubt upon the suggestion that the cow-calf unit is the basic social grouping. Estrous herds (an estrous female and several males) are common short-lived social units. Manatees aggregate, often in large numbers, at warm-water refuges during cold weather (Campbell, 1976). The gestation period is not certain; a period of about 385-400 days has been suggested by Hartman (1971). Usually, only a single calf is born, but twins have been reported (Hartman, 1971). The bond between cow and calf may last from one to two years, and it is estimated that sexual maturity is attained between age four and age six. Cows probably breed every 2.5 to three years (Hartman, 1971). Manatee longevity in the wild is not known, but captive manatees have lived for more than twenty-five years (Campbell, 1976; Husar, in press).

The total population size of the species is unknown, but is probably declining over most of its range. A recent winter survey of Florida manatees located a total of at least 748 animals (Irving and Campbell, personal communication). Campbell and Powell (1976) state that other recent survey information suggests that there are at least 1 000 manatees remaining in the United States. Other recent data indicate that Caribbean manatees are still found in all other countries in which they have been known to occur; however, local population sizes and distribution require documentation.

The principle cause of the decline of the Caribbean manatee has been overhunting for meat and hides, which began in the Caribbean region in the seventeenth century. Although the species is legally protected throughout much of its range, effective enforcement is difficult. The extent of mortality through accidental captures in commercial fishing nets is, as with other manatees, unknown. In Florida, nearly 25 % of all documented mortalities have resulted from collissions with boats or barges (Campbell and Powell, 1976). A small number of deaths result from vandalism, from being crushed in canal locks and from other accidents. Manatees are also occasionally killed by severe cold weather (Campbell and Powell, 1976; IUCN, 1976).

2.4 Amazonian Manatee

The Amazonian manatee occurs in the Amazon basin. It has been recorded below falls in most tributaries of the Amazon River in Peru, Brazil and Colombia. Its possible occurrence in the Orinoco basin has not been confirmed. (D. Magor, personal communication).

The average adult weight of the species is estimated to be 250 kg. The Amazonian manatee was thought to be fairly sedentary, but new information indicates that seasonal migration may be extensive (D. Magor, personal communication). Salinity, temperature and rapids and falls may directly or indirectly limit distribution. Large herds were reported in lakes and rivers in the middle Amazon basin. However, large aggregations are probably now extremely rare because of drastic population reductions through commercial hunting. Groups of four to eight Amazonian manatees have been seen in feeding areas (D. Magor, personal communication). The bond between cow and calf may last more than two years, although the period of suckling is not known. Amazonian manatees apparently communicate by frequent and simple vocalizations (D. Magor, personal communication).

On the basic of past and recent commercial exploitation (Ferreira, 1903; Mendes, 1938; Pereira, 1947) and recent catch data from certain localities (D. Magor, personal communication), an estimated minimum population of 10 000 manatees is thought to be sparsely distributed throughout the Amazon basin. The *Red Data Book* (IUCN) states that no population estimates exist, but that numbers have been greatly reduced, first by commercial hunting for meat and hides, which continued until recently, and then due to continued exploitation by local subsistence hunters. A summary of the history of exploitation of this species follows.

Dutch traders reportedly exported up to twenty shiploads of salted manatee meat per year from the lower Amazon to Europe and Surinam in the eighteenth century (Mendes, 1938). Overexploitation was reported from the Rio Tapajo (lower Amazon) in the 1770's. An active commercial fishery for manatee meat and oil resulted in serious depletion or apparent elimination of the species from several lakes in that region (Ferreira, 1903). The canning and export of *mixira* (manatee meat fried in its own fat) was an important commercial venture from the mid seventeenth century to the nineteenth century (Pereira, 1947). Fluctuations in quantities of meat reportedly processed may reflect serious over-exploitation. A method of tanning manatee skins was developed about 1934. Over a five-year period (1938-42) 6 549 skins were exported from Manaus to southern Brazil and Europe (Pereira, 1947). The total number of hides taken in the state of Amazonas, Brazil, decreased from 38 013 in 1950 to 5 509 in 1954. Although animals up to four metres in length were reported in the early Brazilian literature, reliable reports of individuals larger than 3.1 m have not been received recently. While herds of over 100 animals were reported in the 1940s, groups of only four to eight manatees have been seen recently 1973) in feeding areas in the middle Amazon (D. Magor, personal communication), and single animals are more commonly found.

In 1963, the lowest Amazonian river levels of the century resulted in large-scale massacres of manatees in most areas due to the animals' increased vulnerability during such times. For example, up to sixty manatees per day were taken for fifteen days in October 1963 on the Rio Urubu. Only the fat was removed for oil production; the hides were not used and there was more meat than the people could consume or sell (D. Magor, personal communication).

The species in now legally protected in Brazil, Colombia and Peru but enforcement is difficult in isolated areas. Complete legal protection for the manatee was not enacted in Brazil until 1968, and large-scale hunting has only been reduced since 1970. No fines or jail terms have yet been imposed for the capture, sale or purchase of manatees or their products in Amazonas. Legislation is effective in at least two towns in the state of Para where local fishing co-operatives enforce the law among their own members. High water levels since 1969 are primarily responsible for the present protection of the species, since they reduce the availability of manatees to hunters. This factor and the low population densities due to a long period of overhunting have resulted in diminishing returns per unit of hunting effort. There are some indications that manatees may be making a slow recovery from the 1963 slaughter (D. Magor, personal communication). Since there are only six wildlife inspectors for the Brazilian states of Amazonas and Rondonia, another dry year would allow large numbers of animals to be taken, possibly seriously threatening several populations; increased state and local enforcement of existing legislation is, therefore, urgently needed. An ongoing status survey, including documentation of trends in exploitation and population abundance, was begun in August 1973 in the central Amazon. Public education programmes were also initiated in 1976 by the National Institute for Amazonian Research and the Brazilian fisheries service (SUDEPE).

3. ENVIRONMENTAL CONSIDERATIONS

3.1 Trophic Relations

3.1.1 Dugong

Dugongs normally feed on seagrasses (Potamogetonaceae and Hydrocharitaceae) (Heinsohn, Wake, Marsh and Spain, in press). Qualitative estimates of the species eaten are given by Heinsohn and Birch (1972) and limited quantitative data is given by Wake (1975). If seagrasses are scarce or not available, dugongs will feed on attached algae such as *Sargassum* sp. (Spain and Heinsohn, 1973). Invertebrate animals are sometimes taken (Hirasaka, 1932; Pfeffer, 1963; Spain and Heinsohn, 1973; Wake, 1975). Although these are probably eaten incidentally with seagrasses, the possibility exists that they form a necessary part of the diet. The species of seagrasses and their world-wide distribution have been well documented by Hartog (1970). Seagrass community studies and dry-weight biomass estimates have been made for six seagrass study areas located in important dugong feeding grounds in tropical Queensland (Wake, 1975). It appears that dugongs graze heaviest on seagrass beds of moderate to low density. Figures on seagrass removal from dugong feeding trails are given by Wake (1975), Heinsohn (1975) and Heinsohn, Wake, Marsh and Spain (1976). The quantity of food required by dugongs under natural conditions is not known, although two captive animals ate fifty to fifty-five kg of seagrass (wet-weight) per day (Jones, 1967). Oke (1967) and Aung (1967) also give data on food consumption by captive dugongs. Data on the apparent digestibilities of nitrogen, phosphorous, neutral detergent fibre and acid detergent fibre in seagrasses are given by Murray, Marsh, Heinsohn and Spain (1976). The metabolic requirements of the species are unknown. The calorific values and ionic concentrations of seagrass species from dugong feeding areas in North Queensland have been determined (Birch, 1975); Wake (1975) has obtained additional data on the calorific values, chemical composition and digestibilities of seagrasses on which dugongs feed.

3.1.2 West African Manatee

The West African manatee is both marine and riverine in distribution, occurring up to several hundred miles inland

(Sikes, 1974). Aquatic vascular plants, mangrove leaves and bank grasses are eaten (Dorst and Dandelot, 1969; Cadenat, 1957; Beal, 1939). A 1.8 m captive male consumed twelve kg of vegetables per day; upon reaching two to four m, the daily intake increased to seventeen to eighteen kg (Gizen, 1963). The food and metabolic requirements of this species and the temporal and spatial distribution, caloric value and chemical composition of its food species, have not been studied.

3.1.3 Caribbean Manatee

The Caribbean manatee feeds on submerged and emergent aquatic vegetation; the species' food habits have been described by Hartman (1971) for the Crystal River area of Florida and by Allsopp (1969) for Guyana. In Florida, food species are distributed in fresh, marine and estuarine waters without apparent seasonal fluctuations (Hartman, 1971). Spatial distributions of food in relation to manatee feeding are not known, nor are quantitative data available on the composition of its diet. The efficiency of food utilization in the species and the food requirements of wild manatees are also unknown. At the Miami Seaquarium, manatees are fed about thirteen to fourteen kg (wet-weight) of lettuce per animal, per day, or about 3 % of body weight per day; the animals are healthy and have been maintained on this diet for about fifteen years. Scholander and Irving (1941) calculated basic metabolic rates. Metabolic requirements are low. Chemical composition, caloric values and conversion efficiency for freshwater plant species eaten by manatees are currently under study in Florida.

3.1.4 Amazonian Manatee

Food habits have been described by Pereira (1947) for the Amazonian manatee in Brazil. Shore- and bottom-rooted grasses (e.g. *Paspalum, Echinochloa*), floating aquatics (e.g., *Utricularia, Pistia* and *Limnobium*) and at least two submerged plants constitute the main food sources. Leaves from low-hanging vines are cropped in blackwater lakes and rivers. Young animals graze on green algae and on the roots of floating plants, and appear to have food preferences different from those of older animals. They may also ingest considerable quantities of mud and sand while feeding (D. Magor, personal communication). References have been made to the consumption of floating palm fruits (Pereira, 1947). A captive fifty kg male, at least 3.5 years old, is maintaining body weight while consuming, per day, 2.5 kg (wet-weight) of *Cabomba* and three kg of *Panicum*, both preferred foods in captivity. Figures are also available for a young captive female (D. Magor, personal communication). Most food plants undergo seasonal fluctuations and their seasonal distributions are largely controlled by PH and nutrient availability. In addition, seasonal fluctuations in river levels make different plants accessible to manatees at different times of year. Proportional food requirements, efficiency of utilization, metabolic requirements and caloric value and chemical composition of food plants are as yet unknown for this species, but feeding studies and food plant analyses are underway in Brazil (D. Magor, personal communication).

3.2 Interactions of Sirenians with Other Species

The interactions of dugongs with other species of benefit to man was discussed by Heinsohn (1975); much of this discussion also applies to manatees. These interactions basically involve the effects that sirenians have on the species compositions, structures and biomasses of the aquatic plant communities in which they feed. Included are the direct consequences on the aquatic plant species proper and indirect effects on other animals through competition for plants as food and through removal of plants as a source of shelter and substrate.

The rôle and importance of sirenians in nutrient recycling are unknown; they may have positive effects on lower food-chain organisms in nutrient-poor lakes. (Such effects have been demonstrated for caymans by Fittkau, (1973)). Seagrass-based food webs are primarily detrital (Thayer, Wolfe and Williams, 1975). The presence in abundance of large herbivores, such as dugongs or manatees, changes this situation through the diversion of secondary productivity away from detritus food chains. Heavy grazing by dugongs and manatees could reduce the value of seagrass communities as nursery areas and as shelter for small and juvenile fish and a variety of invertebrates, including species important to commercial and sport fisheries. The production of detritus, reduced by grazing, is also important for food chains of commercially valuable fish. It should be pointed out that a given biomass of seagrass or other aquatic vegetation could support a higher biomass of a primary consumer, such as dugongs or manatees, than that of most commercial fish, the latter being carnivores. These and other effects of sirenians on the species compositions and productivities of their aquatic communities need further study.

Competition between dugongs and marine turtles is probably not very great (Heinsohn, 1975). Of the five species of sea turtles occurring within the range of the dugong, the loggerhead (*Caretta caretta*) is carnivorous and the others appear to be omnivorous (Bustard, 1972). Because the food habits of these omnivorous turtles are not well known, very little can be said about competition between them and other animals for food. Although the green turtle (*Chelonia mydas*) feeds extensively on seagrasses (Bustard, 1972; Hirth, Klikoff and Harper, 1973), the species has less-selective food preference than dugongs, uses different feeding methods and utilizes a wider range of habitats (Heinsohn, 1975); consequently, competition between the two species is probably not very significant. A similar relation probably exists between the Caribbean manatee and the green turtle.

Manatees could produce negative effects on human activities (e.g., reduced stocks of sport fish) and aesthetic values, by depletion of aquatic vegetation in restricted areas. This is not yet a problem but may be anticipated if aggregations of manatees are encouraged in sanctuaries or preserves of limited size. Expensive supplemental feeding of manatees may also be required. The determination of manatee carrying capacity for varied habitats is thus critical to evaluating this potential problem.

3.3 Incidental Netting

Incidental netting and subsequent drowning from entanglement in fishing and shark nets is a second major cause of mortality of sirenians. There are records of West African manatees being taken in fixed shark nets set between Dakar and Bathurst (Cadenat, 1957; Bertram and Bertram, 1973; Husar, Unpubl. MS), and, in the Unites States, manatees are occasionally taken in shrimp trawling operations (H.W. Campbell, personal communication). Incidental capture of Amazonian manatee calves in commercial fishing nets is increasing, due primarily to increased numbers of commercial fishing boats and larger and stronger nets (D. Magor, personal communication). Although these examples exist, the extent of losses through incidental capture in commercial fishing operation is unknown for all three species of manatees.

The extreme risks of mortality to dugongs from netting operations are described by Heinsohn, March and Spain (1976). Dugongs are known to have been taken in gill nets, although the full extent of these kills is not known. Tended fish nets are less likely to catch and drown dugongs than are set nets, as the activity of persons working the nets tends to frighten the animals away from the areas being fished (G. Heinsohn, personal communication); monofilament nylon fish nets are considered to be much more destructive than are multifilament nets. The use of shark tangle nets in Kenya has greatly reduced the number of dugongs in that region (P. Shaw, personal communication). Bertram and Bertram (1973) state that the serious progressive decrease of dugongs in the waters of Sri Lanka was likewise a result of accidental drowning in commercial fish nets.

Shark nets set off swimming beaches to help protect swimmers have been responsible for the killing of large numbers of dugongs in Queensland (Heinsohn, 1972; Heinsohn and Spain, 1974). In general, such shark netting should be halted or reduced in areas of dugong abundance, in favour of other shark control methods (e.g., use of drum lines and the building of large swimming enclosures). In all cases, management of sirenian populations will have to include consideration of the effects of net fishing operations (e.g., where nets are set, types of nets used and fishing procedures).

3.4 Alteration of Habitats, Pollution and Other Human Disturbances

Campbell and Powell (1976) report that in Miami, Florida, many manatees are landlocked in the city's canal system. These animals represent an isolated population and suffer high mortality from vandalism and accidents in canal locks.

Recreational use of sheltered bays and inlets may discourage sirenians from using these areas, which are important as refuges during storms and periods of strong prevailing winds. The total environmental impact of coastal developments should be evaluated and protection of sirenians should not be compromised for recreational ends.

Introduced plant species have replaced many indigenous plants in various areas thus altering food resources. In many regions (e.g., Florida), some of these introduced plants, such as hydrilla (*Hydrilla verticillata*) and water hyacinth (*Eichhornia crassipes*), are more abundant than native species and thus represent an increased food source (Hartman, 1971).

3.4.1 Alteration of Habitats

Human activities may affect the sizes of marine mammal populations by altering critical habitats. Critical habitats can be defined as those areas, including resources, that are required to sustain viable populations of a species. Alterations of these need not be destructive; human developments may create new habitats or sources of required resources. Manatees have been affected both positively and negatively. Marinas have provided new sources of freshwater which may be necessary for the survival of the Caribbean manatee in marine areas of Florida. However, marinas also restrict available useable habitats, lower productivity and increase the danger of injury from power boat propellers (Hartman, 1971). Dams may also create new manatee habitats, for example, in West Africa (Cansdale, 1964), and in Florida (D. Odell, personal communication); however, construction of dams and similar projects may restructure and, in some cases, restrict movement patterns of sirenians, resulting in lessened gene flow.

3.4.2 Pollution

Pollution can harm sirenians through direct toxic effects, or indirectly through various forms of habitat alteration. The lake, river and inshore marine habitats of these animals are particularly vulnerable to human disturbances. Seagrass communities on which sirenians depend can be harmed by siltation, toxic and thermal wastes, oil spillage and sewage (Thayer, Wolfe and Williams, 1975). The effects of such disturbances depend, in part, upon the location and nature of the habitat components affected.

Areas of seagrass beds have been destroyed in Moreton Bay (the southernmost critical habitat of dugongs in eastern Australia) through deposition of sediments (Young, 1975). Near Townsville, Queensland, harbour dredging has likewise damaged seagrass beds through increased siltation (G.E. Heinsohn, personal communication). Large-scale clearing of land and overgrazing by livestock can also result in extensive erosion and the deposition of sediments onto inshore marine habitats; mining activities may have similar effects. Seagrass beds in Hinchinbrook Channel, an important dugong habitat in northern Queensland, may have been adversely affected by dredge spoil from tin mines which is being carried into the sea by the Herbert River (Heinshohn, 1975). (Heavy freshwater runoff may also affect dugong populations through destruction of seagrass beds (Heinsohn and Spain, 1974).

The direct effects of toxic substances, such as biocides,

petroleum derivatives and heavy metals, on seagrasses are mostly unknown (Thayer, Wolfe and Williams, 1975). Such wastes usually affect animals more directly than plants. Pesticides, herbicide and trace metal residues may accumulate in sirenian tissues to a point where they could kill or weaken the animals or have adverse effects on biological functions such as reproduction. The long-term effects of heavy metals on marine organisms are being studied at James Cook University, Queensland (C. Burdon-Jones and G. Denton, personal communication). The concentrations of ten heavy metals in organs from dugongs caught near Townsville have been determined. Very high iron concentrations have been found in dugong livers; these could be derived from food sources, as seagrasses collected near Townsville are also very high in iron (G. Denton, personal communication). Accumulation of other heavy metals in seagrasses could also have toxic effects. Effluent being dumped into the sea from a recently completed nickel refinery could cause such pollution near Townsville.

Throughout the range of manatees, herbicides have been used in an effort to control aquatic weeds, in particular, water hyacinth, a manatee food plant (National Science Research Council of Guyana, 1973). In the St. John's River of Florida 2-4-D has been used in large quantities; it breaks down rapidly, but the effects on manatees are as yet unknown (H. Campbell, personal communication). Copper sulphate and sulphuric acid have been used as herbicides in Crystal River, Florida (Hartman, 1972), but, again, no effects on manatees have been determined. Tissue samples from manatee carcasses in Florida are being analysed by the U.S. National Fish and Wildlife Laboratory for insecticide, herbicide and heavy metal residues.

Other forms of pollution also affect sirenians, sometimes, perhaps, beneficially. Sewage and fertilizer-rich runoff from agricultural areas pose the threat of eutrophication of food resources, although low concentrations may instead fertilize food plants and stimulate growth (Hartman, 1971). Thermal pollution from power plants may alter local food resources but also provides beneficial warm-water refuges for manatees during periods of cold weather near the northern extremes of their range in Florida (Campbell and Powell, 1976). The unreliability and recreational uses of these areas, however, may pose additional long-term problems for manatees.

3.4.3 Power Boats

Intense use of power boats in areas where sirenians are present may cause further problems. A main threat to manatees in Florida is collision with speeding motor boats and powerful barges (Campbell and Powell, 1976). Local regulations to slow boats in particular restricted areas during times when manatees are most abundant is all that may be required to reduce boat collisions to a level that can be tolerated by manatee populations. In some areas of northern Australia, power boats may disturb breeding, shelter and feeding areas of dugongs, and open up previously remote areas to human disturbance.

3.4.4 Other Activities

Several additional human activities can affect the sizes and distributions of sirenian populations. Detonation of explosive material for the purpose of munitions disposal, gunnery practise and seismic testing can cause death and, if carried out intensively, can change local distribution patterns. Vandalism and poaching result in a few manatee deaths every year in Florida; even though state and federal laws are very stringent with stiff penalties being provided, no cases have ever been prosecuted. Children who are unaware of laws and their consequence appear to be the main offenders, and an active educational programme is recommended (Campbell and Powell, 1976). Mortality due to harassment by skin and scuba divers has been documented in Florida, reported in both Mexico and Belize and probably occurs wherever manatees and divers are found together.

4. VALUES TO MAN

Sirenians are valuable to man not only in their intrinsic interest and too frequent rarity, but in their importance as the only mammals which are both fully aquatic and herbivorous. They are worthwhile in scientific, ecological, economic and aesthetic ways.

The scientific value of sirenians covers a broad spectrum of research disciplines. Areas of immediate interest include natural history and ecology. The evolutionary relations among the living species and their origin and relationships to other subungulates, the order's anatomical and physiological adaptations to the aquatic environment and comparisons with other groups of marine mammals, are also important subjects of study.

The ecological significance of the sirenians to the stability and productivity of their habitats has not been determined, but appears to be of considerable importance. Manatees consume large quantities of the abundant macrophytes found in freshwater systems of Amazonia, excreting nutrients which have been fixed in these plants for several months (W. Junk, personal communication). Since Amazonian waters have been found to be generally poor in electrolytes, addition of even small amounts of nutrients can have a profound fertilization effect, stimulating production by phytoplankton and zooplankton. These organizms ultimately provide the nutritional base on which the commercially valuable food fish of Amazonia depend.

Sirenians are important to subsistence hunters as sources of high quality meat and oil for consumption and local sale. Research should be conducted on the past, present and potential importance of sirenians as regards these productivities and economic values. The composition of sirenian carcasses in terms of useable meat, oil, leather and other products need to be determined. The useable meat on dugongs is roughly comparable to that on some breeds of cattle: 20-26 % of total body weight (G.E. Heinsohn, H. Marsh and A.V. Spain, personal communication) compared to 30 % muscle for

British breeds of cattle and 35 % for Brahman breeds (Springell, Butterfield, Johnson and Seebeck, 1968). Percentage values of total weight for dugong skin and skeleton were found to be 25 % and 7 %, respectively (G.E. Heinsohn, H. Marsh and A.V. Spain, personal communication). The internal fat of an adult dugong yields four to five gallons of oil, which was regarded as having curative powers by some of its native users. The tanned hide provided good leather, and the bones have been said to make good charcoal for sugar refining (Troughton, 1958). Manatees have also been heavily exploited for meat and hides (National Science Research Council of Guyana, 1974; Peterson, 1974).

Manatees are of potential value for aquatic weed control in tropical waterways (National Science Research Council of Guyana, 1973, 1974); They have also been considered for control of mosquitos (McLaren, 1967). Control of aquatic weed growth and consequent oxygen-consuming weed decomposition may be essential to increase fish production in freshwater lakes of many developing tropical countries. However, considerable research will be required before any extensive use of manatees for these purposes can be attempted. The logistic problems associated with the transport of manatees, problems of food preferences, the nutritional values of the weeds to be controlled and the biological needs of manatees relative to confinement in weed control areas all must be resolved. Wild manatee stocks are too depleted to support the removal of animals for weed control programmes. Captive reproducing stocks might be developed to insure a supply of manatees for this purpose and wild populations could also be managed to benefit weed control programmes. In any case, several decades may be required to develop effective weed control using manatees — especially involving captive animals — as basic reproductive biology and physiology must be determined to support such a venture. The importance of this possibility has already received considerable international attention. The whole problem of aquatic weed control, including the possible use of manatees, was discussed by a workshop on aquatic weed control held in Guyana (National Science Research Council of Guyana, 1973). Further to this, another workshop was held in Guyana to discuss and initiate arrangements for the establishment of the International Centre for Manatees Research in Guyana. The objectives of this centre would be (i) to sponsor, promote and coordinate activities that will advance knowledge of manatee biology, (ii) to assess the effectiveness of using manatees as aquatic weed control agents, (iii) to promote manatee conservation and (iv) to provide guidance in planning and in techniques of advanced mammalian research (National Science Research Council of Guyana, 1974).

Two other conferences relevant to this subject have recently been held: the U.S. National Academy of Science Conference on Use and Control of Aquatic Weeds, Gainesville, Florida, 1975, and the Second World Conference on Breeding Endangered Species in Captivity, London, July, 1976 (Bertram, in press).

Live sirenians have considerable value to people as interesting and important wildlife to be seen either in the wild or in captivity. In many regions, they are among the most spectacular wildlife species to be seen. Manatees can be approached, observed and photographed in the wild (e.g., Hartman, 1969); this is also the case with dugongs (Barnett and Johns, 1976; P.K. Anderson, A. Birtles and G.E. Heinsohn, personal communication). There are also reports of wild dugongs and manatees coming into swimming areas and associating with people. Sirenians also have importance as subjects of interest, entertainment and education through books, magazines, television, films and other communications media.

Captive sirenians kept in zoos and aquaria are of great public interest and value. Very few dugongs have been held in captivity and breeding of captive animals has never been known to have occurred, although the opportunities have been minimal. Manatees have only bred in captivity on rare occasions (Barbour, 1937; W. Zeiller, personal communication). Concern was expressed that there is a danger of zoos and oceanaria adding dugongs and manatees to their collection for prestige purposes and so further diminishing wild stocks of these rare animals. However, there may be instances where captive specimens may make an important contribution to the local education of people unaware of their own rare fauna: the displays of manatees in Guyana and Nigeria serve as examples where captive animals have increased interest and thereby provided better protection of local wild stocks.

Finally sirenians play an important rôle in the folklore and mythology of many peoples. These animals, in particular dugongs, are undoubtedly a source of mermaid legends.

5. MANAGEMENT AND RESEARCH

The most important activities responsible for the reduction of sirenian populations have been identified. Declining stocks indicate that management as currently practised is inadequate and that more effective guidelines are needed. Primary problems in sirenian management are lack of adequate knowledge of current utilization, lack of basic population and other bilogical data and high variability in the protection afforded to the species throughout the different countries within their ranges. Even in countries which afford sirenians full or partial protection, there are wide discrepancies in the effectiveness of law enforcement efforts. Given the subsistence level of existence of human populations over much of the range of sirenians, full protection or even carefully managed exploitation may be an unreasonable goal for the immediate future. Efforts are now required to prevent further decline until basic research on the states of species and populations has been completed to provide proper guidance for the development of management practices; in particular, expanded international commerce in any species should be discouraged until the results of such research are available and have been evaluated.

The most important management objective should be the conservation of the sirenians over their entire ranges. In areas where species are rare or thought to be close to extinction, management should be immediately directed at increasing population sizes.

5.1 Direct Exploitation

The greatest declines in sirenian stocks have occurred in those areas where there has been an increased demand for sirenian products, especially meat. In most areas, traditional hunting methods are still used, but power boats, monofilament nets and the introduction of the non-traditional methods and equipment, have contributed to increased hunting efficiency for dugongs in some areas. The increased demand for sirenian products may result from commercial interests and/or rapid human population growth, the latter often being further associated with poverty, protein deficiency and lack of funds and administration to enforce protective legislation. In such regions, sirenians are generally listed as being rare or in danger of extinction (Bertram and Bertram, 1973). In some areas where human populations have not increased at such high rates and where traditional hunting methods supplying only local consumption are still used, such severe declines in sirenian stocks have not been recorded — for example, in Papua New Guinea (Hudson, 1976) and northern Australia (Heinsohn, Wake, Marsh and Spain, in press).

While commercial demands for sirenians have diminished or stopped in some areas (e.g., the dugong oil industry in Queensland; large scale *mixira* export in South America), local pressures for meat remain substantial. Although the rate of direct exploitation, by aborigines in northern Australia, for example, could be declining as traditions and hunting skills are gradually lost and as native peoples become less dependent on traditional food resources, this can be offset through the use of modern technology, such as fast boats. Other technological innovations which pose a serious threat to all sirenians include rifles and nylon nets for hunting. Where management of dugongs and manatees allows exploitation for food and other products, the methods by which sirenians are taken should therefore be given very strong consideration — for example, new legislation in Papua New Guinea requires that dugongs only be taken by traditional methods and used for traditional purposes (Hudson, 1976).

With growing education and sophistication of native peoples, the variety of superstitious uses of sirenian products (e.g., as aphrodisiacs, cure-alls and antidotes for poisons) should decline. It is recommended that governments of countries where sirenians are found initiate educational programmes to rectify the wrong and superstitious ideas about sirenian products.

5.2 Sanctuaries

Protection of sirenians by means of sanctuaries has been proposed and attempted with varying success in several countries. An example of an effective manatee sanctuary is the reserve recently established by the Florida Department of Natural Resources at Blue Springs; the protected area serves as a warm-water refuge. Restrictions include prohibition of boats in the sanctuary and reduced speed limits nearby. About eight manatees are frequent year-round visitors and at least twenty-two others are seasonal visitors. The sanctuary has no food resources for manatees and no individuals are permanently resident. A full-time observation and research programme is in progress. Visitors to the reserve can observe manatees and engage in other outdoor recreation as well. Additional manatee reserves are being proposed for other areas of Florida.

Manatee are known to occur in national parks and reserves as follows: the Caribbean manatee in the Everglades National Park, U.S.A., the Rio Dulce National Park, Guatemala, and the Tortugera National Park, Costa Rica; the West African manatee in the Oiseaux du Djoudi and Basse-Casamance National Parks in Senegal and the Faunal Reserve of Lere-Binder in Chad; the Amazonian manatee is found in the Pacaya National Reserve, Peru. The West African manatee is also thought to occur in the Digya National Park in Ghana and will be included in the proposed Ibi National Park in Nigeria. Dugongs are believed to be found in some marine reserves such as Malindi and Watamu Marine Parks in Kenya (IUCN, 1976). A dugong refuge project begun at Mandaman Camp in India was discontinued (S. Jones, 1976). Information was not available on proposed dugong reserves in Sri Lanka, Tanzania and the Palau Islands. This list of sanctuaries is far from complete; however, only one of them, the Everglades National Park, is possibly large enough to encompass the normal movements of even part of its sirenian population and thereby offer year-round protection. All other sanctuaries are used only periodically or seasonally.

The creation of marine and freshwater parks and sanctuaries is of the greatest importance in any long-term protection scheme for sirenian populations. The establishment of sanctuaries should be based on research on, inter alia, sirenian distribution, movement patterns [1], and habitat utilization and carrying capacities, in order that reserves are of sufficient size, include a full range of sirenian habitats and, if practicable, harbour year-round residents. Reserves should totally protect sirenians and their habitats. Netting should be prohibited and restrictions on boating and diving imposed where necessary. Sirenian reserves that are publicized must be adequately patrolled by rangers. However, it is immediately necessary to set aside areas of important coastal habitats even if there are insufficient funds at present for proper management and protection.

An extensive series of reserves that would include resident sirenians and also serve as refuges for migratory animals should be established. For example, Australia, with long stretches of uninhabited coastal areas harbouring an abund-

[1] Information on the movements of sirenians is especially important when establishing reserves. At present, very little is known; evidence based on aerial survey studies indicates that sirenians undergo extensive migrations either in response to seasonal changes, food availability or both. If these animals do engage in long migrations along coasts, each critical habitat area is of especial importance to the survival of the species because of the presence of long stretches of coastline not suitable for sirenians. Research on methods of capturing and marking sirenians (including telemetry) to help determine their movements is being conducted by the U.S. National Fish and Wildlife Laboratory. Development of tagging techniques will be conducted in collaboration with sirenian investigators in other parts of the world.

ance of dugongs, is a prime area for such a system. Queensland has state habitat reserves that contain dugong populations, but national parks and other more rigorously protected sanctuaries are needed. Possible locations in Queensland include parts of Moreton Bay, the Fraser Island area, the Hinchinbrook Island area and parts of northern Cape York and the Gulf of Carpentaria. Aerial surveys are being conducted to determine suitable reserve areas (Heinsohn, Spain and Anderson, 1976; Heinsohn and Wake, 1976). Surveys of coastal areas not recently studied in Australia and other countries also need to be carried out.

5.3 Research

Large gaps exist in the knowledge of sirenian biology; there are insufficient data upon which to base population models for any of the four species. The most urgent of the pre-management requirements are:

(i) Stocks and habitat assessments for all species, covering present status, distribution and population abundance trends (information on the west African manatee is especially lacking).
(ii) Assessments of extent and seasonality of movements.
(iii) Determination of basic habitat requirements for maintenance or increase of present population levels.

Additional necessary research is needed on reproductive biology, growth rates and nutritional requirements. Evaluation of the current high-consumptive uses of sirenians is also needed to help future trends in exploitation.

The specific research needs and practical arrangements necessary for management depend upon the management objective, or combination of objectives, chosen. Three general possibilities are apparent:

(i) Management of wild populations without consideration for high-consumptive and other utilitarian objectives.
(ii) Management of wild populations for utilitarian ends (e.g., weed control or meat production).
(iii) Development of captive and/or semi-domesticated stocks for utilitarian ends.

Requirements for the former objective include the enactment and enforcement of protective legislation, public education, the monitoring of the effectiveness of these measures and research on habitats, reproductive biology and population dynamics, especially recruitment and mortality. Both objectives which take account of utilitarian considerations include the need to determine the potential of sirenians for the practical ends in view, as well as the potential economic and social profits and economic and ecological costs. Pursuance of the third objective further requires the determination of the suitability and practicality of sirenians for captivity and/or semi-domestication through, in part, studies of nutrition, growth rates, husbandry and reproductive biology, and also requires the insurance of adequate funding, space and technical assistance that such a programme would demand.

6. REFERENCES

ACMRR *Ad hoc* Group II - Small Cetaceans and Sirenians. 1976a Report. Presented to the ACMRR(FAO) Scientific Consultation on the Conservation and Management of Marine Mammals and their Environment. Bergen, Norway, 31 August-9 September, 1976. Rome, FAO, ACMRR/MM/SC/3.

ACMRR *Ad hoc* Group II - Small Cetaceans and Sirenians. 1976b Report, Supplement 1 (General Conclusions). Presented to the ACMRR(FAO) Scientific Consultation on the Conservation and Management of Marine Mammals and their Environment. Bergen, Norway, 31 August-9 September, 1976. Rome, FAO, ACMRR/MM/SC/3 Suppl. 1.

ALLSOPP, W.H.L., Aquatic weed control by manatees - its 1969 prospects and problems. *In* Man-made lakes, edited by L.E. Obeng. Accra, Ghana University Press, pp. 344-51.

—, A manatee research centre for Guyana: is it feasible and 1974 desirable? *In* Proceedings of the Manatee Workshop held in Georgetown, Guyana, February, 1974. Georgetown, Guyana, National Science Research Council.

AMINUL HAQUE, A.K.M., Observations on the occurrence of 1976 the dugong, *Dugong dugon*, in Bangladesh. Paper presented to the ACMRR(FAO) Scientific Consultation on the Conservation and Management of Marine Mammals and their Environment. Bergen, Norway, 31 August-9 September, 1976. Rome, FAO, ACMRR/MM/SC/129.

AUNG, S.H., A brief note on dugongs at Rangoon ZOO. *Int.* 1967 *Zoo Yearb.*, 7:221.

BARBOUR, T., Birth of a manatee. *J. Mammal.*, 18(1):106-7. 1937

BARNETT, C., and D. JOHNS, Underwater observations of du- 1976 gong in northern Queensland, Australia, with notes on dugong hunting and recommendations for future research. Paper presented to the ACMRR(FAO) Scientific Consultation on the Conservation and Management of Marine Mammals and their Environment. Bergen, Norway, 31 August-9 September, 1976. Rome, FAO, ACMRR/MM/SC/106.

BEAL, W.P., The manatee as a food animal. *Niger. Field*, 1939 8(3):124-6.

BERTRAM, G.C.L., Increased interest in Sirenia. Paper pre- 1976 sented to the ACMRR(FAO) Scientific Consultation on the Conservation and Management of Marine Mammals and their Environment. Bergen. Norway, 31 August-9 September, 1976. Rome, FAO, ACMRR/MM/SC/94.

—, Status and husbandry of manatees. *Int. Zoo Yearb.*, (17) (in press).

BERTRAM, G.C.L., and C.K. BERTRAM, The modern Sirenia:
1973 their distribution and status. *Biol. J. Linn. Soc.*, 5:297-338.

BIRCH, W.R., Some chemical and calorific properties of ma-
1975 rine angiosperms compared with those of other plants. *J. Appl. Ecol.*, 12:201-12.

BOUVEIGNES, O. de, Ce que les modernes savent du lamantin.
1952 *Zooleo*, 14(4):237-44.

BUSTARD, R., Sea turtles. Natural history and conservation.
1972 London, Collins, 220 p.

CADENAT, J., Observations de cétacés, siréniens, chéloniens et
1957 sauriens en 1955-1956. *Bull. Inst. Fr. Afr. Noire(A)*, 19(4):1358-83.

CAMPBELL, H.W., and J.A. POWELL, Endangered species: the
1976 manatee. *Fla. Nat.*, April issue: 15-20. Paper presented to the ACMRR(FAO) Scientific Consultation on the Conservation and Management of Marine Mammals and their Environment. Bergen, Norway, 31 August-9 September, 1976. Rome, FAO, ACMRR/MM/WG 4.8.

CANSDALE, G., The Volta Dam may help wildlife in Ghana.
1964 *Oryx*, 7(4):168-71.

DOMNING, D.P., Steller's sea cow and the origin of North
1972 Pacific aboriginal whaling. *Syesis*, 5187-9.

—, An ecological model for late tertiary sirenian evolution in the North Pacific Ocean. *System. Zool.*, (in press).

DORST, J., and P. DANDELOT, A field guide to the larger
1969 mammals of Africa. Boston, Houghton Mifflin Co., 287 p.

FERREIRA, A.R., Memoria sobre o peixe-boy y do uso que lhe
1903 dao no Estado do Frao Para. *Arch. Mus. Nac. Rio de Jan.*, 1903.

FITTKAU, E.J., Crocodiles and the nutrient metabolism of
1973 Amazonian waters. *Amazonia*, 4(1):103-33.

GIZEN, A., Au cours de huit années de séjour au Zoo, Huka
1963 notre lamantin n'a fait que croître et prospérer. *Zoo, Antwerp*, 28:194.

HARTMAN, D.S., Florida's manatees, mermaids in peril. *Natl.*
1969 *Geogr. Mag.*, 136(3):342-53.

—, Behaviour and ecology of the Florida manatee, *Trichechus*
1971 *manatus latirostris* (Harlan) at Crystal River, Citrus County. Ph.D. Thesis (Zoology), Cornell University, 285 p.

—, Manatees. *Sierra Club Bull.*, 57(3):20-2.
1972

—, Project 922 status survey of the manatee.
1974

—, Distribution, status and conservation of the manatee in the
1974 United States. Unpubl. M.S. 247 p.

HARTOG, C. DEN, The sea-grasses of the world. Amsterdam,
1970 North-Holland Publishing Co., 275 p.

HEINSOHN, G.E., A study of dugongs (*Dugong dugon*) in nor-
1972 thern Queensland, Australia. *Biol. Conserv.*, 4(3):205-13.

—, The dugong (*Dugong dugon* (Müller)): ecosystem rela-
1975 tions, species inter-actions, and effects of human activities. Paper presented to the FAO/ACMRR Working Party on Marine Mammals, *ad hoc* Group IV, Monaco. Background paper, 24 p. (unpubl.).

—, Report on aerial surveys of dugongs in northern Australian
1976a waters. Canberra, Australia, Department of Environment, Housing and Community Development, 14 p. (unpubl. rep.).

—, WG.4 Sirenians - Draft Report. Paper presented to the
1976b ACMRR(FAO) Scientific Consultation on the Conservation and Management of Marine Mammals and their Environment. Bergen, Norway, 31 August-9 September, 1976. Rome, FAO, ACMRR/MM/SC/WG4.1.

HEINSOHN, G.E., and W.R. BIRCH, Foods and feeding habits
1972 of the dugong, *Dugong dugon* (Erxleben), in northern Queensland, Australia. *Mammalia*, 36(3):414-22.

HEINSOHN, G.E., and A.V. SPAIN, Effects of a tropical cyclone
1974 on littoral and sub-littoral biotic communities and on a population of dugongs (*Dugong dugon* (Müller)). *Biol. Conserv.*, 6(2):143-52.

HEINSOHN, G.E., and J. WAKE, The importance of the Fraser
1976 Island region to dugongs. *Operculum* 5(1):15-8. Paper presented to the ACMRR(FAO) Scientific Consultation on the Conservation and Management of Marine Mammals and their Environment.

Bergen, Norway, 31 August-9 September, 1976. Rome, FAO, ACMRR/MM/SC/WG4.11.

HEINSOHN, G.E., H. MARCH and A.V. SPAIN, Extreme risk of mortality to dugongs (Mammalia: Sirenia): from netting operations. *Aust. J. Wildl. Res.*, 3(7) (in press). Paper presented to the ACMRR(FAO) Scientific Consultation on the Conservation and Management of Marine Mammals and their Environment. Bergen, Norway, 31 August-9 September, 1976. Rome, FAO, ACMRR/MM/SC/WG4.9.

HEINSOHN, G.E., A.V. SPAIN and P.K. ANDERSON, Populations of dugongs (Mammalia: Sirenia): aerial survey over the inshore waters of tropical Australia. *Biol. Conserv.*, 9:21-3. Paper presented to the ACMRR(FAO) Scientific Consultation on the Conservation and Management of Marine Mammals and their Environment. Bergen, Norway, 31 August-9 September, 1976. Rome, FAO, ACMRR/MM/SC/WG4.12.

HEINSOHN, G.E., J. WAKE, H. MARSH and A.V. SPAIN, The dugong (*Dugong dugon* (Müller)) in the seagrass system. *Aquaculture* (in press).

HIRASAKA, K., The occurrence of the dugong in Formosa.
1932 *Mem. Fac. Sci. Agric. Taihoka Imp. Univ.*, 7:1-4.

—, On the distribution of sirenians in the Pacific. *Proc. Pacif.*
1934 *Sci. Congr.*, 5:4221-2.

HIRTH, H.F., L.G. KLIKOFF, and K.T. HARPER, Sea grasses at
1973 Khor Umaira, People's Democratic Republic of Yemen, with reference to their role in the diet of the green turtle, *Chelonia mydas*. *Fish. Bull., NOAA/NMFS*, 71(4):1093-7.

HUDSON, B.E.T., Dugongs: distribution, hunting, protective
1976 legislation and cultural significance in Papua New Guinea. Paper presented to the ACMRR(FAO) Scientific Consultation on the Conservation and Management of Marine Mammals and their Environment. Bergen, Norway, 31 August-9 September, 1976. Rome, FAO, ACMRR/MM/SC/86.

HUGHES, G.R., and OXLEY-OXLAND, A survey of dugong
1971 (*Dugong dugon*) in and around Antonio Enes, northern Mozambique. *Biol. Conserv.*, 3:229:331.

HUSAR, S.L., A review of the literature of the dugong (*Dugong*
1975 *dugon*). *Wildl. Res. Rep. Fish. Wildl. Serv. U.S.*, (4):30 p. Paper presented to the ACMRR(FAO) Scientific Consultation on the Conservation and Management of Marine Mammals and their Environment. Bergen, Norway, 31 August-9 September, 1976. Rome, FAO, ACMRR/MM/SC/WG4.2.

—, [A review of the literature of the West Indian manatee (*Trichechus manatus*).] *Wildl. Res. Rep. Fish Wildl. Serv. U.S.* (7) (in press).

—, Survey of the order Sirenia. Part 3. The Amazonian manatee (*Trichechus inunguis*). Part 4. The African manatee (*Trichechus senegalensis*). Washington, D.C., U.S. National Fish and Wildlife Laboratory, National Museum of Natural History (unpubl. MS).

ILANI, G., More about dugongs. *Israel Land Nat.*, 1(4):161.
1976 Paper presented to the ACMRR(FAO) Scientific Consultation on the Conservation and Management of Marine Mammals and their Environment. Bergen. Norway, 31 August-9 September, 1976. Rome, FAO, ACMRR/MM/SC/WG4.7.

IUCN, Red Data Book. Morges, Switzerland, IUCN.
1976

JONES, S., The dugong - its present status in the seas around
1967 India with observations on its behaviour in captivity. *Int. Zoo Yearb.*, 7:215-20.

—, The present status of the dugong, *Dugong dugon* (Müller)
1976 in the Indo-Pacific and problems of its conservation. Paper presented to the ACMRR(FAO) Scientific Consultation on the Conservation. Paper presented to the ACMRR(FAO) Scientific Consultation on the Conservation and Management of Marine Mammals and their Environment. Bergen, Norway, 31 August-9 September, 1976. Rome, FAO, ACMRR/MM/SC/26.

LIGON, S.H., A survey of dugongs (*Dugong dugon*) in
1976a Queensland. *J. Mammal*, 57(3):580-2.

—, Aerial survey of the dugong in Kenya. Paper presented to
1976 the ACMRR(FAO) Scientific Consultation on the Conservation and Management of Marine Mammals and their Environment. Bergen, Norway, 31 August-9 September, 1976. Rome, FAO, ACMRR/MM/SC/107.

LIGON, S.H., and B.E.T. HUDSON, Aerial survey of the dugong
1976 (*Dugong dugon*) in Papua New Guinea. Paper presented to the ACMRR(FAO) Scientific Consultation on the Conservation and Management of Marine Mammals and their Environment. Bergen, Norway, 31 August-9 September, 1976. Rome, FAO, ACMRR/MM/SC/89.

LIPKIN, Y., Food of the Red Sea *Dugong* (Mammalia: Sirenia)
1976 from Sinai. *Israel J. Zool.*, 24(1975):81-98.

LOUGHMAN, D.W., F.L. FRYE and E.S. HERALD, The chro-
1970 mosomes of a male manatee, *Trichechus inunguis*. *Int. Zoo Yearb.*, 10:151-2.

McLaren, J.P., Manatees as a naturalistic biological mosquito control method. *Mosquito News*, 27(3)387-93.
1967

Meester, J., and H.W. Sitzer (Eds), The mammals of Africa. Washington, D.C., Smithsonian Institution Press.
1971

Mendes, A., As pescarias amazonicas e a piscicultura no Brasil. Sao Paulo, L+R, 181 p. (after Padre A. Vierra).
1938

Mitchell, J., Age determination in the dugong, *Dugong dugon* (Müller). *Biol. Conserv.*, 9(1):25-8.
1976

Murray, R.M., H. Marsh, G.E. Heinsohn and A.V. Spain, The role of the midgut caecum and large intestine in the digestion of sea grasses by the dugong (Mammalia: Sirenia). *Comp. Biochem. Physiol. (A Comp. Physiol.)*, 54. (in press). Paper presented to the ACMRR(FAO) Scientific Consultation on the Conservation and Management of Marine Mammals and their Environment. Bergen, Norway, 31 August-9 September, 1976. Rome, FAO, ACMRR/MM/SC/WG4.10.

National Scientific Research Council of Guyana, Some prospects for aquatic weed management in Guyana. *In* Workshop on aquatic weed management and utilization. Georgetown, Guyana, National Scientific Research Council of Guyana, 39 p.
1973

National Scientific Research Council of Guyana, An international centre for manatee research. Georgetown, Guyana, National Scientific Research Council of Guyana, 34 p.
1974

Oke, V.R., A brief note on the dugong at Cairns Oceanarium. *Int. Zoo Yearb.*, 7:220-1.
1967

Pereira, N., O peixe-boi da Amazonia. Manaus, Brasil, Imprensa Oficial, Tecnico da Divisão de Caça e Pesca do Ministerio da Agricultura.
1947

Peterson, S.L., Man's relationship with the Florida manatee, *Trichechus manatus latirostris* (Harlan): an historical perspective. M.A. thesis, Univ. Michigan, 78 p.
1974

Pfeffer, P., Remarques sur la nomenclature du dugong, *Dugong dugon* (Erxleben) et son statut actuel en Indonésie. *Mammalia*, 27(1).
1963

Poche, R.W., Niger's threatened park. *Oryx*, 12(2):216-22.
1973

Por, F.D., A sea cow captured near Elat. *Sci. Notes Heins Steinitz Mar. Biol. Lab. Elat*, 2:12-3.
1972

Reinhart, R.H., A review of the Sirenia and Desmostylia. *Univ. Calif. Publ. Geol. Sci.*, 36(1):1-146.
1959

Robinson, P.T., Wildlife trends in Liberia and Sierra Leone. *Oryx*, 11(2-3):117-21.
1971

Romer, A.S., Vertebrate paleontology. Chicago, University of Chicago Press, 468 p.
1966

Scholander, P.F. and L. Irving, Experimental investigations of the respiration and diving of the Florida manatee. *J. Cell Comp. Physiol.*, 17:169-91.
1941

Sikes, S., How to save the mermaids. *Oryx*, 12(4):465-70.
1974

Simpson, G.G., The principles of classification and a classification of mammals. *Bull. Am. Mus. Nat. Hist.*, 85:350 p.
1945

Spain, A.V., and G.E. Heinsohn, Cyclone associated feeding changes in the dugong (Mammalia: Sirenia). *Mammalia*, 37(4):678-80.
1973

—, Size and weight allometry in a North Queensland population of *Dugong Dugon* (Müller) (Mammalia: Sirenia). *Aust. J. Zool.*, 23:159-68.
1975

Springell, P.H., R.M. Butterfield, E.R. Johnson and R.M. Seebeck, The use of body weight, total body water and red cell volume to predict muscle weight of beef cattle. *Proc. Aust. Soc. Anim. Prod.*, 7:314-7.
1968

Tadjalli-Pour, M., Les mammifères marins d'Iran. Paper presented to the ACMRR(FAO) Scientific Consultation on the Conservation and Management of Marine Mammals and their Environment. Bergen, Norway, 31 August-9 September, 1976. Rome, FAO, ACMRR/MM/SC/125/Rev.1.
1976

Thayer, G.W., D.A. Wolfe and R.B. Williams, The impact of man on seagrass system. *Am. Sci.*, 63(3):288-96.
1975

Tranngocloi, N.T., Capture d'un dugong au Viet Nam. *Mammalia*, 26:451-2.
1962

Troughton, E. le G., Dugong. *In* The Australia encyclopaedia. Sydney, Angus and Robertson, vol. 3:307.
1958

Wake, J., A study of the habitat requirements and feeding biology of the dugong, *Dugong dugon* (Müller). Thesis, James Cook University, 99 p.
1975

White, J.R., D.R. Harkness, R.E. Isaacks and D.A. Duffield, Some studies on blood of the Florida manatee, *Trichechus manatus latirostris*. *Comp. Biochem. Physiol.*, 55(4A):413-7.
1976

Young, P.C., Fraser Island environmental enquiry. Submitted to the Fraser Island Environmental Inquiry, Brisbane, 14 p. (Unpubl.).
1975

FAO SALES AGENTS AND BOOKSELLERS

Algeria	Société nationale d'édition et de diffusion, 92, rue Didouche Mourad, Algiers.
Argentina	Editorial Hemisferio Sur S.A., Librería Agropecuaria, Pasteur 743, 1028 Buenos Aires.
Australia	Hunter Publications, 58A Gipps Street, Collingwood, Vic. 3066; Australian Government Publishing Service, Publishing Branch, P.O. Box 84, Canberra, A.C.T. 2600; and Australian Government Publications and Inquiry Centres in Canberra, Melbourne, Sydney, Perth, Adelaide and Hobart.
Austria	Gerold & Co., Buchhandlung und Verlag, Graben 31, 1011 Vienna.
Bangladesh	ADAB, 79 Road 11A, P.O. Box 5045, Dhanmondi, Dacca.
Belgium	Service des publications de la FAO, M.J. de Lannoy, 202, avenue du Roi, 1060 Brussels. CCP 000-0808993-13.
Bolivia	Los Amigos del Libro, Perú 3712, Casilla 450, Cochabamba; Mercado 1315, La Paz; René Moreno 26, Santa Cruz; Junín esq. 6 de Octubre, Oruro.
Brazil	Livraria Mestre Jou, Rua Guaipá 518, São Paulo 10; Rua Senador Dantas 19-S205/206, 20.031 Rio de Janeiro; PRODIL, Promoção e Dist. de Livros Ltda., Av. Venâncio Aires 196, Caixa Postal 4005, 90.000 Porto Alegre; A NOSSA LIVRARIA, CLS 104, Bloco C, Lojas 18/19, 70.000 Brasilia, D.F.
Brunei	SST Trading Sdn. Bhd., Bangunan Tekno No. 385, Jln 5/59, P.O. Box 227, Petaling Jaya, Selangor.
Canada	Renouf Publishing Co. Ltd, 2182 Catherine St. West, Montreal, Que. H3H 1M7.
Chile	Tecnolibro S.A., Merced 753, entrepiso 15, Santiago.
China	China National Publications Import Corporation, P.O. Box 88, Beijing.
Colombia	Litexsa Colombiana Ltda., Calle 55, N° 16-44, Apartado Aéreo 51340, Bogotá D.E.
Costa Rica	Librería, Imprenta y Litografía Lehmann S.A., Apartado 10011, San José.
Cuba	Empresa de Comercio Exterior de Publicaciones, O'Reilly 407 Bajos entre Aguacate y Compostela, Havana.
Cyprus	MAM, P.O. Box 1722, Nicosia.
Czechoslovakia	ARTIA, Ve Smeckach 30, P.O. Box 790, 111 27 Praha 1.
Denmark	Munksgaard Boghandel, Norregade 6, 1165 Copenhagen K.
Dominican Rep.	Fundación Dominicana de Desarrollo, Casa de las Gárgolas, Mercedes 4, Apartado 857, Zona Postal 1, Santo Domingo.
Ecuador	Su Librería Cía. Ltda., García Moreno 1172 y Mejía, Apartado 2556, Quito; Chimborazo 416, Apartado 3565, Guayaquil.
El Salvador	Librería Cultural Salvadoreña S.A. de C.V., Calle Arce 423, Apartado Postal 2296, San Salvador.
Finland	Akateeminen Kirjakauppa, 1 Keskuskatu, P.O. Box 128, 00101 Helsinki 10.
France	Editions A. Pedone, 13, rue Soufflot, 75005 Paris.
Germany, F.R.	Alexander Horn Internationale Buchhandlung, Spiegelgasse 9, Postfach 3340, 6200 Wiesbaden.
Ghana	Fides Enterprises, P.O. Box 1628, Accra; Ghana Publishing Corporation, P.O. Box 3632, Accra.
Greece	G.C. Eleftheroudakis S.A., International Bookstore, 4 Nikis Street, Athens (T-126); John Mihalopoulos & Son, International Booksellers, 75 Hermou Street, P.O. Box 73, Thessaloniki.
Guatemala	Distribuciones Culturales y Técnicas "Artemis", 5a. Avenida 12-11, Zona 1, Apartado Postal 2923, Guatemala.
Guinea-Bissau	Conselho Nacional da Cultura, Avenida da Unidade Africana, C.P. 294, Bissau.
Guyana	Guyana National Trading Corporation Ltd, 45-47 Water Street, P.O. Box 308, Georgetown.
Haiti	Librairie "A la Caravelle", 26, rue Bonne Foi, B.P. 111, Port-au-Prince.
Hong Kong	Swindon Book Co., 13-15 Lock Road, Kowloon.
Hungary	Kultura, P.O. Box 149, 1389 Budapest 62.
Iceland	Snaebjörn Jónsson and Co. h.f., Hafnarstraeti 9, P.O. Box 1131, 101 Reykjavik.
India	Oxford Book and Stationery Co., Scindia House, New Delhi 110001; 17 Park Street, Calcutta 700016.
Indonesia	P.T. Sari Agung, 94 Kebon Sirih, P.O. Box 411, Djakarta.
Iran	Iran Book Co. Ltd, 127 Nadershah Avenue, P.O. Box 14-1532, Teheran.
Iraq	National House for Publishing, Distributing and Advertising, Jamhuria Street, Baghdad.
Ireland	The Controller, Stationery Office, Dublin 4.
Italy	Distribution and Sales Section, Food and Agriculture Organization of the United Nations, Via delle Terme di Caracalla, 00100 Rome; Libreria Scientifica Dott. Lucio de Biasio "Aeiou", Via Meravigli 16, 20123 Milan; Libreria Commissionaria Sansoni S.p.A. "Licosa", Via Lamarmora 45, C.P. 552, 50121 Florence.
Jamaica	Teacher Book Centre Ltd, 95 Church Street, Kingston.
Japan	Maruzen Company Ltd, P.O. Box 5050, Tokyo International 100-31.
Kenya	Text Book Centre Ltd, Kijabe Street, P.O. Box 47540, Nairobi.

FAO SALES AGENTS AND BOOKSELLERS

Korea, Rep. of	Eul-Yoo Publishing Co. Ltd, 112 Kwanchul-Dong, Chong-ro, P.O. Box Kwang-Whamoon No. 363, Seoul.
Kuwait	Saeed & Samir Bookstore Co. Ltd, P.O. Box 5445, Kuwait.
Luxembourg	Service des publications de la FAO, M.J. de Lannoy, 202, avenue du Roi, 1060 Brussels (Belgium).
Malaysia	SST Trading Sdn. Bhd., Bangunan Tekno No. 385, Jln 5/59, P.O. Box 227, Petaling Jaya, Selangor.
Mauritius	Nalanda Company Limited, 30 Bourbon Street, Port Louis.
Mexico	Dilitsa S.A., Puebla 182-D, Apartado 24-448, Mexico 7, D.F.
Morocco	Librairie " Aux Belles Images ", 281, avenue Mohammed V, Rabat.
Netherlands	Keesing Boeken B.V., Hondecoeterstraat 16, 1017 LS Amsterdam.
New Zealand	Government Printing Office: Government Bookshops at Rutland Street, P.O. Box 5344, Auckland; Alma Street, P.O. Box 857, Hamilton; Mulgrave Street, Private Bag, Wellington; 130 Oxford Terrace, P.O. Box 1721, Christchurch; Princes Street, P.O. Box 1104, Dunedin.
Nigeria	University Bookshop (Nigeria) Limited, University of Ibadan, Ibadan.
Norway	Johan Grundt Tanum Bokhandel, Karl Johansgate 41-43, P.O. Box 1177 Sentrum, Oslo 1.
Pakistan	Mirza Book Agency, 65 Shahrah-e-Quaid-e-Azam, P.O. Box 729, Lahore 3.
Panama	Distribuidora Lewis S.A., Edificio Dorasol, Calle 25 y Avenida Balboa, Apartado 1634, Panama 1.
Paraguay	Agencia de Librerías Nizza S.A., Tacuarí 144, Asunción.
Peru	Librería Distribuidora " Santa Rosa ", Jirón Apurímac 375, Casilla 4937, Lima 1.
Philippines	The Modern Book Company Inc., 926 Rizal Avenue, P.O. Box 632, Manila.
Poland	Ars Polona, Krakowskie Przedmiescie 7, 00-068 Warsaw.
Portugal	Livraria Bertrand, S.A.R.L., Rua João de Deus, Venda Nova, Apartado 37, Amadora; Livraria Portugal, Dias y Andrade Ltda., Rua do Carmo 70-74, Apartado 2681, 1117 Lisbon Codex; Edições ITAU, Avda. da República 46/A-r/c Esqdo., Lisbon 1.
Romania	Ilexim, Calea Grivitei N° 64-66, B.P. 2001, Bucharest.
Saudi Arabia	University Bookshop, Airport Street, P.O. Box 394, Riyadh.
Senegal	Librairie Africa, 58, avenue Georges Pompidou, B.P. 1240, Dakar.
Singapore	MPH Distributors (S) Pte. Ltd, 71/77 Stamford Road, Singapore 6; Select Books Pte. Ltd, 215 Tanglin Shopping Centre, Tanglin Road, Singapore 1024; SST Trading Sdn. Bhd., Bangunan Tekno No. 385, Jln 5/59, P.O. Box 227, Petaling Jaya, Selangor.
Somalia	" Samater's ", P.O. Box 936, Mogadishu.
Spain	Mundi Prensa Libros S.A., Castelló 37, Madrid 1; Librería Agrícola, Fernando VI 2, Madrid 4.
Sri Lanka	M.D. Gunasena & Co. Ltd, 217 Olcott Mawatha, P.O. Box 246, Colombo 11.
Sudan	University Bookshop, University of Khartoum, P.O. Box 321, Khartoum.
Suriname	VACO n.v. in Suriname, Dominee Straat 26, P.O. Box 1841, Paramaribo.
Sweden	C.E. Fritzes Kungl. Hovbokhandel, Regeringsgatan 12, P.O. Box 16356, 103 27 Stockholm.
Switzerland	Librairie Payot S.A., Lausanne et Genève; Buchhandlung und Antiquariat Heinimann & Co., Kirchgasse 17, 8001 Zurich.
Tanzania	Dar es-Salaam Bookshop, P.O. Box 9030, Dar es-Salaam; Bookshop, University of Dar es-Salaam, P.O. Box 893, Morogoro.
Thailand	Suksapan Panit, Mansion 9, Rajadamnern Avenue, Bangkok.
Togo	Librairie du Bon Pasteur, B.P. 1164, Lomé.
Trinidad and Tobago	The Book Shop, 22 Queens Park West, Port of Spain.
Tunisia	Société tunisienne de diffusion, 5, avenue de Carthage, Tunis.
United Kingdom	Her Majesty's Stationery Office, 49 High Holborn, London WC1V 6HB (callers only); P.O. Box 569, London SE1 9NH (trade and London area mail orders); 13a Castle Street, Edinburgh EH2 3AR; 41 The Hayes, Cardiff CF1 1JW; 80 Chichester Street, Belfast BT1 4JY; Brazennose Street, Manchester M60 8AS; 258 Broad Street, Birmingham B1 2HE; Southey House, Wine Street, Bristol BS1 2BQ.
United States of America	UNIPUB, 345 Park Avenue South, New York, N.Y. 10010.
Uruguay	Librería Editorial Juan Angel Peri, Alzaibar 1328, Casilla de Correos 1755, Montevideo.
Venezuela	Blume Distribuidora S.A., Gran Avenida de Sabana Grande, Residencias Caroni, Local 5, Apartado 70.017, Caracas.
Yugoslavia	Jugoslovenska Knjiga, Trg. Republike 5/8, P.O. Box 36, 11001 Belgrade; Cankarjeva Zalozba, P.O. Box 201-IV, 61001 Ljubljana; Prosveta, Terazije 16, P.O. Box 555, 11001 Belgrade.
Zambia	Kingstons (Zambia) Ltd, Kingstons Building, President Avenue, P.O. Box 139, Ndola.
Other countries	Requests from countries where sales agents have not yet been appointed may be sent to: Distribution and Sales Section, Food and Agriculture Organization of the United Nations, Via delle Terme di Caracalla, 00100 Rome, Italy.

This volume was designed by Ferruccio Martellacci

Finito di stampare con i tipi della fotocomposizione della tipo-lito SAGRAF - Napoli

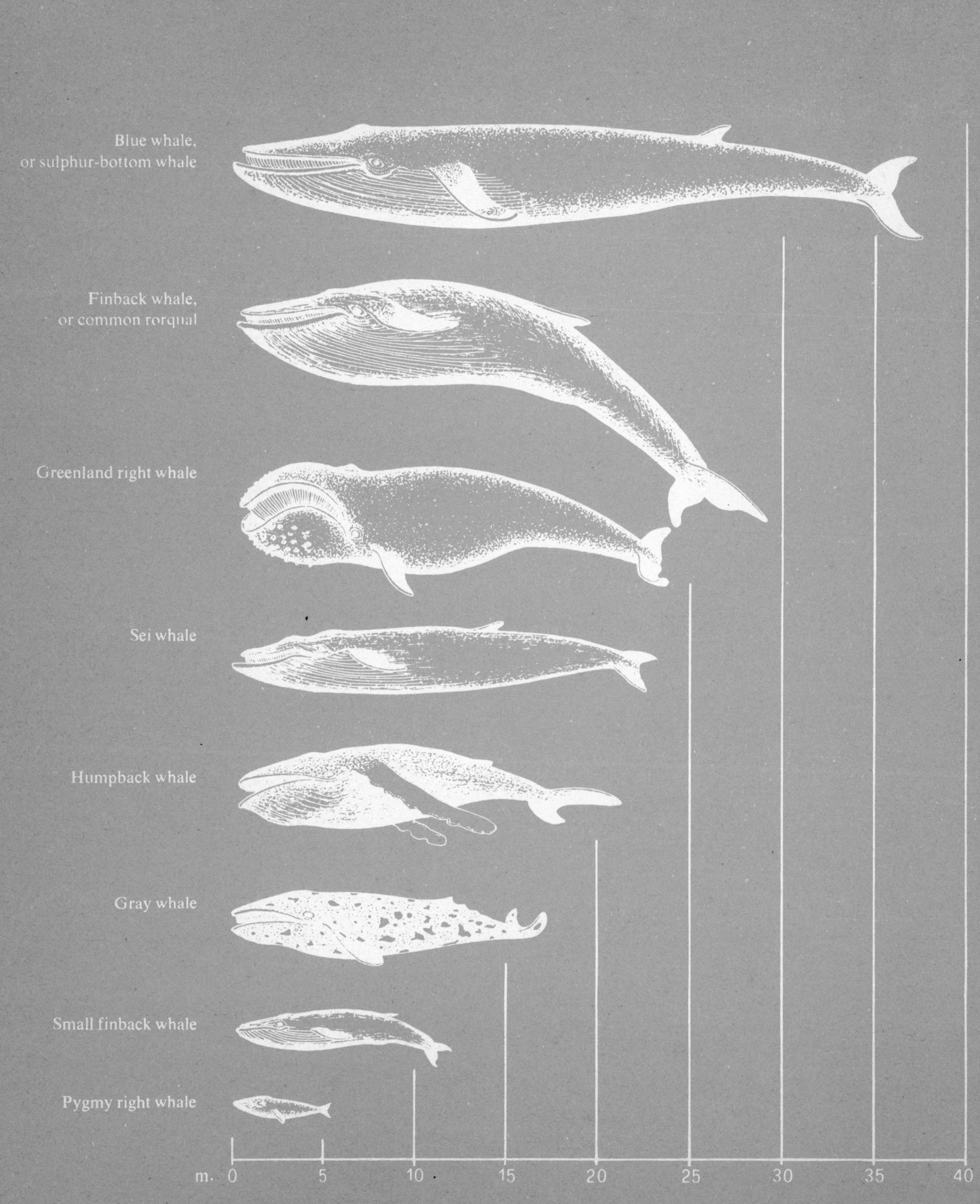
Blue whale,
or sulphur-bottom whale
Finback whale,
or common rorqual
Greenland right whale
Sei whale
Humpback whale
Gray whale
Small finback whale
Pygmy right whale
m. 0 5 10 15 20 25 30 35 40